THE KEYNESIAN THEORY OF
ECONOMIC DEVELOPMENT

THE KEYNESIAN THEORY

OF

ECONOMIC DEVELOPMENT

Kenneth K. Kurihara
Rutgers University

COLUMBIA UNIVERSITY PRESS

NEW YORK

1959

First published 1959 by
George Allen & Unwin Ltd., London

Library of Congress Catalog Card Number: 58-13724

Printed in Great Britain

PREFACE

THIS book is intended to clarify the technical possibilities and limitations of economic growth in general and of the economic development of underdeveloped countries in particular. To sharpen the issue, I have deliberately made comparative analyses of divers growth problems of underdeveloped and developed economies throughout this volume. My principal concern has been to elucidate the operationally significant mechanisms of economic development in given socio-cultural conditions. Accordingly I have selected those relations between measurable variables on which the growth of per capita real incomes most strategically depends—to be analysed on assumptions plausible yet simple enough to yield useful results. Separate chapters, though incomplete in and by themselves, have been arranged so as to constitute an integrated theoretical whole and to facilitate an overall scheme of industrialization programming in less developed countries.

By way of acknowledgment may I justify my predilection for the Keynesian frame of reference expressed in the title of this book, on several grounds. First, and contemporaneously, this book is very deeply indebted to Mr. R. F. Harrod and Mrs. Joan Robinson who, as one might expect of distinguished pupils of Keynes, have done most to secularize and dynamize Keynes's short-run theory. Specifically this book could not have been written without Mr. Harrod's path-breaking apparatus of growth analysis and without Mrs. Robinson's challenging suggestion about the possible application of Keynesian dynamics to underdeveloped countries.* However, I have not hesitated to disagree with the specific tools of analysis in their writings, as the reader will see subsequently. Though written in the same *post*-Keynesian spirit of Mr. Harrod and Mrs. Robinson, this book is entitled 'Keynesian' in order to distinguish it from

*Mrs. Robinson's suggestion will be found in her 'Mr. Harrod's Dynamics', *Economic Journal* (March 1949). I had already written the bulk of this book when Mrs. Robinson's new book, *The Accumulation of Capital*, came to my attention. However, my belated reactions to her new book will be found in Chapter 4 of this volume. I need hardly mention Mr. Harrod's well-known *Towards a Dynamic Economics*.

other books that are specifically 'neo-Classical', 'Marxian', or 'Schumpeterian'.

Second, this writing owes its initial conception and its basic inspiration to the vision of Keynes as epitomized by his technical, multinational, nonpartisan attitude toward the economic development of less developed countries—a rare vision that is permanently embodied in the general principles of the International Bank for Reconstruction and Development, of which Keynes was the recognized intellectual architect. Third, economic development as an object of pragmatic analysis and policy seems to call for a volume that is in keeping with 'Keynesian operationalism', which Professor A. C. Pigou has so aptly characterized as the kind of model-building 'designed to stand in close relation to facts susceptible of statistical measurement; to help forecasts and guide policies'. Fourth, the national income analysis and national economic statecraft associated with the name of Keynes have rendered the short-run problem of unstable effective demand largely surmountable without too drastic a departure from the traditions, so that every mixed public–private economy may now confidently tackle the long-run problem of achieving and maintaining its target rate of progress within technical limits but without the fear of being inevitably upset by cyclical instability.

Lastly, Keynes' social philosophy outlined in the concluding chapter of the *General Theory* would appear to be an indispensable lighthouse for guiding that pattern of economic development which is firmly based on overflowing enthusiasm for speedy industrialization tempered with underlying sensibilities toward human values—a pattern of global economic development which Keynes envisaged in 'the new democracy of nations which after this war [World War II] will come into existence'.

Many other economists have stimulated, if not influenced, my own thinking on the subject, as the reader may surmise from the precursors delineated in the introductory chapter of this book as well as from the bibliography attached at the end. However, I wish to express my special appreciation to a few individuals who have been personally helpful in my latest endeavour to extend and implement Keynes. I am most indebted, as so often, to Professor William Vickrey of Columbia University for his careful and helpful criticisms on technical details. Professor Broadus Mitchell of Rutgers University has kindled my imagination with his instructive tales of early American development under the leadership of Alexander Hamilton, while Professor Robert Alexander has confronted my theories at all stages with his empirical data on Latin American developing economies. Professor Gerhard Tintner of Iowa State College has given me the benefit of his criticism on a number of technical points. Professors Hideo Aoyama and Shinichi Ichimura, respectively of Kyoto University Research Centre for Economic Development and Osaka University Institute of Social and Economic Research, have given me valuable suggestions in the light of their intimate knowledge of Japan's industrial advance. President Howard Bowen of Grinnell College has given me warm encouragement, as always. My wife, Kay, has given me the sort of sympathy and support every author needs most in the turbulent course of serious writing.

To all these friends and colleagues I owe very much, but of course none of them should be held responsible for whatever failings the reader may discover in this volume. To the editors of the following journals I wish to express my thanks for permission to reproduce here all or part of my contributions: the *Indian Journal of Economics*, the *Indian Economic Journal*, the *Metroeconomica*, the *Finances Publiques* (Netherlands), the *Economic Studies Quarterly* (Japan), and the *Economic Weekly* (India).

KENNETH K. KURIHARA

Rutgers University

CONTENTS

CHAPTER I

CLASSICAL AND POST-CLASSICAL PRECURSORS

THE modern theory of economic development, like every other branch of economic theory, has a unique history of its own that is at once retrospective of present-day development theorizing and prospective of surrealistic model building. The subjective history of economic thought in this particular field is a good first approximation to the objective history of economic evolution in varying circumstances. By way of providing a broader perspective this introductory chapter will delineate the classical and post-classical insights into the nature and causes of economic development in historically heterogeneous yet essentially homogeneous human societies. The following selection of precursors is intended to indicate only the greatest classical and post-classical influences on contemporary thinking and programming in the specialized field of economic development.

CLASSICAL INSIGHTS AND FORESIGHTS

Adam Smith (1723–1790)
It is no accident that Adam Smith, the founder of the classical school in the already most advanced industrial nation of the world—Great Britain—should have been also the first to outline the general nature of economic progress and the particular causes of capitalistic development. The former generality is a matter of greater importance than the latter particularity, inasmuch as contemporary development theorists are much more interested in the *technical* conditions of economic progress to be satisfied than in its *ideological* implications to be welcomed or feared. Adam Smith's failing on this score was that he did not clearly distinguish between what would prove valid for all times and places and what would hold good for the limiting case of 'Individualistic Capitalism'.

Thus his *laissez-faire*, maximum competition, free trade,

the entrepreneur as the harmonizer of private and public interests, and parsimony as an individual and national virtue would appear to present-day theorists to be suitable guide-posts for economic development along the lines of pure 'Individualistic Capitalism'. Yet it would be amiss to dismiss Adam Smith's *Wealth of Nations* as irrevelant to the economic development of contemporary societies without much attachment to any particular form of economic organization. For that book advances, among other things, the general proposition that the growth of national wealth depends on (a) the productivity of labour associated with the technologically determined 'division of labour' and (b) the accumulation of capital associated with the institutionally determined extent of 'parsimony'. Few would challenge the broad validity of this proposition, though many might today question Adam Smith's reliance on the 'invisible hand' for assuring such technological advance and capital accumulation as to entail the automatic and undisturbed growth of national wealth. This proposition of Adam Smith anticipates Keynes's retrospection that the slow rate of progress in the pre-capitalistic period was due to two retarding factors, namely, (a) 'the remarkable absence of important technical improvements' and (b) 'the failure of capital to accumulate'.[1] Thus Adam Smith may be credited with giving a pioneering emphasis to the crucial role played by the quantity and quality of capital in national industrialization.

Thomas Robert Malthus (1766–1835)

Like Adam Smith but unlike David Ricardo (who was mainly concerned with the *distribution* of a given output), Robert Malthus, 'the first of the Cambridge economists', was preoccupied with the *volume* of output, with 'the immediate causes of the progress of wealth'. Malthus, however, differed from Smith in perceiving the technical possibility of economic progress with 'irregular movements' ('cyclical growth', in modern jargon), when and where the accumulation of savings, on which that progress largely depends, is allowed to proceed

[1] See J. M. Keynes, *Essays in Persuasion*, Rupert Hart-Davis, London, 1952, p. 360.

so rapidly as to diminish consumption-demand and so to impair 'the usual motives to production'. Such, in a nutshell, is Malthus's view of unsteady uneasy 'progress of wealth' in societies whose effective demand does not behave in the manner described by Say's Law of Markets. This view is expressed in Malthus's *Principles of Political Economy*, a view which has come to be generally known largely through Keynes's efforts.[1]

More interesting from the standpoint of underdeveloped economies is Malthus's other major work, *An Essay on the Principle of Population, as it Affects the Future Improvement of Society*, in which he advanced the startling idea that the growth of population could outrun the growth of capital (hence of means of subsistence) in the circumstances where the former was left uncontrolled and the latter left to *laissez-faire*. Here Malthus anticipates Marx's theory of the 'industrial reserve army' (structural underemployment), for 'Marx's reasons for holding this view are by no means without interest, being in fact closely akin to Malthus's own theory that "effective demand" may fail in a capitalist society to keep pace with output', as Keynes pointed out.[2] Unlike Marx, however, Malthus considered the rational control of the rate of births, not the abolition of *laissez-faire* capital accumulation, as the right remedy for the so-called 'overpopulation problem'. Be that as it may, Malthus was the first to give a 'smashing emphasis' (in Keynes's phraseology) to the dynamic treatment of population as a *variable* in long-run economic analysis instead of as a given datum—a treatment that is of particular significance for overpopulated underdeveloped economies.

Friedrich List (1789–1846)

Representing as he did the industrially backward Germany of his day, Friedrich List became the principal champion of industrialization through economic nationalism in general and through protectionism in particular. His theory of economic development still has a powerful appeal to present-day under-

---

[1] See Keynes's charming and penetrating biography of Malthus in *Essays in Biography*, Horizon Press, N.Y., 1951, pp. 81–124.

[2] Keynes, *ibid.*, pp. 107–8.

developed economies that are politically independent but economically dominated by advanced economies.[1] In his book, *Das nationale System der politischen Ökonomie*, List contributed a new element to the theory of economic development, namely, a theoretical justification of protective tariffs specifically designed to encourage the growth of indigenous 'infant industries' until those industries can compete with foreign industries on the basis of comparative advantage. List's theory of industrialization through protectionism, via his intellectual child Henry C. Carey,[2] played a pioneering role in the sheltered development of American manufacturing industry, albeit beyond the historical justification of the 'infant industry' argument in some cases.

List, while he provided no concrete safeguards against the danger of protected industries becoming self-defeating marginal industries, nevertheless called attention to the *element of nationalism* as a crucial driving force in the economic development of 'young' nations—an element which had been overlooked by Adam Smith and other 'free traders' who tacitly assumed the existence of universal full employment and full development. For his original insight into the incompatibility of under*development* and free trade List occupies a rather unique place in the history of international economics, just as Keynes does for his demonstration of the incompatibility of under*employment* and free trade. The technical weakness of protection as a particular implementation should not be exaggerated to the point of missing List's broader contributions such as indicated above.

Karl Marx (1818–1883)

Marx contributed to the theory of economic development in three respects, namely, in the broad respect of providing an economic interpretation of history, in the narrower respect of specifying the motivating forces of capitalistic development,

---

[1] For List's influence on present-day underdeveloped economies see, e.g. *Niveles de Vida y Dessarrollo Economico* (a symposium on economic development), National School of Economics of the University of Mexico, 1953.

[2] My colleague Professor Broadus Mitchell kindly informed me that List was an intimate friend of Mathew Carey, the father of Henry Carey, and that Mathew Carey enlisted the intellectual support of List, who had come to America, for American industrialization through protective tariffs.

and in the final respect of suggesting an alternative path of planned economic development. As one writer puts it, 'the efforts of Karl Marx to reach an integrated theory of economic and social evolution surpassed in ambition anything that had been attempted by the classical economists'.[1]

In the preface of his *Critique of Political Economy* Marx outlined his 'materialistic' conception of historical evolution, according to which economic institutions, while they are products of social evolution, are themselves capable of influencing the course of social progress. This point of view may have inspired Schumpeter's method of treating historical events and social institutions as endogenous variables in economic analysis instead of exogenous parameters.[2] More generally, the same point of view underlines the broader 'inter-disciplinary' approaches of contemporary writings.[3] It is in his major work, *Capital*, that Marx makes the turbulent process of capitalistic development depend on (a) profit-takers' savings at the expense of wage-earners' consumption, (b) the investment of those savings in new capital propelled by the competition for profits but inhibited by the disappearance of investment opportunities as a result of both underconsumption and overinvestment, and (c) the sociologically given size and technologically given productivity of the labour population.[4] This Marxian theory of capitalistic development anticipates many modern long-run theories, namely, the stagnation theories of Keynes and Hansen,[5] the dynamic theories of Harrod and Domar,[6] the 'cyclical growth' theories of Schumpeter, Kalecki, Kaldor, and

[1] See T. Haavelmo. *A Study in the Theory of Economic Evolution*, North-Holland Publishing Co., Amsterdam, 1954, p. 12.

[2] For his tacitly approving discussion of Marx's methodology, see J. A. Schumpeter, *Capitalism, Socialism and Democracy*, Harper & Brothers, N.Y., 1942, and *Ten Great Economists: From Marx to Keynes*, Oxford, N.Y., 1954.

[3] Such as one sees in the pages of the University of Chicago's *Economic Development and Cultural Change*.

[4] For a modern Marxian interpretation, see P. Sweezy, *The Theory of Capitalist Development*, Oxford, N.Y., 1944.

[5] See J. M. Keynes, '*Some Economic Consequences of a Declining Population*', *Eugenics Review*, April, 1937; A. H. Hansen, 'Economic Progress and Declining Population Growth', *American Economic Review*, March 1939.

[6] R. F. Harrod, *Towards a Dynamic Economics*, Macmillan, London, 1948; E. D. Domar, 'Expansion and Employment', *American Economic Review*, March, 1947.

Goodwin,[1] and Mrs. Joan Robinson's theory of structural underemployment.[2]

Ironically, however, it is Marx's perception of planned development expressed in his minor writings which presumably has had a greater impact on the actual economic development of countries such as Soviet Russia and Mainland China. Marx's notion of planned development also seems to appeal to those backward countries which are in a great hurry to industrialize even at the risk of excessive national 'belt-tightening' and of unnecessary isolation from advanced countries.[3] It remains to be seen whether the future generations will learn more or less from the spirit of Marx which regards the State *ownership* of the instruments of production as a historically necessary condition of planned development[4] than from the spirit of Keynes which views the State *control* of those instruments as an economically desirable condition of it.[5]

POST-CLASSICAL DOCTRINES

John Maynard Keynes (1883–1946)

To those who remember the name of Keynes only by his short-run dictum that 'in the long run we are all dead' it may come as a bit of surprise to discover that he had anything at all to say about the long run. True, Keynes made his greatest theoretical contribution in the field of short-run economic analysis, but his short run was never too short to let him take wings into the long run, as the reader of his varied writings knows. Moreover, Keynes's insights and theories will be found

---

[1] J. A. Schumpeter, *Business Cycles*, McGraw-Hill, N.Y., 1938, M. Kalecki, *Theory of Economic Dynamics*, Rinehart, N.Y., 1951 (esp. Part 6); N. Kaldor, 'The Relation of Economic Growth and Cyclical Fluctuation', *Economic Journal*, March 1954; R. M. Goodwin, 'A Model of Cyclical Growth', *The Business Cycle in the Post-War World* (E. Lundberg, ed.), Macmillan, London, 1955.

[2] See 'Marx and Keynes', in her *Collected Economic Papers*, Kelley, N.Y., 1951; also her *An Essay in Marxian Economics*, London, 1942.

[3] Cf., M. Bronfenbrenner, 'The Appeal of Confiscation in Economic Development', *Economic Development and Cultural Change*, April 1955.

[4] For a helpful summary of these speculative ideas of Marx as well as his definitive economic theories, see E. Roll, *A History of Economic Thought* (3rd ed.), Prentice-Hall, N.Y., 1956, Chap. 6.

[5] For his reasons for preferring control to ownership, see *General Theory*, pp. 378–81.

to have greater relevance to underdeveloped economies than is commonly supposed, particularly to those which are inclined to develop along democratic rather than authoritarian lines.[1] What exactly, then, are Keynes's contributions to the theory of economic development? The following is at least one answer.

Let us begin with Keynes's broader insights. In his essay entitled 'Economic Possibilities for Our Grandchildren' (1930) Keynes suggested that the future rate of economic progress would depend on (a) 'our power to control population', (b) 'our determination to avoid wars and civil dissensions', (c) 'our willingness to entrust to science the direction of those matters which are properly the concern of science', and (d) 'the rate of accumulation as fixed by the margin between our production and our consumption'.[2] Here we have the most comprehensive outline of the fundamental conditions of economic progress, embracing as it does all the wisdom of classical thinkers and underlining as it does all the complicated growth models of contemporary writers. How to make such broad intuitive insights operationally significant is a task that was left for post-Keynesian economists to fulfill. But Keynes himself made a significant start in the direction of measurable and testable hypotheses about the determinate rate of economic progress, as we shall see presently.

Keynes made no systematic analysis of capitalistic development, but in his *General Theory* he made a number of sporadic and digressive observations which it is interesting to compare with Marx's views already mentioned as well as with Schumpeter's theory discussed subsequently. If Marx was a prophet of doom, Keynes can be said to have been a prophet of boom, as far as the future possibilities of capitalism are concerned. For Keynes viewed capitalism essentially as a *mechanism* capable of being repaired and improved so as to help rather than hinder human progress toward that 'destination of economic bliss' when 'the accumulation of wealth is no longer of high social

---

[1] For an unmistakable impact of Keynes on underdeveloped economies, see Indian Economic Association, *Keynesian Economics in Relation to Underdeveloped Countries*, Japipur, December 1953: also the issue of *Indian Journal of Economics* published in commemoration of the 10th death anniversary of Lord Keynes (July 1956).

[2] See his *Essays in Persuasion*, p. 373.

importance' and when the pursuit of spiritual and artistic improvements can have free play. By contrast, Marx (and Schumpeter) regarded capitalism essentially as an *organism* that grows only to decay and die out of existence, presumably carrying within itself the seeds of self-destruction. However, Keynes's theory of stagnation gave modern expression to some endogenous elements stressed in Marx's 'breakdown' theory, such as chronic underconsumption, general over-production, and the secularly declining rate of profit.[1] The important practical difference between them, though, is that Keynes sought the remedy in the modification of *laissez-faire* capitalism through 'deliberate State action', whereas Marx dogmatically dismissed any and all such State actions as inevitably and invariably benefiting only 'the capitalist class' instead of the economy as a whole.

Turning now to more technical aspects of Keynes, first and above all, there is his theory of effective demand, without which Harrod's growth theory might not have seen the light. For it is but a step from Keynes's static condition of saving–investment equilibrium in terms of levels to go logically to Harrod's dynamic condition of saving–investment equilibrium in terms of ratios, as J. R. Hicks pointed out[2] and hence to Harrod's 'warranted' rate of growth, as will be discussed in subsequent chapters. Harrod's original dynamic essay[3] is remarkable, both because Harrod had the imagination and foresight to turn to very important long-run considerations at a time when most of his contemporaries were still engrossed in short-run considerations, and because Keynes as the editor of *Economic Journal* apparently had the generosity and sagacity to encourage the publication of his pupil's essay which stressed the capacity-increasing aspect of saving in contradistinction to its demand-decreasing aspect which he had been emphasizing. In a growth model similar to Harrod's, Domar also made an attempt to synthesize Keynes's multiplier theory (the demand

[1] Compare S. Tsuru, 'Keynes versus Marx: The Methodology of Aggregates', in *Post-Keynesian Economics* (K. Kurihara, ed.) Rutgers Univ. Press and Allen & Unwin, 1954.

[2] See his 'Mr Harrod's Dynamic Theory', *Economica*, May 1949.

[3] See his 'An Essay in Dynamic Theory', *Economic Journal*, March 1939.

or 'income effect' of investment) and the classical theory of productivity (the 'sigma effect' of investment).[1]

Once the level of output is determined by effective demand in given conditions of supply (esp. with a constant stock of capital), as in Keynes's short-run theory, the next logical question to ask is: what would happen to that output if the stock of capital increased to change the conditions of supply?, as is asked and answered in dynamic economics. Apropos, Mrs. Joan Robinson parenthetically states: 'This explains the paradox that although Keynes's *General Theory* is strictly static in form, it has opened the way for a great outburst of analysis of dynamic problems'.[2] It is also significant that Nurkse,[3] together with Mrs. Robinson,[4] shifted the direction of dynamic economics to underdeveloped economies, both stressing the causal importance of investment-*demand* as well as of capital accumulation for developing economies. It remains to be argued out whether the growth of capital is impossible without reducing consumption, as classical economists believed, or impossible without simultaneously increasing consumption, as Keynes taught, or yet possible without changing consumption, as Nurkse has it.[5]

Keynes's national income analysis is a minimal base of reference for development programming and a technical basis for estimating saving, consumption, investment, employment, and other operationally significant variables of economic development. This simple fact is mentioned only because it is often overlooked by the practical men of affairs who care not whence the theoretical basis of national income accounting comes. One cannot begin discussing economic development in an operationally significant way without reference to the quantities and functional relations stressed in Keynes's *General Theory*,

[1] Domar, *op. cit.*

[2] In the preface of her *The Rate of Interest and Other Essays*, Macmillan, London, 1952.

[3] R. Nurkse, *Problems of Capital formation in Underdeveloped Countries*, Blackwell, Oxford, 1953.

[4] J. Robinson, 'Mr Harrod's Dynamics', *Economic Journal*, March 1949; also *The Rate of Interest*, etc.

[5] Nurkse's position will be discussed in some detail in connection with disguised unemployment as a 'saving potential'. See Chapter 6. For an overall appraisal of Nurkse's theory of 'balanced growth' see Chapter 11.

though those variables must be supplemented by what Harrod calls 'fundamental conditions' such as population, technology, and resources in any long-run analysis. Moreover, Keynes's national income *analysis* is a constant reminder that the mere accumulation of statistical data and the refinement of measuring techniques are not very useful *without theory*, without some plausible hypotheses to facilitate the meaningful interpretation of the behaviour of national income components (e.g. consumption and investment), and particularly to guide the fruitful industrialization of actual underdeveloped economies within technical limits.

Last but not least is Keynes's contributions to the idea and establishment of a World Bank for Reconstruction and Development so colourfully described in Harrod's biography of Keynes.[1] Here Keynes flatly contradicted Marx and his followers who considered international heterogeneity in the economic field as a permanent way in which advanced capitalistic nations exploited backward nations,[2] for Keynes looked upon international economic homogenization as a path to universal prosperity and lasting world peace. He deemed the World Bank to be a proper instrumentality for making the saving propensities of the world's richer members compatible with the development needs of its poorer members. It is not the detail of its lending operations, which may have to be revised and improved from time to time, but the *idea* of a World Bank for the specific purposes of reconstruction and development that is both novel and significant. For that idea owes much to Keynes's bold imagination and genuine internationalism, and promises a far-reaching influence on the future conduct of divers nations in general and on the future economic development of underdeveloped countries in particular.[3]

Joseph A. Schumpeter (1883–1950)

Schumpeter was the first among modern economists to cut out economic development as a specialized area of economic

---

[1] See his *The Life of John Maynard Keynes*, Harcourt, Brace & Co., N.Y., 1951.

[2] Cf., E. Heimann, 'Marxism and Underdeveloped Countries', *Social Research*, Sept. 1952.

[3] See United Nations, *Measures for the Economic Development of Underdeveloped Countries*, N.Y., 1951. Also see the appendix to this volume.

analysis. This he did in his then little heeded book, *The Theory of Economic Development*, published in German in 1911. Even the appearance of its English edition twenty-three years later did not make much of an impression, for the world was much too preoccupied with the pressing short-run problems of depression and mass unemployment to pay serious attention to long-run problems. It is only in the present post-war period of reconstruction and development, given effect by the diminution of cyclical problems,[1] that economists are beginning to take a 'new look' at Schumpeter's theory of economic development. However, the ideological and institutional overtones of Schumpeter's theory[2] weaken its technical value and limit its practical applicability.

According to Schumpeter, capitalism develops by jerks owing to the erratic interaction of the entrepreneur (innovator), innovation, and credit, and is destined to give way to some form of socialism owing to its successful achievements such as mass production, mass education, and big business as well as to its inevitable accompaniments such as government regulation, intellectual resentment, and trade unionism. Here Schumpeter shares Marx's conviction about the 'inevitable' breakdown of capitalism,[3] though the former ascribes it to the very *success* of capitalism while the latter attributes it to its *failure*. Be that as it may, few would doubt the descriptive value of the entrepreneur, innovation, and credit as institutionally realistic explanatory variables of historical economic development. For the lack of private initiative and risk-taking, the absence of innovational ingenuity, and the primitive state of banking facilities and capital markets are common institutional characteristics of underdeveloped market economies even today.

Yet Schumpeter's interpretation of the innovator exclusively in terms of the private entrepreneur may be thrown into question in this day and age of mixed economies.[4] Even more

---

[1] For some of the reasons for this diminution, see *The Business Cycle in the Post-War World*, op. cit.

[2] Especially as extended in his later work, *Capitalism, Socialism and Democracy*.

[3] See Shumpeter's last message 'The March into Socialism', *American Economic Review*, May 1950.

[4] See W. A. Lewis, *The Theory of Economic Growth*, Allen & Unwin, London, 1955.

controversial is his over-optimistic notion of innovation, as far as underdeveloped economies are concerned. If innovation takes the form of improved techniques of production, it has the advantage of increasing the productivity of labour without necessarily changing the existing stock of capital. Such an improvement in labour productivity would certainly be welcome in a capital-poor economy, to be sure. But if a capital-poor economy represents also a community with rapid population growth, the adoption of techniques requiring less labour relatively to the given stock of capital may aggravate the problem of unemployment. If, on the other hand, innovation takes the form of expanded plant and equipment, it has the advantage of increasing the productivity of labour without necessarily changing techniques of production. But then an underdeveloped economy may not save enough to realize the desired 'innovational investment' in new plant and equipment. Insofar, moreover, as innovational investment depends on the private expectation of profit and the capital-using state of technology, an underdeveloped economy may not find such investment to be a very reliable way to accumulate capital for rapid economic development. For the vagaries of profit and the dynamics of technology are not always such as to encourage innovational investment in quantities that an underdeveloped economy may desire.[1]

Schumpeter's emphasis on the role of private credit, while it correctly reflects the historical role of bank credits and corporate debt-equity financings in the development of capitalism, nevertheless not only obscures the real basis of such monetary instruments (i.e. real savings arising from production minus consumption) but abstracts out public credit, deficit financing, budgetary savings, and other fiscal operations of the government. Moreover, it is merely a truism to say that industrialization is aided by the development of banking facilities, for it is repeating the classical observation that 'money and banking' institutions expedite the transition from a barter economy to an exchange economy. It would be more helpful for development programming to suggest what measures

[1] See S. Yoshida, 'Schumpeterian System and Monopoly', and K. Shibayama, 'Monopoly and Economic Development', *Economic Studies Quarterly*, June 1957.

of fiscal–monetary policy would increase the rate of growth of output or promote the stable growth of output at a given rate.

All the same, Schumpeter will probably go down in the history of economic thought as one who more than anyone else stressed the *dynamics of technology* both as the most important single cause of economic development in general and as the key explanation for the cyclical growth of capitalism in particular. Because of his emphasis on institutional factors, Schumpeter's theory of economic development is, contrary to his intentions, likely to appeal to those less developed economies which are inclined to make a drastic break with the tradition.

CHAPTER II

THE STRUCTURE OF AN UNDER-DEVELOPED ECONOMY

STRUCTURAL analysis is an indispensable preliminary to any behavioural analysis. So that we may gain deeper insight into the fundamental problems common to all underdeveloped economies, let us begin with a description of the structural characteristics and determinants of an underdeveloped economy. In so doing we shall, however, select only those characteristics and determinants which seem operationally most significant and economically most important. To sharpen the issue, we shall contrast underdeveloped economies with advanced economies in this survey chapter.

INDICATORS OF ECONOMIC UNDERDEVELOPMENT

Low Per Capita Real Income

Perhaps the most serviceable single indicator of an underdeveloped economy is low per capita real income,[1] whatever else may be said to characterize such an economy. The qualifying phrase 'per capita' puts a welfare content into an otherwise non-normative indicator, for it immediately suggests that an underdeveloped economy also represents a community whose material well-being in terms of consumption per head remains unimproved year after year and decade after decade. It also suggests that an economy may be underdeveloped, not necessarily because its propensity to procreate is too strong relative to its capacity to produce, but possibly because its capacity to produce is too weak relative to its propensity to

---

[1] Per capita national income is defined in the form $y = Y_r/P$, where y is average income, Y_r real national income, and P the size of population. As such, per capita national income is a good measure of economic *progress*, in contradistinction to economic *growth*. This distinction is important because there can be no economic progress if the growth of population exceeds the growth of output so that each person is worse off than before.

procreate. Thus the 'per capita' qualification would take care of the case of 'underpopulated' underdeveloped economies as well as the more common case of 'overpopulated' ones.

As for the 'real' income[1] involved in the above indicator, it helps to distinguish between the physical volume of output and its monetary value. It is the former, not the latter, which is a true measure of productivity and welfare in terms of physical goods produced and consumed. Moreover, the concept of real income safeguards one against the myopic mistake of viewing pecuniary profitability as if it represented physical productivity—a mistake that conceivably might lead to a serious misdirection of productive resources to the possible detriment of long-term economic growth.

Deficient Natural Resources

Another operational indicator of an underdeveloped economy is deficient natural resources in relation to the size of population.[2] So important or human well-being did this non-reproducible exhaustive material wealth appear to be, especially in the absence of counterbalancing technology, that classical economists established 'land' as a separate and distinct factor of production, on a par with reproducible 'capital' and 'labour'. So impressed were some of those classical economists by the inelasticity of total 'land' relative to rapid population growth that they reached the 'dismal' conclusion that the 'law of diminishing returns' would always operate to keep the standard of life depressed. Although the economies technologically advanced have greatly benefited by 'economies of mass production' instead, the technologically backward economies with rapidly growing populations but without sufficient natural resources still remain peculiarly susceptible to the relentless operation of the law of diminishing returns.

With the exception of a few, most of the actual underdeveloped economies are confronted with the problem of 'over-

---

[1] Real national income is expressible in the form $Y_r = Y_m/P(t)$, where Y_m is money income and $P(t)$ the average price at time t (as compared with the base period chosen). It is the behaviour of real income, as such, that is significant for long-run analysis.

[2] Cf., W. S. & E. S. Woytinsky, *World Population and Production*, Twentieth Century Fund, N.Y., 1953.

population' precisely because the per capita amount of principal natural resources[1] (e.g. arable land, coal deposits, oil deposits, iron deposits, and forest) is too small to aid substantial industrialization and so to overcome a 'superfluous population'. It is to be emphasized, however, than an economy with abundant natural resources but without the necessary technology or capital to develop them is almost as 'poor' as one without those resources. Yet the opulence of natural resources is *per se* a condition favourable to technological progress. Thus viewed, an underdeveloped economy is likely to represent also an 'overpopulated' nation if for no other reason than that the paucity of natural resources serves to stress the didactic significance of Malthus's warning even for present-day underdeveloped economies, especially the technologically backward.

Insufficient Capital Equipment

The insufficient amount of physical capital in existence is so characteristic a feature in all underdeveloped economies that they are often called simply 'capital-poor' economies. Not only that, but so strategically important is the role of capital in economic development that some writers discuss little else.[2] Since the stock of physical capital existing at any point of time is the result of past saving and investment, an underdeveloped economy with a relatively small stock of capital may be said to represent also a low-saving, low-investing community. This latter low-saving, low-investing state of affairs may in turn be attributed to low family incomes, the smallness of the thrifty middle-class, poorly organized capital markets and saving institutions, 'conspicuous consumption' among the well-to-do, and other factors affecting saving habits. It is to be noticed that low saving as a measure of the insufficient supply of

[1] To the extent that an economy possesses relatively abundant resources other than agricultural land, it is capable of overcoming the Malthusian problem of 'overpopulation' more easily by developing domestic manufacturing and exporting goods in exchange for foodstuffs. This seems to be what Great Britain did yesterday and what Mainland China is trying to do today. But if an economy is lacking in both arable land and other natural resources relative to a growing population, the Malthusian problem is all the more serious. This is actually the case in Japan, though she is a highly industrialized nation. Japan might not be less developed than Western economies were it not for her deficient natural resources.

[2] See, e.g. R. Nurkse, *Problems of Capital Formation in Underdeveloped Countries.*

capital is a common problem peculiar to all underdeveloped economies, whereas the demand for capital (investment, *ex ante*) presents a problem not alone for underdeveloped economies.

If what the community saves is assumed to materialize in an equal amount of investment, it is possible to classify three patterns of economic development according as the community's stock of capital is increasing, constant, or decreasing.[1] Thus we have a *progressing* economy if the community consumes less than its net production so as to permit a net addition to the existing stock of capital, that is, net investment.[2] Next we have a *static* economy if the community consumes as much as its net production so as to get zero net investment, that is, to leave the existing stock of capital unchanged. Lastly we have a *retrogressing* economy if the community consumes more than its net production so as to permit negative net investment, that is, to let the existing stock of capital decrease without replacement. Thus if a country has only a small constant stock of capital, this creates a presumption against the existence of rapid economic development.

Technological Backwardness

Still another operational indicator can be seen in the backward state of technology, as measured in terms of the average cost of production or of the high ratio of labour or capital to output. The total real cost of production (i.e. an input of capital, labour, and other factors required to produce an output) is generally higher in the economies technologically retarded than in the economies technologically advanced. It is in this 'real' sense that an underdeveloped economy is said to represent a high-cost area, despite low money wages entering the money cost of production. Conversely, an advanced

---

[1] These patterns may be represented symbolically as follows:
Progressing economy: $(dY/dt) > 0$ due to $(dK/dt) > 0$, $(Y > C, S = I > 0)$.
Static economy: $(dY/dt) = 0$ due to $(dK/dt) = 0$, $(Y = C, S = I = 0)$.
Retrogressing economy: $(dY/dt) < 0$ due to $(dK/dt) < 0$, $(Y < C, S = I < 0)$.
Here Y is net national product, K real capital, C consumption, S savings, I net investment, and t time.

[2] Apropos, present-day underdeveloped economies' net investment runs at the rate of 3 per cent. to 5 per cent. of national product and advanced economies, at the rate of 10 per cent. to 15 per cent., according to S. Kuznets. (See his 'Economic Growth and Income Inequality', *American Economic Review*, March 1955).

economy with 'economies of mass production' can be said to represent a low-cost area, despite high money costs of labour services that prevail in that economy.

Moreover, a technologically backward economy is likely to have both a high labour-output ratio and a high capital-output ratio as a rule and on the average,[1] given constant factor prices (wages, interest, etc.), thus reflecting a generally low productivity of labour and a generally low productivity of capital. Backward conditions of technology are reflected in the preponderance of unskilled, untrained workers. Accordingly, with the given stock of capital equipment, more labour is required per unit of output than if the workers involved were technically better trained. Thus technological backwardness tends to increase the ratio of labour to output for the whole economy. Backward conditions of technology are also reflected in the large amount of capital equipment required to produce a national output. For if inadequate know-how causes labour productivity Y/N to rise in smaller proportion than the capital-labour ratio K/N, the capital-output ratio will rise via $K/Y = (KN)/(YN)$.[2] Technological backwardness is at least one important factor tending to increase the capital-output ratio of an underdeveloped economy. The extent to which flexible factor prices can be relied upon for reversing this tendency remains yet to be discussed.

Structural Underemployment

Structural underemployment is another characteristic of underdeveloped economies. This type of unemployment arises from the insufficiency of capital equipment even when fully utilized, and even if effective demand is sufficient. It is useful to distinguish among *available* labour (the existing labour force governed by population growth), *employed* labour (that part of the labour force actually employed in response to changing effective demand, given the stock of capital), and *required* labour (that maximum potential amount of labour which is employable by fully utilizing the existing equipment at the

---

[1] For details see Chapter 5 of this book.

[2] For controversial points of view see the subsection entitled 'The Capital Output Ratio as a Policy Parameter' in Chapter 5 (esp. n. 8).

given pattern of effective demand, and which is capable of changing as a result of a change in capital equipment or in the productivity of capital). Then underdeveloped economies will be found to have, as a rule and on the average, the excess of available labour over required labour, the difference between them being a measure of *structural underemployment*.

The existence of structural underemployment in underdeveloped economies is due primarily to the chronic shortage of capital relative to a growing labour population. By contrast, mass unemployment in developed economies arises mainly from the cyclical shortage of effective demand relative to both the given population and capital stock. The following illustration may be useful in passing. Let $N =$ available labour, N_e = employed labour, and N_r = required labour, as parenthetically defined above. Then it is possible to classify the major types of unemployment broadly as: (a) total unemployment in *any* economy = $N - N_e$, (b) structural underemployment in an *underdeveloped* economy = $N - N_r$, and (c) cyclical unemployment in an *advanced* economy = $N_r - N_e$. However, an actual underdeveloped economy is likely to experience both types of unemployment simultaneously, as will be elaborated in a later chapter. The excess of available labour (N) over required labour (N_r) means that the existing stock of capital when fully utilized is still insufficient to absorb all the labour available in productive employment. On the other hand, the excess of required labour (N_r) over employed labour (N_e) means that the actually employed part of available labour is smaller than if the existing stock of capital were fully utilized (as when effective demand is sufficient). A more rigorous and dynamic treatment of these different types of unemployment will have to be postponed until we come to discuss the dual unemployment of underdeveloped economies (Chapter 6).

Extreme Income Disparities

Another operational earmark of an underdeveloped economy can be found in an extremely high degree of income inequality, as measured by the deviation from the perfect line of equality in the Lorenz-curve sense. The Lorenz curve for a typical underdeveloped economy should be expected to be much farther away from the 45° line of equality than is the curve for a typical developed economy, indicating that the income of the 10 per cent. of the population with the lowest incomes falls short of 10 per cent. of total income by a much greater amount in the case of underdeveloped countries than in that of developed countries. This accords with the common observation that the gap between wealth and poverty is exceedingly wide in most underdeveloped economies, with the virtual absence of the 'middle class'. To be sure, in some exceptional cases extreme income inequalities are not permitted to prevail as a matter of political principle or humanitarian philosophy. But such exceptions do not alter the fundamental fact that income disparities are greater in underdeveloped economies as a whole than in developed ones and during the industrializing phase of a particular economy than during its industrial maturity.[1] Two general reasons for this fact may be mentioned here.

First, industrializing underdeveloped economies are under strong economic compulsion to maintain, if reluctantly, a high degree of income inequality for the purpose of speeding up capital accumulation.[2] For since the wealthy usually have higher marginal propensities to save than do the poor, the community's propensity to save would be the higher, and the supply of capital the greater, the larger is the proportion of families falling far above and far below the average family income. Whether extreme income disparities are or are not really conducive to economic development is another matter, however. Second, in underdeveloped economies the level and rate of increase of real income are so low that they lack the economic basis necessary for developing, on a significant and increasing scale, such equalizing forces as progressive taxation, social insurance, trade unionism, mass education, mass production, anti-monopoly legislation, and occupational mobility. For unless the size of the national income pie itself is enlarged, the relative share of any particular income group cannot be

[1] For some past and recent empirical data see S. Kuznets, 'Economic Growth and Income Inequality', *op. cit.*

[2] This compulsion does not seem to exist in those underdeveloped economies which let their governments serve as the chief saving agency, and seems to exist to a less extent in others with free and easy access to foreign capital.

augmented except at the expense of another, thereby leaving room for the effective operation of equalizing forces.

External Indebtedness

The last characteristic to be mentioned is the long-run debtor position of an underdeveloped economy considered as an 'open' system with foreign-trade relations. Persistent external indebtedness on the part of any nation fundamentally reflects its weak export capacity relatively to its strong import needs. We may express an underdeveloped economy's long-run debtor position in the form $B = P + M - E$, where B is net foreign borrowing, P net foreign payments on capital account, M real imports, and E real exports. The equation indicates that net foreign borrowing tends to rise as a result of an increase in imports or of a decrease in exports. It also indicates that a rise in net foreign payments would necessitate further borrowing unless such a rise in net foreign payments is offset by an equal rise in exports or by an equal fall in imports. Thus viewed, it is no accident that most of the now developed economies went through the so-called 'borrowing stage' of their industrialization. For that matter, even the United States had been a debtor nation before World War I.

If an underdeveloped economy represented also a long-run debtor nation in the past, is there any reason why it should continue to represent one in the future? Several answers may be given tentatively. For one thing, most underdeveloped economies are so far behind advanced economies technologically as to suffer competitive disadvantages in a world market, thereby rendering themselves susceptible to import surpluses and hence to net foreign borrowing on a continuing basis. Another answer is that present-day underdeveloped economies seem less concerned with the short-run problem of external payments than with the long-run implications of foreign borrowing or their economic development. Furthermore, the possibility of financing the necessary imports in excess of exports through gold sales or foreign gifts is at best limited to a short period and at worst closed to most underdeveloped economies even in a longer period. Lastly, there is today the widespread realization that the economic development of underdeveloped

c

countries should not be left to the accident of *laissez-faire*
international capital movements but should be deliberately
aided by the World Bank for Reconstruction and Development
and other international agencies whose policy it is to make
long-term developmental loans at liberal terms and on a
technical basis. Such planned multinational lending and
borrowing have the advantages of inducing capital-rich nations
to lend abroad without the epithet of 'imperialists' being
hurled at them and persuading capital-poor nations to
borrow abroad without the traditional fear of 'political
strings' and without the necessity of undue national 'belt-
tightening'.

The above outline may have provided a useful set of criteria
by which to distinguish a typical underdeveloped economy
from a typical advanced economy, although some actual
underdeveloped economies fall in the marginal category
between them.

STRUCTURAL DETERMINANTS OF DEVELOPMENT

Having seen the measurable manifestations of an underdeveloped economy, we may now proceed to draw a general
sketch of the causal factors underlying those manifestations.
The limited intention here is to make a preliminary survey of
the general nature and significance of certain technical factors
affecting both the pattern and speed of economic development
in any modern society. Thus the basic determinants to be discussed here apply to developed as well as underdeveloped
economies, though obviously with greater or less force.

Labour Population

The real income of an economy considered as a 'closed'
system fundamentally depends on the technical relations of
labour population, capital stock, and technological advance.
Taking the stock of capital and the state of technology as
given, we can concentrate on the role of labour population in
economic development. To illustrate, let Y = national output,
N = labour population, and H = average labour productivity. Then we have the equivalents:

(1)   National output: $Y = H \cdot N$
(2)   Labour population: $N = Y/H$
(3)   Labour productivity: $H = Y/N$.

Here Y is potential output from full employment, N the labour population when fully employed, and H the technologically determined ratio of total output to total labour.[1]

The above equivalents indicate that national output is capable of increasing if the labour population employed increases relatively to the constant productivity of labour or if the productivity of labour rises relatively to the constant labour population. If the ratio of output to labour (H) is technologically fixed, we have the simplest case of output growing *pari passu* with the increasing number of hands, as it were. But an increase in the number of hands is complicated by an increase in the number of mouths to feed. For if the entire population (not just the labour population) should grow faster than does total output, economic progress in terms of rising per capita real income would not occur despite the fact that output grows as a result of a growing labour force. This implies that labour productivity (H) would have to be increased if there is to be economic progress along with output growth. The main point is that, given the culturally determined (e.g. the choice between work and leisure) fraction of the total population that is ready and willing to work, the speed of the growth of national output depends, among other things, on the quantity and quality (productivity) of employed labour.

The Stock of Real Capital
Another basic determinant of economic development is the quantity of real capital available. In the present context the term 'capital' refers to man-made physical instruments of

---

[1] Let, e.g. $Y = \$40$ billion (in constant prices), $N = 40$ million (workers), and total man-hours per unit of labour per year $= 2,000$ (on the assumption of a forty-hour week and fifty weeks a year). Then $Y/N = 40,000/40 \times 2,000 = 4/8 = 0.5$. If the average working hours per week were more than forty, output per man-hour (H) would of course be smaller than 0.5. Also, actual unemployment would reduce the value of N and hence that of Y, unless otherwise offset by an increase in H.

production which normally come into being as a result of net production exceeding physical consumption,[1] that is, of positive real saving and net investment. The historical role played by the accumulation of capital, as such, in the industrialization of nations has been so singularly crucial as to have distinguished their methods of production, if not their whole economic systems, as 'capitalistic' or 'round-about'. To isolate the effect of a change in the stock of capital, it is convenient to hold the supply of labour constant. Then it is possible to consider the following relations:

(4)   National output: $Y = J \cdot K$
(5)   Capital stock: $K = Y/J$
(6)   Capital productivity: $J = Y/K.$

Here K is real capital and J the average productivity of capital.

The above relations (4)–(6) show the theoretical possibility of output growing as a result of an increase in real capital or in the productivity of capital or in both. If the productivity of capital (J) is considered technically given, then one way to increase output is by augmenting the stock of real capital (K). The question naturally arises as to why the stock of capital increases at the average rate of 5 per cent. in an underdeveloped economy and at 15 per cent. in an advanced economy. This question may best be answered by separate reference to the propensity to save representing the supply of capital and to the propensity to invest representing the demand for capital. The general determinants of the demand and supply of capital are well known, but one must, in the particular case of underdeveloped economies, allow for the possibilities of 'forced saving' (via e.g. budgetary surpluses, priority allocations, austerity rationing, compulsory saving-bond programmes, inter-governmental borrowing, and foreign-exchange controls)

---

[1] Some consider it appropriate to broaden the concept of net investment to include such outlays as might be made for 'increasing the efficiency of the workers by health and sanitation programmes, expansion of educational facilities to reduce illiteracy or provide technical training,' etc. (See N. S. Buchanan and H. S Ellis, *Approaches to Economic Development*, Twentieth Century Fund, 1955, p. 68.) However, such outlays do not *directly* result in the accumulation of capital in our sense.

supplementing deficient 'voluntary saving' and public investment complementing private investment.

Technological Advance

Technology is the last internal determinant to be mentioned in this preliminary survey. To treat technology in an operationally meaningful way, it is convenient to express it in terms of certain technological parameters, such as the labour-output ratio and the capital-output ratio. Then a decrease in either of these co-efficients can be taken to mean technological advance in the economic field, for a fall in the labour-output ratio or the capital-output ratio implies a rise in the average productivity of labour or of capital. This can be illustrated in the following reformulations of equations (3) and (6):

(7) $\qquad (1/H) = (N/Y)$ (labour-output ratio)

(8) $\qquad (1/J) = (K/Y)$ (capital-output ratio).

National output can be shown to grow as a result of a fall in the labour-output ratio (a rise in labour productivity) or a fall in the capital-output ratio (a rise in capital productivity), other things remaining equal. An interesting question to ask, at this juncture, is: what forces make for lower labour-output and capital-output ratios reflecting higher productivities of labour and capital? It is tempting to answer this question in purely technological terms, but the temptation must be resisted if human motives, market conditions, deliberate actions, and other interdependent forces are not to be lost sight of. Accordingly a secular fall in the labour-output ratio might be attributed to a combination of such forces as the greater division of labour, the technical and financial ease with which other factors can be substituted for labour, the increasing adoption of 'labour-saving' devices, higher-wage movements, and slow population growth. As for the technological and other forces making for a secular decline in the capital-output ratio, one might mention capital-saving inventions and innovations, the greater durability structure of capital, high long-term interest rates, the structural shift from more capital-intensive to less capital-intensive industries, and the long-run elasticity of substitution of capital for other productive factors. These secular changes in the technological parameters may be of a predominantly autonomous nature, as Marx and Schumpeter were inclined to view them, or of a predominantly induced nature (induced by market conditions including relative factor prices), as the traditional analysis has it.

External Determinants

Two basic external determinants of internal growth are a nation's capacity to export and its ability and willingness to import capital. The first of these determinants is crucial in the long run, since the ability to pay for a stustained import surplus (i.e. a net addition to national output) depends ultimately on a nation's capacity to produce and export the kinds of goods and services desired by other nations and at a competitively advantageous cost. The second determinant is important especially in the early stage of a nation's industrialization during which its ability to export to pay for needed imports is technically limited and therefore must be supplemented by foreign borrowing.

We have learned from modern analysis that foreign trade variables have contradictory effects on domestic income and domestic productivity. For exports exert an inflationary influence on domestic income but a deflationary one on domestic productivity, while imports have a deflationary effect on domestic income but an inflationary effect on domestic productivity. Thus it is important to investigate both the multiplier effect of foreign trade and the productivity effect of it, especially if one is interested in the possibility of achieving and maintaining stable growth without inflation and imbalance. Such an investigation will be made in great detail later. Suffice it here to say that, as far as an underdeveloped economy is concerned, the productivity effect of foreign trade must supersede the multiplier effect of it if that economy is to grow secularly without being upset by persistent inflation and imbalance. We have also learned from modern analysis that the classical assumption of full employment must be dropped, thus implying that the income rather than price mechanism is what we must study in order to understand the equilibrium process in a predominantly underemployed and underdeveloped world economy.

This means that traditional preoccupation with the terms of trade and price elasticities must, in modern conditions, give way increasingly to the analysis of marginal propensities to import, the export-income ratio, the import-income ratio, productivities of export-biased and import-biased domestic industries, and other non-price factors.

The long-run significance of foreign borrowing, whether incident to an adverse balance of payments or as a result of autonomous capital imports, lies in the possibility that the borrowing nation may use the proceeds productively so as to increase domestic real income by more than the annual debt obligations involved. Whether or not nations can finance an import surplus in this way depends not only on their propensities to import but also on others' willingness to lend abroad. If borrowing nations are thus enabled to develop their productive resources, they may eventually cease to be deficit and debtor nations and begin to be surplus and creditor nations, as the history of international trade and finance indicates. As far as the majority of underdeveloped economies are concerned, it is as debtors and borrowers rather than as creditors and lenders that they are most likely to benefit by international capital movements.

On the other hand, the long-run importance of foreign lending lies in the possibility of building up an array of overseas earning-assets with an ultimate view to achieving an import surplus with the net earnings from those assets. This possibility may be illustrated by expressing the long-run creditor position of a developing economy in the form $L = E - M + R$, where L is net foreign lending and R net foreign receipts on capital account, E and M being real exports and real imports as before. This equation indicates that if net foreign receipts are very small, as they are likely to be in the early stage of foreign lending, there is no basic way to increase foreign lending except by achieving an export surplus. If foreign lending is thus increased, the lending nation will sooner or later earn more abroad on capital account (an increase in R). If, further, net foreign receipts on capital account exceed current lending abroad, $R > L$, then imports can exceed exports, $M > E$, as the above equation implies. In this respect, it is not hard to imagine that Great Britain's industrial progress might have been quite different had it not been for her position as the world's greatest creditor up to World War I. If Great Britain and other nations who lost a large part or all of their overseas earning-assets as a result of World War II are to re-accumulate such overseas assets, they will find it increasingly necessary to achieve and maintain a persistent export surplus and so to lend abroad an amount equal to or less than that trade surplus. The resulting net foreign receipts on capital account in excess of current lending can then be used to finance an import surplus, if necessary.

With this outline, let us now proceed to analyze the nature and process of economic development more precisely, more deeply, and in an operationally more significant way.

CHAPTER III

THE SOCIALLY OPTIMAL RATE
OF GROWTH

DEVELOPMENT programming requires, first and above all, some central standard of reference, that is, some ideal index of economic progress as a general base of reference. This chapter therefore will explore the concept and determination of what might be called 'the socially optimal rate of growth'. Once such a target rate of growth is clearly defined and agreed upon, the rest will be matters of refinement and implementation. Specifically this chapter will discuss the socially optimal rate of growth with reference to (a) the relation of population growth and living standards, and (b) the rate of capital accumulation required for the realization and maintenance of an ideal line of advance consistent with the economic needs of a growing population as well as with the technological possibilities of a developing economy.

POPULATION GROWTH AND LIVING STANDARDS

The population of any economy is at once the ultimate object of utility-satisfaction and a fundamental condition of utility-creation. This double character of a population is inherent in the dual role of 'economic man' as a consumer and as a producer. In its capacity as a consuming public, a population desires a higher and higher standard of living. In its capacity as a working force, a population lays an economic basis for realizing the higher standard of living desired. Accordingly it is necessary to analyze the relation of population growth and living standards from the standpoint of both consumer welfare and labour productivity.

Employable Population
Let us begin with the broader question of the reasons why (a) the rate of population growth and (b) the proportion of

employable labour to a given total population vary both in time and space. The 'natural increase' in the size of population (excluding immigration and emigration) depends on the rate of births exceeding the rate of deaths. These latter rates in turn may be influenced by a combination of economic and non-economic factors. Among the factors affecting the *birth* rate, one hears the following most frequently mentioned by population experts: the average marriage age, the state of obstetrics, birth-control knowledge and practice, open or hidden abortions, government family subsidies, family fedundity, per capita real income, tax burdens on family incomes, and prospective economic opportunities for children. As for the *death* rate, it is believed to be influenced by such factors as the degree of population density (population relative to disposable resources), the state of medical science and public hygiene, the frequency of wars (international and civil), natural calamities, epidemics, famines, and health insurance systems.

Numerous as the demographic determinants are, an economically meaningful interpretation of population growth might be found in the simplifying assumption that the rate of growth of population takes the following form:

$$\frac{\Delta P}{P} = B\left(\frac{P}{K}\right) - D\left(\frac{P}{C}\right), \qquad (1)$$

where $\Delta P/P$ is the rate of growth of population, B the rate of births, D the rate of deaths, K/P the stock of capital per head, C/P the means of consumption per head, $B(P/K)$ the propensity to procreate based on the assumption that the birth rate varies inversely with the stock of capital per head (the greater the amount of capital resources and capital products, the more strongly will the average family be inclined to prefer a new 'car to a baby'), and $D(P/C)$ the population density on the assumption that the death rate varies inversely with the means of consumption per head.

Turning now to the reasons why a definite fraction of the total population is always ready and willing to work, the answer depends on a number of socio-economic factors. One might mention such factors as the community's choice between work

and leisure, family and educational systems, social strati-
fications, property relations, the legal limitations on child and
women labour, work incentives, inheritance-death duties, and
even climatic conditions. For these reasons the labour force
may normally make up half of the total population in one
economy and one third in another. Generally speaking, the
more industrialized is the economy, the smaller is the proportion of the labour force to the total population. For a highly
industrialized society is more capable of supporting a large
'leisure class' than is a less industrialized one.

For simplicity let us subsume all these underlying influences
in a coefficient measuring the community's choice between
work and leisure. Such a coefficient relates an employable
labour force to a total population. If the community's choice
between work and leisure determines a fixed ratio (α) between
an employable labour force (N) and a total population (P),
we have $N/P = \alpha = $ constant. From this relation we have
the rate of growth of labour population

$$\frac{\Delta N}{N} = \frac{\alpha \Delta P}{N} = \frac{\alpha \Delta P}{\Delta P} = \frac{\Delta P}{P}. \tag{2}$$

It is the rate of growth of labour population determined by
equation (2) that forms one analytical foundation for building
an edifice called 'the socially optimal rate of growth'. If the
size of population is determined in the manner indicated by
equation (1), the size of *labour* population must grow at the
same rate as the rate of population growth, provided that the
ratio of the labour force and the total population remains constant, according to equation (2). There is one more analytical
foundation, namely, the standard of living desired by the
population. Let us turn to this other foundation.

The Attainable Standard of Living
The standard of living is usually measured by per capita real
income, but here it may be treated in a somewhat restricted
way. Since per capita real income depends, in the final analysis,
on the average productivity of labour, we may understand by
the standard of living real income per 'bread-winner'. This
double role of labour productivity is easy to see when it is

recalled that average labour productivity $(H = Y/N)$ also represents average labour income, the actual correspondence between the two depending on institutional arrangements of a concrete society. The main point to be stressed here is that the average productivity of labour constitutes the *ultimate technical* justification of a higher or lower standard of living per 'bread-winner' everywhere and anytime.

To desire a higher standard of living would be, in effect, to desire such improvements in methods of production as to increase output per unit of labour, that is, the average productivity of labour. Fundamentally, a technologically backward economy may realistically aspire to a higher standard of living only by overcoming its technological backwardness. Suppose that such an economy can, by its own technological progress, increase the average productivity of labour at the rate

$$\frac{\Delta H}{H} = h, \tag{3}$$

where H stands for the ratio of output to fully employed labour. Then $h > 0$ means a rising standard of living, $h < 0$ a falling standard of living, and $h = 0$ a stationary standard of living. It will be found that these three patterns of living standards depend on the margin between the rate of growth of production and the rate of growth of population. Thus the *attainable* standard of living depends on population and productivity. We are now ready to tackle the concept of 'the socially optimal rate of growth' itself.

The Concept of the Socially Optimal Rate

In the light of the foregoing discussion, a rate of growth of real income that may be considered 'socially optimal' need not refer to Cockaigne even if it reflects a growing population's subjective desires for full employment and for a rising standard of living. For the socially optimal rate of growth in the present context refers to a maximum rate of growth of output consistent with the full employment of a growing labour population and the rising trend of labour productivity. The actual realization and maintenance of such a maximum rate of growth will be found to depend on there being the same rate of capital accumulation, thus implying a possible conflict between a desire for full employment (of labour) and a desire for full utilization (of capital) as well as between a desire for higher consumption and a desire for higher saving. We shall return to these implications later. Meanwhile we may, as a first approximation,[1] think of the socially optimal rate of growth as the sum of the rate of growth of employable labour force and the rate of growth of labour productivity:

$$\frac{\Delta Y}{Y} = \frac{\Delta N}{N} + \frac{\Delta H}{H}, \qquad (4)$$

where $\Delta Y/Y$ is the maximum rate of growth of output, which is consistent with population growth and technological advance as specified above. Equation (4) indicates that the maximum target rate attainable will be the higher, the higher is the rate of growth of labour productivity ($\Delta H/H$) to reduce employed labour per unit of output and the higher is the rate of growth of labour population ($\Delta N/N$) to be absorbed in productive employment.

Putting $G_m = \Delta Y/Y$, $n = \Delta N/N$, and $h = \Delta H/H$, we may illustrate the magnitudes involved in equation (4), as follows:

If $n = 0.01$, $h = 0.04$, then $G_m = 0.05$
(an advanced economy).

If $n = 0.015$, $h = 0.02$, then $G_m = 0.035$
(an intermediate economy).

If $n = 0.02$, $h = 0.005$, then $G_m = 0.025$
(an underdeveloped economy).

These examples indicate that an economy can realistically aim at a high target rate of growth by maximizing the rate

---

[1] Let $Y = HN$, where Y is net national output, H average labour productivity, and N labour population. This implies $\Delta Y = H\Delta N + N\Delta H$. For letting $y = \Delta Y/Y$, $h = \Delta H/H$, and $n = \Delta N/N$, we have

$$Y(1+y) = H(1+h)N(1+n)$$
$$Y+yY = (H+hH)(N+nN)$$
$$= HN + HnN + hHN + hHnN$$
$$y = (nHN/Y) + (hHN/Y) + (hnNH/Y).$$

Omitting the last term hn as negligibly small yields

$$y = n+h,$$

which represents our notion of the *socially optimal* rate of growth, $y = G_m$.

of growth of labour productivity (h) and by minimizing the rate of growth of labour population (n). The implication for an underdeveloped economy is that if its labour population is growing at the rate of 2 per cent., the only way to attain as high a rate of growth of output consistent with population growth as 5 per cent. associated with an advanced economy would be by increasing its labour productivity at the rate of 3 per cent., instead of $\frac{1}{2}$ per cent. This leads us to the relation between production and population, the margin of which determines the standard of living.

Production vs. Population

Equation (4) carries with it the important implication that output must grow at a rate exceeding the rate of growth of labour population, if the standard of living per 'bread-winner' is to improve secularly. This implication is clearly seen in the transposed equation

$$\frac{\Delta H}{H} = \frac{\Delta Y}{Y} - \frac{\Delta N}{N}, \tag{5}$$

where $\Delta H/H$ is a measure of the standard of living in a dynamic setting, as indicated before. Equation (5) may be illustrated in terms of three trends of living standards, as follows:

If $G_m - n > 0$, then $h > 0$ (a rising standard of living).
If $G_m - n = 0$, then $h = 0$ (a stationary standard of living).
If $G_m - n < 0$, then $h < 0$ (a declining standard of living).

These examples indicate that the standard of living (per 'bread-winner') can be improved secularly by increasing the rate of growth of output (G_m) by decreasing the rate of growth of population (n), or by doing both. They also present some difficult questions regarding the relation of population growth and production growth, which determines the secular standard of living.

If, for instance, an economy aspires to a higher standard of living than what current output and population trends allow, as in the temporal inequality of the form $h_{t+1} > (G_m - n)_t$, it is confronted with the practical difficulty of choosing between slowing down population growth and stepping up production growth.[1] In this connection we are reminded of the classical conflict of opinion between Malthus and Marx concerning the remedy for the 'overpopulation problem', to which conflict Keynes alludes.[2] In the light of Keynes's already cited comment on the Malthus-Marx controversy, a more sensible position to take seems to be that the population problem, especially in the narrower sense of living standards, should be attacked on both fronts, that is, by concentrating on efforts to increase the rate of growth of production in shorter periods *and* by making long-range efforts to control the rate of growth of population.

Harrod's 'Natural' Growth Rate

At this juncture it seems useful to compare our 'socially optimal' growth rate with Harrod's 'natural' growth rate. Harrod defines his 'natural' rate as 'the rate of advance which the increase of population and technological improvements allow', and which 'represents the line of output at each point on which producers of all kinds will be satisfied that they are making a correct balance between work and leisure'.[3] Moreover, he precludes 'involuntary unemployment' from his concept of the 'natural' rate, so that an economy advancing at the 'natural' rate is always associated with full employment. Lastly Harrod suggests that no growth rate can be higher than the 'natural' rate in the long run, so that Mrs. Joan Robinson has interpreted it as the 'maximum feasible' rate of growth.[4]

Harrod contemplates an economy in which the 'natural' rate of growth (i.e. the rate consistent with population growth

[1] Apropos, the World Population Conference (Italy, August 1954) was reportedly divided into the diametrically opposed 'pessimistic' and 'optimistic' schools of thought. The pessimistic school expressed grave apprehensions lest the world's population should outgrow its resources, the great promise of nuclear science notwithstanding. The optimistic school, by contrast, seemed to argue simply: 'If your shoes are killing you, why not get a larger pair of shoes to fit your big feet, instead of foolishly cutting off your toes to fit your small shoes?' (See M. Tachi and K. Akamatsu, 'A Report on the World Population Conference', *Riron Keizaigaku* (Economic Studies Quarterly), Japan, March 1955. On the pessimistic side will be found also H. H. Villard, 'Some Notes on Population and Living Levels', *Review of Economics and Statistics*, May 1955.

[2] Keynes, *Essays in Biography*, pp. 107–8.
[3] *Dynamic Economics*, p. 87.
[4] See her *The Rate of Interest*, etc., p. 160.

and technological advance) tends to fall behind the 'warranted' rate of growth which is the rate consistent with the savers' desire and the investors' profit-motive, and then proposes the remedy therefor. In other words, he deals with an advanced economy whose capital accumulation tends to outrun its population growth so as to make for secular stagnation. Thus Harrod's concept of the 'natural' rate is a significant tool of analysis for explaining the secular instability (esp. downward) of advanced capitalism.[1] This *application* of the 'natural' rate has been challenged by Mrs. Robinson on the ground that a more typical situation than that which is contemplated by Harrod is one in which population growth tends to outrun capital accumulation, not the other way around.[2]

The question of application apart, Harrod's *concept* of the 'natural' rate itself is problematical, for a number of reasons. First, he makes it depend partly on 'the increase of population', whereas his reference to the community's choice between work and leisure suggests a *labour* population instead of the whole population. In this latter event Harrod would have to determine the growth of labour population in the manner indicated by equation (2) above. Second, Harrod leaves unspecified both the nature and influence of 'technological improvements' on which his natural rate partly depends. By arbitrarily defining labour-saving inventions as synonymous with capital-using technology,[3] Harrod seems to contemplate a constant

[1] This significance is entirely missed by W. Fellner when he complains that 'the "natural rate of growth" in Mr. Harrod's sense is not a definite magnitude because there exists no such thing as a unique rate of growth made possible by "natural" factors.' (See Fellner, 'The Capital-Output Ratio in Dynamic Economics', in *Money, Trade and Economic Growth*, Macmillan, N.Y., 1951, p. 113). Nevertheless, Fellner's objection points up the vague character of Harrod's 'natural' rate. Had Harrod determined his 'natural' growth rate precisely by relating it to more *determinate* 'natural' factors, much of its mysterious characters would have disappeared.

[2] Thus Mrs. Robinson, apparently having a 'capital-poor' world in mind, criticizes Harrod's onesided application by saying: 'A community whose only problem was that they have all the capital that there is any use for, would not really have a great deal to worry about, and we need not wring our hearts by contemplating their troubles.' (See her *The Rate of Interest*, etc., p. 161). However, Mrs. Robinson is not disagreeing with Harrod's concept of the 'natural' rate itself but only with its *application*.

[3] *Dynamic Economics*, pp. 26–7.

labour-output ratio as well as a constant capital-output ratio. Thus he states that 'it is not my impression that inventions have been predominantly labour-saving in the sense defined.'[1] But it is a meaningless tautology to consider 'labour-saving' only those inventions which are 'capital-using',[2] for labour per unit of output can decrease or, what is the same, output per unit of labour can increase, without thereby causing more capital to be used per unit of output, contrary to what is implied by Harrod's definition of labour-saving inventions. The reason for this contrary view is that output constantly increases as a result of labour-saving technological progress, thereby decreasing the capital-output ratio (K/Y) via an increase in its denominator (Y). Accordingly one may not simply adduce labour-saving technology from capital-using technology.

If, however, the labour-output ratio is assumed to be technologically fixed, irrespective of whatever may be happening to the capital-output ratio, so that $N/Y = \beta =$ constant, output needs to grow at the same rate as the rate of growth of labour population, that is,

$$G_n = \frac{\Delta Y}{Y} = \frac{\Delta N/\beta}{N/\beta} = \frac{\Delta N}{N} = n. \qquad (6)$$

Thus G_n given by equation (6) seems to approximate Harrod's notion of the 'natural' growth rate required to keep a growing labour population fully employed.

If G_n approximates Harrod's 'natural' rate, it is less than 'socially optimal' in our sense. For Harrod's 'natural' rate, as such, while it guarantees full employment, nevertheless does not admit of a secularly rising standard of living (per breadwinner). Exclusion of an explicit variable representing the standard of living is due to the constant labour-output ratio which Harrod seems to assume. If, however, the labour-output ratio is decreasing over time (if, that is, the average

---

[1] *Ibid*, p. 28.

[2] On this point of criticism, see Y. Takata, 'A Reflection on Growth Rates', in *Studies in Growth Economics* (Y. Takata, ed.), Osaka Univ. Institute of Social and Economic Research, 1954.

D

productivity of labour is increasing) according to $H_t = H_0(1 + h)t$, output must grow at the rate of G_m given by equation (4) in order to avoid otherwise inevitable 'technological unemployment' and to improve the standard of living secularly. Introduction of the rate of growth of labour productivity (h) as specifically expressing 'technological improvements' would make Harrod's 'natural' rate identifiable with our 'socially optimal' rate, so that $G_n = G_m$. Despite the rather vague form in which it is expressed, Harrod's concept of the 'natural' growth rate is important for the insight it provides into such fundamental categories as population and technology and for the light it, in conjunction with his 'warranted' rate, throws on the secular instability of a growing capitalistic economy.

REQUIRED CAPITAL ACCUMULATION

The socially optimal rate of growth, while it tells us a possible line of advance consistent with the population's desires for fuller employment and better life, cannot by itself tell us whether or not such a line of advance will be actually realized and continuously maintained. This is where we must turn to the consideration of 'required' capital accumulation. If the socially optimal rate of growth expressed by equation (4) is taken as sociologically and technologically given, it is possible and necessary to determine the required rate of capital accumulation. It is necessary because there must be a growing stock of capital to equip a growing labour population and to realize a rising standard of living. It is possible because the amount of real capital required (demanded) is some function of output. If the rate of capital accumulation required for the socially optimal growth is determined, then the next logical question might be whether or not the population is able and willing to supply savings at the same rate[1] and at the possible sacrifice of desired consumption.

---

[1] This is the sort of question Harrod poses in his *Dynamic Economics* (p. 87). His own answer is that the rate of investment consistent with the 'natural' rate of growth of output may or may not be consistent with the savers' desire. Thus he writes $G_n C_r = $ or $\neq s$, where G_n is the 'natural' rate, C_r the required capital-output ratio, and s the saving ratio.

The Required Investment Ratio

To determine the rate of growth of capital necessary for the socially optimal growth, it is necessary first to make clear the relation between capital and output. Writing K for real capital and Y for output, we may express the amount of real capital required to produce a given output in the form $K = bY$, where b is the capital-output ratio subject to change as a result of technological progress and/or relative factor-price movements. The above relation implies that if socially optimal output increases by ΔY, capital must also increase by an amount equal to $\Delta K = b\Delta Y + Y\Delta b$, where the term $Y\Delta b$ expresses the possible effect of a variable capital-output ratio on any level of output and hence on the amount of additional real capital required. Alternatively we can say that socially optimal output is capable of expanding by an amount equal to $\Delta Y = \Delta K/b + Y\Delta b/b$. If, therefore, an economy is to grow at the rate of G_m, that is, at the socially optimal rate, capital must also grow at the same rate of G_m. For from $K = bY$, and neglecting the term $Y\Delta b$ for simplicity, we have

$$\frac{\Delta K}{K} = \frac{b\Delta K}{K} = \frac{b\Delta Y}{bY} = \frac{\Delta Y}{Y} \equiv G_m, \tag{7}$$

where $\Delta K/K$ is the 'required' rate of growth of capital, which may not be related to the savers' attitude.

So that the required rate of growth of capital given by equation (7) may conform to the familiar saving-investment theory, it is convenient to reduce that required rate to terms of the required investment ratio by putting $\Delta K/K = \gamma$, as follows:

$$\frac{I^r}{Y} = \frac{\Delta K}{Y} = \frac{\gamma K}{Y} = \gamma b = G_m b, \tag{8}$$

where I^r/Y stands for the required investment ratio.

If the required investment ratio is given by equation (8), the population must save in terms of real income at the same rate, that is,

$$s^r = \frac{I^r}{Y} = G_m b, \tag{9}$$

where s^r stands for the *required* saving ratio. Considering s^r as a measure of the supply of real capital required for the socially optimal growth, the operational significance of equations (7)–(9) can be exemplified, as follows:

If $G_m = 0.05$, $b = 3$, then $s^r = 0.15$
(an advanced economy).
If $G_m = 0.035$, $b = 3.5$, then $s^r = 0.1225$
(an intermediate economy).
If $G_m = 0.025$, $b = 4$, then $s^r = 0.10$
(an underdeveloped economy).

The different values of the socially optimal growth rate in the above models are due to the different rates of growth of population and of productivity assumed, as indicated earlier. As for the divers values of the capital-output ratio, they are based on the assumption that the higher the stage of economic development, the smaller is the amount of capital required per unit of output or, what is the same in effect, the greater is the average productivity of capital. On these assumptions, it can be seen that an underdeveloped economy would have to save at the constant rate of 10 per cent. of its net national output in order to realize and maintain its socially optimal growth rate, while an advanced economy would have to save at the constant rate of 15 per cent. and an intermediate economy at the constant rate of $12\frac{1}{4}$ per cent. The question naturally arises as to whether each type of economy does or does not *actually* save at the required rate. Let us answer this question with particular reference to an underdeveloped economy.

The Required vs. Actual Saving Ratio

If most present-day underdeveloped economies can actually save from only 3 per cent. to 5 per cent. of net national output, as available data suggest, it may prove practically difficult for them to satisfy the condition specified by equation (9). Suppose that an underdeveloped economy has a 2 per cent. rate of growth of labour population and a $\frac{1}{2}$ per cent. rate of growth of labour productivity so that it can realistically aim at a $2\frac{1}{2}$ per cent. socially optimal rate of growth of output to be realized and maintained, as in the above case of $G_m = 0.025$. Then the required saving ratio is 10 per cent. according to equation (9). If, however, the institutional-psychological complex of the underdeveloped economy in question is such as to provide actual savings at the rate of, say, 5 per cent. instead, there will be a short supply of savings equal to $(s^r - s)\Upsilon$, where s stands for the *actual* saving ratio. Unless this shortage of savings is made good somehow, the underdeveloped economy may not be able to realize, much less maintain secularly, the $2\frac{1}{2}$ per cent. rate of growth of output consistent with the needs and productivity of its growing population—for lack of capital.

Faced with a shortage of capital relative to the required optimal growth, an underdeveloped economy has two basic choices, namely, either to reduce the required investment ratio through the downward adjustment of n or/and h or to raise the actual saving ratio via appropriate changes in the institutional-psychological complex. However, there are other possibilities. First, in an open system with foreign-trade relations, there is always the theoretical possibility of wiping out the gap between the required and actual saving ratios through capital imports. Second, irrespective of the savers' attitude, an underdeveloped economy may increase the *capacity* to produce capital goods (in contradistinction to the supply of savings) by making such improvements in the structure of industry as greater resource mobility, greater equipment standardization, greater output homogeneity, and greater factor substitutability.[1]

The foregoing analysis has shown the technical possibilities and difficulties of realizing and maintaining the socially optimal rate of growth. Since population, technology, and capital all have their own independent laws of growth to obey, there is no reason to suppose that the socially optimal growth rate and other growth rates always coincide, except by chance or by design. If so, there is a strong likelihood that the productive capacity of labour may be wasted and the standard of living retarded for lack of capital, as far as underdeveloped economies are concerned.

[1] For detailed discussion of the capacity to produce capital goods, as distinguished from the supply of savings, see my *Introduction to Keynesian Dynamics*, Allen & Unwin, London, and Columbia Univ. Press, N.Y., 1956, p. 201 ff.

CHAPTER IV

CAPITAL ACCUMULATION AND PRODUCTIVE CAPACITY

THE accumulation of capital is the key to the industrialization of any economy, for capital is the only factor of production that possesses the unique property of indefinite expansibility. This unique property of capital is the fundamental *raison d'être* of relying mainly on the expansion of capital rather than of land or labour for industrialization. Moreover, it is as increasing an economy's productive capacity rather than as generating its effective demand that an underdeveloped economy contemplates the accumulation of capital. Specifically, it is as actually realizing and maintaining the socially optimal rate of growth of output that we shall now consider the technical relation of capital accumulation and productive capacity. To sharpen the issue, we shall also make some critical observations on the Harrod-Domar models involving the interaction of productive capacity and effective demand and on Mrs. Joan Robinson's theory of capital accumulation.

THE CAPACITY-CREATING PROCESS

The potential productive capacity of an economy consists in the aggregate supply of goods and services obtainable by fully utilizing all the productive resources available within the limits of given technology. It can increase as a result of technological improvements and resource discoveries, but these influences can be expressed in the productivity of capital or of labour. If, moreover, we take labour as given, we may consider productive capacity as a unique function of the quantity and quality of capital, that is, on the assumption that the shortage of labour is not a serious bottleneck to the full utilization of available productive capital. Then the growth of productive capicity will be found to depend on the technical relation of (a) an investment ratio and (b) a productivity of investment. Let us see exactly why and how the growth of productive capacity is determined between them.

The Growth of Capital and Capacity
Given a level of effective demand high enough to justify the full utilization of real capital in existence, net investment (I), that is, an increase in real capital $(I = \Delta K)$ must mean an increase in productive capacity:

$$\Delta Y' = \sigma \Delta K = \sigma I, \tag{1}$$

where Y' is capacity output, K real capital, and σ the productivity of investment given by the prevailing state of technology.

Given the composition of output and the structure of industry, net investment is related to capacity in

$$\frac{I}{Y'} = \delta, \tag{2}$$

where δ is the investment ratio whose value differs from one economy to another and from one stage of economic development to another. The investment ratio expressed by (2) represents the capacity to produce capital goods, in contradistinction to the saving ratio representing the supply of savings. The significance of this distinction will be made clear a little later.

From equations (1) and (2) we have the rate of growth of productive capacity:

$$\frac{\Delta Y'}{Y'} = \sigma \frac{I}{Y'} = \sigma \delta = G_k, \tag{3}$$

where G_k stands for the rate at which productive capacity can be expanded if the capacity of the investment-goods industries is fully utilized due to net investment. Equation (3) indicates that the rate of growth of productive capacity is capable of varying in direct proportion as the investment ratio (δ) and the productivity of investment (σ) increase. Here the investment ratio represents the *quantity* of capital, while the productivity of investment represents the *quality* of capital. Equation

(3) also implies that both capital and output grow at the same rate and exponentially according to

$$Y'(t) = Y'_0 e^{\sigma \delta t}, \tag{4}$$

and

$$K(t) = K_0 e^{\sigma \delta t}. \tag{5}$$

The operational significance of equation (3) can be exemplified as follows:

> If $\delta = 0.05$, $\sigma = 0.2$, then $G_k = 0.01$
> (underdeveloped economy).
> If $\delta = 0.08$, $\sigma = 0.25$, then $G_k = 0.02$
> (intermediate economy).
> If $\delta = 0.12$, $\sigma = 0.5$, then $G_k = 0.06$
> (advanced economy).

Here the values of σ are inferred from the reciprocals of the capital-output ratios assumed for the three types of economy ($\frac{1}{5} = 0.2$, $\frac{1}{4} = 0.25$, $\frac{1}{2} = 0.5$ on the assumption of $K/Y = 5$ for an underdeveloped economy, of $K/Y = 4$ for an intermediate economy, and of $K/Y = 2$ for an advanced economy). The values of δ are also inferred from the roughly corresponding saving ratios attributed to those types of economy. The above examples indicate that the productive capacity of an underdeveloped economy grows more slowly than that of more developed economies, not only because δ expressing the quantity of capital is smaller but because σ expressing the quality of capital is also smaller. This leads us to inquire as to the concrete reasons why an underdeveloped economy possesses a constantly low investment ratio and a constantly low productivity of investment.

The Low Investment Ratio
Classical economists assumed that the composition of output is so homogeneous and the structure of industry so adjusted that what is not consumed (saved) can always be used as capital goods without difficulty. On this simplifying assumption, it is plausible to argue that if an underdeveloped economy would only try to be more thrifty, it could speed up the growth

of capital and capacity. But then we shall be at a loss to comprehend the anomalous phenomenon that some less developed economies possess a fairly high average propensity to save yet do not possess a great capacity to produce capital goods. It is not that underdeveloped economies are too spendthrift to save at all in terms of real income but that they do not and cannot *invest* in productive equipment even if they have the desire to save, owing to certain technical difficulties which classical economists assumed away in their argument for 'progress through thrift'.

To account for the above anomaly, it is necessary to drop the classical assumption and to recognize the heterogeneous composition of output and the maladjusted structure of industry in the real world. Once this is recognized, what is saved in terms of real income may be found not entirely suitable as capital goods. In other words, non-consumption does not necessarily carry with it the implication that it thereby releases just the kind of human and material resources which can be used to produce capital goods and with nonchalant ease at that. In the concrete context of an underdeveloped economy this means that even if 'the national belt' is tightened to make for more savings in terms of real income, it may not be able to produce more capital goods owing to the specificity of labour, equipment, and raw materials released from the consumer-goods industries. And the more heterogeneous is the composition of output, the greater becomes that specificity of productive factors. For so long as consumer-goods and durable capital-goods are *physically* distinguishable (e.g. wheat and machinery even though they are indistinguishable as inventories), the productive factors used in producing them cannot but help develop a specificity that often defies mutual adaptation.

Thus the heterogeneous composition of output characteristic of a modern economic society is one fundamental explanation for the anomalous phenomenon of the investment ratio being found smaller than the actual saving ratio in an underdeveloped economy. There is yet another fundamental explanation, namely, the greatly maladjusted structure of industry. Let us consider this latter impediment to the capacity to produce capital goods.

The industrial structure of an underdeveloped economy is characterized by the following rigidities and difficulties. First, there is the relative immobility of productive factors as between consumer-goods and capital-goods industries or as between agriculture and industry. Ineffective labour-exchange systems, inefficient transportation-communications facilities, and ill-organized capital markets all contribute to that factor immobility. Second, there are too many small-scale, capital-goods industries using obsolete, and often primitive, plant and equipment. The presence of cheap labour in an over-populated underdeveloped economy has the effect of discouraging the installation of 'streamlined' plant and equipment, even though the latter could be financed internally or externally. Third, there is inordinate capital wastage due to rapid depreciation and obsolescence. The durability structure of capital in an underdeveloped economy is usually such as to require replacement investment at a higher rate than in an advanced economy. For the existing plant and equipment in the former are generally made of so many obsolete, worn-out items that much of new gross investment is just for replacement, thereby leaving little or nothing in the way of a net addition to the capital stock. The average rate of depreciation (in the physical sense) is all the higher in an underdeveloped economy, because capital wastes and losses due to civil wars, natural calamities, large-scale fires, and inadequate storage facilities are inherent in the very underdeveloped nature of the case.

For these reasons the capacity to produce capital goods may fall short of the supply of savings, $\delta < s$. To put the matter differently, the inequality $\delta < s$ indicates an excess of the demand for capital goods over their supply, since $s Y'$ means a demand for capital goods, $(1-s) Y'$ a demand for consumer goods, $\delta Y'$ a supply of capital goods, and $(1-\delta) Y'$ a supply of consumer goods. It follows that $(s-\delta) Y' = (1-\delta) Y' - (1-s) Y'$. This implies that the short supply of capital goods $(s-\delta) Y'$ may, in an open economy with foreign-trade relations, be supplemented by importing that much short capital goods in exchange for the implied excess domestic supply of consumer goods $(1-\delta) Y' - (1-s) Y' > 0$. In the absence of foreign trade the composition of output and/or the structure of industry would have to be adjusted so as to make $\delta = s$. However, even if we had $\delta = s$ on the most favourable assumption about the composition of output and the structure of industry, the rate of growth of capital might still be too slow for the purpose of the optimal growth, owing to a low productivity of investment. This is where we must turn to the consideration of the low productivity of investment in underdeveloped economies.

The Low Productivity of Investment

Broadly speaking, slow capital accumulation and slow technological progress militate against a high productivity of investment. A small and stationary stock of capital does not stimulate technological improvements in the productive quality of capital and other productive factors. It is a bit ironical that an underdeveloped economy must but cannot readily improve the quality of capital because it cannot increase the quantity of capital fast enough, while an advanced economy need not but can greatly improve the quality of capital because it can increase the quantity of capital without difficulty. The insufficient spread of 'roundabout' methods of production throughout the underdeveloped part of the world is a strong presumption against there being more and better capital to increase productive capacity. It is not hard to imagine the difference in productive capacity between an economy relying on hand tools and another depending on automatic equipment (a bicycle vs. a tractor, e.g.). The higher is the level of roundaboutness, the more automatic is likely to be the nature of capital equipment combined with other productive factors. Insufficient roundaboutness may in turn be traced to a high-interest structure or a subsistent level of consumption, both of which tend to discourage the greater use of capital through 'waiting', to use the familiar Marshallian term. Thus technological backwardness and slow capital accumulation are the fundamental forces tending to keep down the productivity of investment in underdeveloped economies.[1]

[1] For some penetrating observations see J. Robinson, 'Notes on the Economics of Technical Progress', in *The Rate of Interest*, etc.

Domar has suggested more specific reasons, some of which are applicable to underdeveloped economies.[1] He considers the shortage of labour as the most important single reason why 'the potential social average productivity of investment' (σ) is lower than 'the productive capacity per dollar invested in the new plants taken by themselves' (s in his notation). Domar apparently contemplates an advanced economy with slow or stationary population growth, so that the supply of labour is so inelastic with respect to output as to cause old plants to curtail further production for lack of labour, thus offsetting an increase in the output of new plants. However, we may rule out his most important reason as least important in the context of an underdeveloped economy with an inherent reserve of unemployed labour. Domar's other reasons seem more applicable in some underdeveloped economies, namely, the case where the new plants cannot produce at full capacity for lack of effective demand and the last case where the old plants cut down their output owing to the competition of the new plants for markets. It is necessary to specify such economies as developing along mainly private-enterprise lines, however. For the possibility of new plants operating at less than capacity for lack of effective demand is much smaller in those under-developed economies which maintain large and growing public investment as a multiplicand.

Granting that the productivity of investment for the whole economy (his aggregate σ) may be lowered by the adverse repercussions of new plants on the output of old plants, it would be amiss to understate the practical importance of 'the productive capacity per dollar invested in the new plants taken by themselves' (his disaggregative s), as far as underdeveloped economies are concerned. For it is a matter of crucial importance to an underdeveloped economy's industrialization programming to avoid the construction of new plants of a pyramid-building kind, whatever their income-effect may be in the short run. Indeed, the observedly low productivity of investment in underdeveloped economies cannot be explained adequately except by specific reference to the *nature* and *types* of 'the new plants taken by themselves'. And the smaller the

[1] E. D. Domar, 'Expansion and Employment', *op. cit.*

investment ratio (δ), the more careful will an underdeveloped economy have to be in selecting those types of new plants and equipment which would expand its productive capacity in the long run, that is, the composition of I involved in $\sigma = \Delta Y/I$.

Capital and Productivity Requirements

Capital accumulation or decumulation is meaningless unless it is related to the desired growth or stability of an economy. Harrod and Domar have properly stressed the relation of capital accumulation and secular *stability* in the context of advanced capitalism. As far, however, as underdeveloped economies are concerned, it is the relation of capital accumulation and the socially optimal *growth* of output which must be stressed. For the purpose of the following discussion, we shall contemplate a situation where the rate of growth of capital is below the socially optimal rate of growth of output, $G_k < G_m$, as in all underdeveloped economies.

To make $G_k = G_m$, it is necessary to increase the investment ratio (δ) or the productivity of investment (σ) or yet both. From $G_k = G_m$ and $G_k = \sigma\delta$ we have the *optimal* investment ratio and the *optimal* productivity of investment in the forms $\delta' = G_m/\sigma$ and $\sigma' = G_m/\delta$. The operational significance of these latter forms may be illustrated, as follows:

> If $G_m = 0 \cdot 05$, $\sigma = 0 \cdot 2$, then $\delta' = 0 \cdot 25$
> (optimal investment ratio).
> If $G_m = 0 \cdot 05$, $\delta = 0 \cdot 1$, then $\sigma' = 0 \cdot 50$
> (optimal *productivity* ratio).

Thus, given a maximum target growth rate of 5 per cent. and an actual investment-productivity ratio of 2 per cent., an underdeveloped economy would have to increase its investment ratio to an *optimal* figure of 25 per cent. Likewise, given the same maximum growth rate and an actual investment ratio of 10 per cent., an underdeveloped economy would have to increase its investment-productivity ratio to an *optimal* figure of 50 per cent. For the inequality $G_k < G_m$ implies that the actual investment ratio and investment-productivity ratios are smaller than what the socially optimal growth requires. A realistic attempt to increase σ or δ, moreover, would take into account those forces making against a large σ or δ which we outlined a little earlier.

The above analysis leads to the conclusion that an underdeveloped economy must satisfy the following condition in order to grow at the socially optimal rate:

$$G_k = \sigma'\delta' = G_m = n+h. \qquad (6)$$

For $G_k < G_m$ signifies that the rate of growth of capital is too low for the underdeveloped economy to realize and maintain an ideal line of advance with a rising standard of living but without structural underemployment due to the shortage of capital.

NOTES ON THE HARROD-DOMAR MODELS

The growth models of Harrod and Domar[1] are addressed to advanced economies, and therefore have been criticized from the standpoint mainly of those economies.[2] We shall, however, appraise their models from the standpoint of underdeveloped economies in order to see clearly what is and what is not relevant to those latter economies.

Harrod's 'Warranted' Rate
In addition to his 'natural' rate referred to earlier, Harrod has another standard of reference, namely, the 'warranted' rate of growth which he defines as 'that over-all rate of advance which, if executed, will leave entrepreneurs in a state of mind in which they are prepared to carry on a similar advance'.[3] To see the exact nature of Harrod's 'warranted' rate (G_w), it is necessary to arrive at it as follows:

$$\frac{S}{Y_w} = s = \text{constant}, \qquad (1')$$

---

[1] Harrod, *Dyanmic Economics*; Domar, 'Expansion and Employment', *op. cit.*

[2] However, the criticisms by Mrs. J. Robinson and R. Eisner contain much that is instructive to underdeveloped economies. (See J. Robinson, 'Mr Harrod's Dynamics', *op. cit.*, and *The Rate of Interest*, etc.; Eisner, 'Underemployment Equilibrium Rates of Growth', *American Economic Review*, March 1952.)

[3] *Dynamic Economics*, p. 82.

$$\frac{\Delta K}{\Delta Y_w} = C_r = \text{constant}, \tag{2'}$$

$$\Delta K = I = C_r \Delta Y_w = s Y_w, \tag{3'}$$

$$G_w = \frac{\Delta Y_w}{Y_w} = \frac{s}{C_r}; \ G_w C_r = s. \tag{4'}$$

Implying

$$\frac{\Delta K}{K} = \frac{s Y_w}{K} = \frac{(s/C_r)K}{K} = \frac{s}{C_r}. \tag{5'}$$

Here Y_w is the 'warranted' level of net national output from the full utilization of capital, K the stock of real capital when fully utilized, I net investment, s the average saving ratio, and C_r the equilibrium value of the capital-output ratio (average = marginal assumed) or the 'required capital co-efficient', in Harrod's terminology.

The above system tells us that if the entrepreneurs invest as much as the community is disposed to save at the full-capacity level of income, and if output keeps on growing as much as the growth of real capital due to that net investment allows, the economy in question will always keep its real capital fully utilized and so advance at the steady rate of G_w. It also indicates the 'required' rate of growth of capital consistent with the savers' desire, as equation (5') implies. Equation (4') makes it clear that Harrod's 'warranted' rate refers to that equilibrium value of productive capacity which is necessary to induce sufficient investment to absorb full-capacity savings, that is, to prevent negative net investment from occurring because of otherwise inevitable idle or excess capacity. Let us proceed to appraise Harrod's model of an economy advancing at the rate of G_w, especially from the standpoint of underdeveloped economies.

1. The 'warranted' rate is Harrod's answer to the fundamental question: what are the conditions necessary to maintain the stable growth of advanced capitalism?—a question which Marx (and Schumpeter later) had raised and answered pessimistically, and which Keynes had revived and tried to answer optimistically. Like Keynes, Harrod contemplates a world in which the propensity to save tends to exceed the

inducement to invest, and in which there is therefore a persistent tendency toward cyclical deflation and chronic stagnation. But unlike Keynes, Harrod gives emphasis to (a) the danger of *productive capacity* outrunning effective demand, (b) the predominant role of *induced* investment, and above all (c) the *instability* of 'progressive equilibrium'. Keynes, it will be recalled, was concerned with the insufficiency of effective demand relative to *given* productive capacity arising from a high marginal propensity to save in relation to inadequate *autonomous* investment (via the multiplier). Moreover, Keynes's equilibrium income associated with the equality of savings and investment is not only static but also stable, whereas Harrod's equilibrium is both *dynamic* and *unstable* in the sense that it has a positive constant rate of change yet does not have the power to restore itself when disturbed.

Despite these differences, Harrod's notion of the 'warranted' rate is firmly based on Keynes's theory of effective demand, and indeed could not be understood except in the context of a Keynesian world of insufficient effective demand and involuntary mass unemployment. Thus Harrod contemplates the possibility of *cyclical* depression arising from the 'actual' rate of growth (G) representing 'trial and error' effective demand falling below the 'warranted' rate representing 'required' productive capacity; and also the possibility of secular stagnation arising from the 'warranted' rate tending to exceed the 'natural' rate (G_n) representing maximum productive capacity consistent with the actual trends of population and technology.[1] In short, Harrod's 'warranted' rate is a tool of analysis to indicate counter-cyclical and counter-stagnation policies, not to guide industrialization programming.

2. What Harrod's 'warranted' rate guarantees is full utilization of *capital*, not necessarily full employment of labour. Even when the saving ratio and the capital-output ratio are arbitrarily related to 'full employment' income, what is meant by the 'warranted' rate, as such,[2] is the problem of 'Keynesian

[1] See *Dynamic Economics*, p. 91; also see my 'Growth Theory and the Problem of Economic Stabilization' in *Economics and the Public Interest* (R. A. Solo, ed.), Rutgers Univ. Press, 1955.

[2] Harrod calls such a rate the warranted rate 'proper'. (See his 'An Essay in Dynamic Theory', *op. cit.*)

unemployment' due to insufficient effective demand. By contrast, the kind of unemployment which exists in underdeveloped economies cannot be met simply by increasing effective demand to a point where it justifies full utilization of available capital. Any other conclusion would be inconsistent with Harrod's fundamental position that 'in Keynesian fashion it [the warranted rate] contemplates the possibility of growing "involuntary" unemployment'.[1] It is not necessary to try, as some writers have tried,[2] to assume a different production function (involving both labour and capital inputs) in order to make Harrod's (and Domar's counterpart) 'warranted' rate take care of full employment as well as full capacity. For Harrod's 'natural' rate, in conjunction with his 'warranted' rate, could do just that, that is, when $G_w = G_n = G$. The main point to be stressed here is that the growth of *even* fully-utilized capital at the rate of G_w cannot overcome the *structural underemployment* of underdeveloped economies occasioned by the accumulation of capital tending to lag behind the growth of population with an increasing productivity.

3. Preclusion of *autonomous* investment renders Harrod's concept of the 'warranted' rate *analytically* inadequate for the purposes of underdeveloped economies. Harrod precludes autonomous investment presumably because he is anxious to demonstrate the instability of a market economy which capriciously expands or contracts investment in response mainly to profit expectations based on income fluctuations. Thus Mrs. Joan Robinson has approvingly observed: 'Mr. Harrod's main point is that the warranted rate cannot normally be achieved in pure *laissez-faire* conditions'.[3] J. R. Hicks, on the other hand, seems to feel that there is too much instability in Harrod's model of an economy advancing at the

[1] *Dynamic Economics*, p. 87.
[2] See e.g. H. Pilvin, 'Full Capacity vs. Full Employment Growth', *Quarterly Journal of Economics*, Nov. 1953.
[3] See her *The Rate of Interest*, etc., p. 160, n.1. This remark she makes by way of defending Harrod against T. C. Schelling's misunderstanding of Harrod's intentions. (See Schelling, 'Capital Growth and Equilibrium', *American Economic Review*, December 1947). This latter misunderstanding might have been spared, however, had Harrod clarified the instability condition that is both necessary and sufficient.

E

'warranted' rate, and so considers it necessary to introduce autonomous investment as a stabilizing force.[1]

Be that as it may, the relevant point is that Harrod (and Hicks) regards autonomous investment merely as a source of *demand* to offset that part of saving which induced investment may not alone absorb. This view of autonomous investment is implicit in Harrod's modified growth equation of the form $GC = s - k$, where G is the 'actual' rate of growth, C the 'trial and error' capital-output ratio, s the ratio of savings to the 'actual' level of income, and k autonomous investment expressed as a fraction of income. Harrod excludes autonomous investment as an explicit variable in his 'warranted' saving-investment equation, $G_w C_r = s$, partly because he apparently wants to give scope to the acceleration principle and partly because he has in view only that kind of autonomous investment which increases demand without at the same time increasing supply (e.g. armaments).[2] For he states that 'in the long run k must disappear, for in the long run all capital outlay is justified by the use to which it is put'.[3]

4. Harrod arbitrarily defines away that sort of autonomous investment which Keynes considered increasingly necessary, namely, public investment based on the State's superior capacity 'to calculate the marginal efficiency of capital on long views and on the basis of the general social advantage'[4]—precisely the sort that is of great *practical* importance to the development of present-day underdeveloped 'mixed' economies. It is indeed difficult to see how underdeveloped economies lacking in private initiative and funds could develop their productive capacity and resources without substantial public investment based on 'long views' and 'the general social advantage', whether it is or is not self-liquidating in the

---

[1] *Trade Cycle*, p. 60. It remains difficult to see how Hicks's kind of autonomous investment based on the self-liquidating principle could be so 'uniform' as to serve as a stabilizer or how it could remain uniform in view of the destabilizing impact of a large and growing stock of capital—unless Hicks's autonomous investment also represents the non-stock raising variety. On this last point of opacity in Hicks's trend-cycle analysis see, e.g. H. Rose, 'Demand, Supply and Price-Level in Macro-Dynamics', *Review of Economic Studies*, V.XX(1), No. 52, 1952–53.

[2] See *Dynamic Economics*, p. 79, where he refers to 'war'.

[3] *Ibid.*

[4] *General Theory*, p. 164.

conventional sense. Moreover, it seems reasonable to assume that growth-conscious underdeveloped economies would gear their autonomous investment, especially of a public nature, to long-term projects of a capacity-increasing character (e.g. highways, harbours, bridges, railways, dams, and the exploitation of natural resources with due regard to conservation). This kind of autonomous investment certainly would not disappear in the long run, even though Harrod's autonomous investment of the armaments variety might. If autonomous investment could be made self-liquidating as well as capacity-increasing (as in the case of America's TVA), there is no reason why it should not be included in the rate of growth of full-capacity output, as our G_k does include. Thus Harrod's 'required capital coefficient' (C_r) relates only induced investment to output, and its reciprocal cannot therefore indicate any productivity that may be associated with autonomous investment of a stock-raising nature. For an underdeveloped economy with a low saving ratio (s) representing, on the most favourable assumption, the supply of capital goods, it is a matter of vital importance that the reciprocal of the capital-output ratio $(1/C_r)$ be kept high by including *productive* autonomous investment, whether private or public.

Domar's 'Full Employment' Rate

We now turn to the consideration of Domar's growth model. Let us begin by amplifying his notion of the 'full employment' rate of growth of net investment, as follows:

$$Y^d = \frac{I}{\alpha}, \tag{1''}$$

(Level of effective demand)

$$Y^s = \sigma K, \tag{2''}$$

(Level of productive capacity)

$$Y^d = Y^s \text{ or } \frac{I}{\alpha} = \sigma K, \tag{3''}$$

(Equilibrium condition)

$$\Delta Y^d = \frac{\Delta I}{\alpha}, \tag{4''}$$

(Increment of demand)

$$\Delta Y^s = \sigma \Delta K = \sigma I, \tag{5''}$$

(Increment of capacity)

$$\Delta Y^d = \Delta Y^s \text{ or } \frac{\Delta I}{\alpha} = \sigma I, \tag{6''}$$

(Equilibrium condition)

$$r = \frac{\Delta I}{I} = \alpha \sigma. \tag{7''}$$

(Growth rate of investment)

Implying

$$\frac{\Delta Y^d}{Y^d} = \frac{\Delta I/\alpha}{Y^d} = \frac{\Delta I/\alpha}{I/\alpha} = \frac{\Delta I}{I} = \alpha \sigma. \tag{8''}$$

(Growth rate of demand)

Here Y^d is the level of net national income or effective demand at full employment, Y^s the level of productive capacity or supply at full employment, I net investment, K real capital, α the marginal propensity to save, and σ the productivity of capital or of net investment.

This system tells us that, given a constant α and a constant σ, net investment will have to grow at the rate r (required rate of growth of net investment) or $\alpha\sigma$, if 'the demand side' of a growing economy given by (4'') and 'the supply side' of it given by (5'') are to be balanced so as to maintain the state of full employment expressed by (6''). It also implies that income or demand must grow at the rate $\alpha\sigma$, as equation (8'') indicates. In sum, the economy must satisfy the condition expressed by (3'') in order to *achieve* full employment and also the condition expressed by (6'') in order to *maintain* full employment. It is important to notice 'the dual character of investment' stressed by Domar. For the numerator of $\Delta I/I$ generates additional demand via equation (4''), as in Keynes's multiplier theory, but then its denominator creates additional capacity via equation (5''), as in Domar's model of a growing economy. The I variable in equation (1'') can generate only a *level* of demand, while the same I variable in equation (5'') can, in due time, create an *increment* of real capital (ΔK). It is an increase in productive capacity (ΔY^s) due to this increment of real capital (ΔK) which must be matched by an equal increase in effective demand (ΔY^d) due to an increment of investment (ΔI), if a growing economy with an expanding stock of capital is to maintain continuous full employment. Let us proceed to appraise Domar's model from the standpoint mainly of underdeveloped economies.[1]

1. The situation envisaged by Domar is essentially the same as that which is contemplated by Harrod, namely, one characterized by a high saving ratio (α) as well as by a high productivity of investment (σ), which is approximately the reciprocal of Harrod's capital-output ratio (C_r). It is a situation where therefore effective demand tends to fall short of productive capacity, $Y^d < Y^s$, as a rule and on the average. To make $Y^d = Y^s$ on a continuing basis, Domar tells us that 'income and capacity should increase at the same rate', that is, $\Delta Y^d = \Delta Y^s$. It is essentially the same world as that which Keynes characterized with the label 'poverty in the midst of plenty'—a world tending to experience 'an insufficiency of effective demand.'[2] For a high saving ratio is indicative of actual 'poverty' due to insufficient demand, while a high productivity of investment is denotative of potential 'plenty' due to sufficient capacity. Domar takes the constancy of a high α and a high σ for granted on institutional and empirical grounds, and then proposes the technological or fiscal adjustment of the rate of growth of net investment ($\Delta I/I$) to the prevailing values of α and σ. But the typical situation found in an underdeveloped economy is the very opposite of what Domar's model seems to describe. For an underdeveloped economy is faced with a low saving ratio as well as a low productivity of investment, thus being exposed to a tendency toward persistent inflation rather than deflation. Such an economy would probably have to adjust its institutional-psychological complex so as to increase the saving ratio, given the values of $\Delta I/I$ and σ ($\alpha = r/\sigma$, where $r = \Delta I/I$), or improve its methods of production so as

[1] For alternative criticisms see R. Eisner, *op. cit.*; T. C. Schelling, 'Capital Expansion and Equilibrium', *American Economic Review*, December 1947; Y. Takata (ed.), *Studies in Growth Economics*.

[2] *General Theory*, p. 30. However, Domar's world is more troublesome than Keynes's, since the former is a dynamic one with a growing stock of capital.

to increase the productivity of investment, given $\Delta I/I$ and α ($\sigma = r/\alpha$).

2. Domar does not take into account the possibility that the rate of growth of net investment, which he considers necessary for 'full employment', may itself generate such destabilizing effects in the long run that the required equilibrium conditions $Y^d = Y^s$ and $\Delta Y^d = \Delta Y^s$ cannot be maintained secularly. In an *advanced* economy, a sustained effort to increase the investment-multiplicand (ΔI) through innovation, as Domar considers preferable, might make for a higher productivity of net investment (σ), only to defeat the required purpose of increasing income without at the same time increasing capacity—unless 'innovational investment' is of a purely income-generating nature. Such a self-defeating consequence is a strong long-run possibility, since innovation tends to reduce the amount of net investment required to produce additional output while tending to open up new investment opportunities and so to increase 'innovational investment' (ΔI). As far as an *underdeveloped* economy is concerned, the above self-defeating consequence is reversed, for a reduction in 'innovational investment' to diminish inflationary demand may be accompanied by a self-defeating fall in the productivity of investment and hence in productive capacity. Moreover, if the productivity of investment is increased as a by-product of an attempt to increase 'innovational investment', the community's thriftiness is likely to be increased so as to increase the saving ratio and hence to decrease income. This is also a strong long-run possibility, since the productivity of investment and the saving ratio tend to move in the same direction. So it is not accidental that σ and α are both higher in advanced economies and both lower in underdeveloped economies. Thus the productivity of investment and the saving ratio (σ, α) may be affected by the long-run course of net investment growing at the rate of $\Delta I/I$ in a way that will upset Domar's equilibrium conditions $Y^d = Y^s$ and $\Delta Y^d = \Delta Y^s$ for reasons neglected by Domar.

3. Perhaps the most serious criticism of Domar's model from the standpoint of an underdeveloped economy is that his 'required' rate of growth of investment fails to solve the

problem of *structural underemployment*. What Domar's 'required' rate of growth meets is the problem of 'Keynesian unemployment' due to an insufficiency of effective demand or, what amounts to the same, an underutilization of capital. Whereas Harrod starts with the assumption of 'involuntary unemployment' and then considers the possibility of reaching a full-employment equilibrium by satisfying the condition $G_w = G_n$, Domar begins by assuming the condition of full employment ($Y^d = Y^s$) and then considers the possibility of maintaining that condition by expanding income and investment at the rate $\alpha\sigma$. Domar's r can no more guarantee both full capacity and full employment than Harrod's G_w alone can. For if the labour population tends to grow faster than capital accumulation, as in most underdeveloped economies, an economy starting out with full employment will sooner or later experience *non-Keynesian* unemployment for lack of capital equipment—unless labour-intensive methods of production can be supposed to avert it without impairing the productivity of labour or unless the initial redundancy of labour can be supposed to reduce the real-wage rate so as to make capital accumulation more profitable. It is an open question whether the adoption of labour-intensive techniques, while they are helpful in reducing non-Keynesian unemployment, nevertheless might militate against the long-run objective of increasing productivity via 'economies of mass production' involving more capital relative to labour. It is also an open question whether labour would submit to the equilibrating reduction in the real-wage rate even in an underdeveloped economy without highly developed trade unionism. Thus the growth of net investment at the rate $\alpha\sigma$, *even if it prevents unused capacity from emerging*, may not be fast enough to absorb a growing labour population. Instead of letting his σ subsume population growth and technological advance, Domar would have to work with an additional rate of growth like Harrod's 'natural' rate, if he is to take care of an underdeveloped economy's non-Keynesian unemployment as well as an advanced economy's Keynesian unemployment. Thus Domar's equilibrium rate of growth, like Harrod's 'warranted' rate, guarantees full utilization of capital, not necessarily full employment of labour—unless some explicit assumption is made concerning the rate of growth of labour population.

4. Finally Domar's attitude toward technology leaves much to be desired. Being preoccupied as he is with an insufficiency of effective demand, Domar looks upon technological progress primarily as 'the creator of investment opportunities'. As far as an underdeveloped economy is concerned, technological progress is desired for its productivity effect (σ), irrespective of whether effective demand is or is not increased thereby. It is necessary, in this connection, to point out that Keynes did not, as Domar supposes, place 'too great' stress on 'the productive qualities of capital' for the reasons which Domar ascribes to Keynes.[1] So enthusiastic was Keynes for technological advance as *the creator of leisure* that he was even inclined to dismiss accompanying 'technological unemployment' as 'a temporary phase of maladjustment'.[2] This welcoming attitude of Keynes toward technological progress as the creator of leisure stands in sharp contrast with Domar's warning attitude toward possibly too high a productivity of investment (σ) that may be associated with technological advance. As far, therefore, as the technologically improvable *quality* of capital (Domar's high σ) is concerned, Keynes had good reason to lay 'great stress' on it.

Nor did Keynes show, as Domar supposes, 'grave concern' over the increasing *quantity* of capital *in the long run*. Quite the contrary, Keynes considered it possible and desirable to increase the quantity of capital to a point where 'the marginal efficiency of capital is zero', and where therefore 'the rentier aspect of capitalism ... will disappear'.[3] Keynes's 'grave concern for the diminishing marginal efficiency of capital', to which Domar refers, occurs only *in the interim circumstances* where the accumulation of capital is left to *laissez-faire*, and where the rate of interest paid on money and debts cannot, for institutional and psychological reasons, fall easily to accommodate itself to a falling marginal efficiency of capital. Thus if the quantity of capital and the rate of interest are independently taken care of, as they would be in a 'properly run community',

---

[1] Domar, *op. cit.*, p. 53.

[2] Keynes, 'Economic Possibilities for our Grandchildren', *op. cit.*

[3] *General Theory*, p. 221, p. 376.

Keynes thought it possible to expect progress to 'result from changes in technique, taste, population and institutions',[1] that is, rather than from capital accumulation. Domar comes close to agreeing with Keynes's conclusion, apparently without realizing it, when he intimates the desirability of promoting technological progress (i.e. increasing σ), provided that excess savings which private innovational investment cannot absorb is 'utilized in other ways (e.g. by government)'.

NOTES ON THE ROBINSON MODEL

The essence of Joan Robinson's theory of capital accumulation[2] is summed up in her central proposition: 'If they have no profit, the entrepreneurs cannot accumulate, and if they do not accumulate they have no profit'.[3] She is interested in explaining the fundamental nature of economic growth according to 'the capitalist rules of the game'. For this purpose she builds a verbal model of a *laissez-faire* closed economy using only capital and labour as productive factors and distributing the whole product to the entrepreneurs and the wage-earners. We shall discuss J. Robinson's basic model, and then indicate its relation to the Harrod-Domar models as well as its place in post-Keynesian growth economics—especially from the standpoint of underdeveloped economies.

To facilitate the following discussion, it seems useful to formalize Robinson's theory of accumulation on appropriate assumptions. Her basic model involves the simplifying assumptions (a) that wage-earners spend all of their wage income on consumption, while profit-takers save and invest all of their profit income, and (b) that capital and labour are combined in fixed proportions to produce a given output. She relaxes the second of these assumptions later to allow for 'the complications of reality'. Her entire argument is conducted in *ex post* terms, but we may interpret it in the *ex ante* spirit of economic theory.

---

[1] *Ibid.*, pp. 220–1.
[2] See her *The Accumulation of Capital*, Irwin, Homewood, 1956 (esp. Book II, Sections 1 and 1).
[3] *Ibid.*, p. 76.

The distribution equation pivotal to J. Robinson's growth theory may be approximated by

$$pY = wN + \pi pK, \tag{1'''}$$

where Y is net national output, N the amount of labour employed, K the amount of capital equipment utilized, p the average price of output as well as of capital equipment, w the money-wage rate, and π the gross profit rate (including the interest rate) required for the normal utilization of the existing stock of real capital. Dividing both sides of equation $(1''')$ by the average price index p, we have the distribution equation in real terms:

$$Y = \frac{w}{p}N + \pi K, \tag{2'''}$$

from which we can obtain the profit rate π. Putting $Y/N = \rho$ and $K/N = \theta$, equation $(2''')$ can be rearranged to yield the profit rate in the form

$$\pi = \frac{Y - \frac{w}{p}N}{K} = \frac{\frac{Y}{N} - \frac{w}{p}}{\frac{K}{N}} = \frac{\rho - \frac{w}{p}}{\theta}, \tag{3'''}$$

which shows that the profit rate depends on the technical relation of labour productivity (ρ), the real-wage rate (w/p), and the capital-labour ratio (θ). In other words, the profit rate is shown as capable of varying directly with the rate of net return to capital $(\rho - w/p)$ and inversely with the coefficient of capital intensity (θ).

The entrepreneurs are presumed to satisfy the profit-maximizing condition

$$\frac{d\left(\frac{\rho - \frac{w}{p}}{\theta}\right)}{d\theta} = 0 \tag{4'''}$$

subject to the production function.

$$Y = F(N, K), \qquad (5''')$$

where K/N is assumed to be constant (for the time being), and where Y is assumed to have the homogeneity of first degree as to K and N (constant returns to scale). We shall later consider the shiftability of this production function. Equation $(5''')$ is the production counterpart of distribution equation $(1''')$.

Turning to the expenditure side, net national real income must, in equilibrium, equal the sum of real consumption expenditure (C) and net real investment (I):

$$Y = C + I; \; S = I, \qquad (6''')$$

which is of course the familiar Keynesian income-expenditure or saving-investment equation. Here consumption (C) and saving (S) are those out of national income, and so must be transformed into forms consistent with Robinson's assumptions thus:

$$C = C_n = \frac{w}{\mathit{p}} N, \qquad (7''')$$

and

$$S = S_k = \pi K. \qquad (8''')$$

Here C_n is consumption expenditure out of wage income and S_k saving out of profit income. As for net investment involved in $(6''')$, it is simply defined as an increase in real capital:

$$I = \Delta K. \qquad (9''')$$

Taking $(8''')$ and $(9''')$ into account, we may rewrite the saving-investment relation expressed by $(6''')$ as

$$\Delta K = \pi K, \qquad (10''')$$

from which, and taking $(3''')$ into consideration, we obtain the rate of growth of capital:

$$\frac{\Delta K}{K} = \frac{\pi K}{K} = \pi = \frac{\rho - \dfrac{w}{p}}{\theta}. \qquad (11''')$$

The rate of growth of capital given by (11''') is the rate which is obtainable by the entrepreneurs following 'the capitalist rules of the game', according to J. Robinson. Equation (11''') indicates that the rate of growth of capital is capable of increasing if the net return to capital $(\rho - w/p)$ rises in greater proportion than the capital-labour ratio. What this means in Ricardian terms is that capital accumulation is strengthened by a fall in the real-wage rate and weakened by a rise in the real-wage rate, when technological conditions remain unchanged (when ρ and θ remain constant, in our instance). So it appears that J. Robinson has brought us back to David Ricardo's theory of economic development, albeit via the Keynesian door. We shall have a little more to say about this later. The main point to notice here is that the rate of growth of capital is, in the Robinsonian scheme of thought, dependent on whatever determines the profit rate (π), 'whatever' presumably referring to the technical relation of the real-wage rate (w/p), labour productivity (ρ) and the capital-labour ratio (θ).

Turning now to J. Robinson's notion of a 'golden age' equilibrium with full employment of labour and full utilization of capital, a basic condition of that equilibrium to be satisfied can be seen in this way: Assuming $K/N = \theta$ = constant in conditions of full employment and full utilization, an increase in the amount of fully employed labour is given by $\Delta N = \Delta K/\theta$. From this last relation we have the rate of growth of fully employed labour:

$$\frac{\Delta N}{N} = \frac{\Delta K/\theta}{N} = \frac{\Delta K/\theta}{K/\theta} = \frac{\Delta K}{K}, \qquad (12''')$$

which tells us that fully employed labour grows at the same rate as the rate of growth of capital, and which implies that capital must grow as fast as labour population when the capital-labour ratio (θ) remains constant. Given a perfectly elastic supply of labour with respect to output, equation (12''') signifies a 'golden age' equilibrium with full employment of both labour and capital.

Then J. Robinson poses the question as to whether the economy possesses any equilibrating mechanism if and when it diverges from the 'golden age' equilibrium for some reason. Suppose that the economy is on a divergent path characterized by the inequality

$$\frac{\Delta N}{N} > \frac{\Delta K}{K},$$

that is, by labour population growing faster than capital accumulation, as in most underdeveloped countries. Whether or not the economy can get back on the path of 'golden age' equilibrium depends, in Robinson's view, on the behaviour of the profit-wage relation. The latent 'progressive underemployment' implied in the above inequality would disappear *if* the redundancy of labour involved generated an equilibrating mechanism. This is a big 'if', inasmuch as the profit-wage relation may or may not behave in an equilibrating manner, depending on market conditions (competitive and monopolistic), the presence or absence of a subsistence-wage floor, and autonomous technical possibilities. Given the state of technology, the above redundancy of labour would sooner or later lead to a reduction in the money-wage rate (w). Such a fall in the money-wage rate would give rise to a fall in the real-wage rate (w/p) if the general price (p) remained constant, as it might in a monopoly-ridden economy. If the real-wage rate is thus reduced, the rate of growth of capital can increase via the increasing effect of the decreased real-wage rate on the profit rate, as equation $(11''')$ indicates. It is possible that the rate of growth of capital would increase to catch up with the constant rate of growth of labour population so as to make $\Delta K/K = \Delta N/N$. If, on the other hand, the real-wage rate fails to fall either because of an intervening subsistence-wage floor or because the general price falls in the same proportion as the money wage-rate (as in a competitive market in the long run), the redundancy of labour involved cannot generate an equilibrating mechanism and 'progressive underemployment' cannot disappear. This latter possibility agrees with Harrod's notion of indefinite instability based on the assumptions of the constancy of technological coefficients and relative factor-price movements.

The converse is true of the case of capital accumulation growing faster than labour population, as in most advanced countries. However, the possibility of advanced economies returning to the path of 'golden age' equilibrium is greater than that of underdeveloped economies, for reasons that are well known to the readers of J. Schumpeter's *Theory of Economic Development* (including J. Robinson herself). For even though the real-wage rate were rigid, a change in labour productivity (ρ) or in the capital-labour ratio (θ) might well be such as to increase the profit rate and hence the rate of growth of capital (or decrease them) in an equilibrating way, as equation ($11'''$) intimates. This is where J. Robinson goes beyond her basic model and becomes more Schumpeterian than Ricardian. This is also where we must reconsider the production function expressed by ($5'''$). The whole production function would shift upward if labour productivity ($Y/N = \rho$) increased for the same capital-labour ratio ($K/N = \theta$) or if the latter ratio decreased for the same value of the former. It is in the Schumpeterian spirit to regard those changes in the technological coefficients as 'autonomous' of market conditions. It is also in that spirit that J. Robinson contemplates technological changes. Equation ($11'''$) suggests that if labour productivity (ρ) rises faster than the real-wage rate for any constant capital-labour ratio ($\theta = \bar{\theta}$), the rate of growth of capital can increase and that if the capital-labour ratio (θ) falls without any accompanying changes in w/p and ρ, the rate of growth of capital can also increase. The trouble may arise if a fall in the coefficient of capital intensity is accompanied by a more than proportionate fall in labour productivity relatively to a given real-wage rate, with the possible result that the rate of growth of capital is decreased rather than increased. This possibility cannot be ruled out, since a fall in the capital-labour ratio represents *less* 'capitalistic' or 'roundabout' methods of production that could otherwise increase labour productivity and the real-wage rate, though not necessarily in the same proportion. Thus viewed, the 'Ricardion effect' mentioned in connection with equation ($11'''$) is a special case of the more general case involving *variable* technological parameters.

The relation of the Robinson model to those of Harrod and

Domar can be seen as follows: Taking equation $(2''')$ into account and rearranging, equation $(3''')$ can be rewritten as

$$\pi = \frac{Y - \dfrac{w}{p}N}{K} = \frac{Y}{K}\left(\frac{Y - \dfrac{w}{p}N}{Y}\right), \qquad (13''')$$

which shows that the profit rate to be proportional to capital productivity $(Y/K = \sigma)$ times the share of profits in national income $[Y - (w/p)N]/Y$. Since $S = \pi K$ and $[Y - (w/p)N]/Y = \pi K/Y = S/Y = s$ and since $b = 1/\sigma$, we have

$$\frac{\Delta K}{K} = \pi = \sigma s \,(\text{Domar}) \text{ or } = \frac{s}{b}\,(\text{Harrod}). \qquad (14''')$$

Thus J. Robinson's growth model comes essentially to the same thing as those of Harrod and Domar. However, the important difference between them lies in the fact that J. Robinson makes capital accumulation depend explicitly on the profit-wage relation (π and w/p) as well as on labour productivity (ρ), thus bringing her theory closer to a real market economy. By contrast, Harrod and Domar, in a more Keynesian manner, makes capital accumulation depend on the saving ratio (related to national income, not to profit income alone) and capital productivity (or its reciprocal) which transcend all economic systems, capitalistic or socialistic. It is not without significance, moreover, that J. Robinson approaches the question of capital accumulation from the standpoint mainly of labour, while Harrod and Domar approach it from that of capital. Thus when J. Robinson talks about capital accumulation according to 'the capitalists rule of the game', she seems to imply that *individualistic* capitalism cannot grow except basically by reducing the price of labour (the real-wage rate) relatively to the price of capital (approximately the profit rate) as well as to labour productivity. This may be her way of saying that an underdeveloped economy would do well not to follow 'the capitalist rules of the game' pure and simple but to adopt the Keynesian technique of a mixed public-private economy with fiscal-monetary policies geared to encouraging 'autonomous' investment (including innovational investment of the Schumpeterian variety).

J. Robinson's chief contribution to post-Keynesian growth economics seems to be that she has integrated classical value and distribution theory and modern Keynesian saving-investment theory into one coherent system. However, this seems to be also the chief drawback, as far as policy application is concerned. For, unlike the Harrod-Domar models, the Robinson model is not capable of being modified so as to introduce fiscal-monetary policy parameters—unless labour productivity, the wage rate, the profit rate, and the capital-labour ratio could be regarded as objects of practical policy—as they might be so regarded in a completely planned economy. Instead of letting redistributions of income (between profits and wages) come about through the parametric role of relative factor prices and so letting capital accumulation be adjusted to given population growth, one might prefer to let income redistributions come about through fiscal policy or to let population growth be adjusted to given capital growth. All the same, J. Robinson's theory greatly deepens our understanding of the fundamental nature of capital accumulation according to the purely 'capitalist rules of the game'. Finally, it must be observed that her growth model, while it is capable of yielding a stable equilibrium solution, nevertheless contains essentially as much instability as do the Harrod-Domar models of a *laissez-faire* economy, judging from J. Robinson's discussion of equilibriating mechanisms 'to be or not to be' operative.

CHAPTER V

THE TECHNOLOGICAL ROLE IN ECONOMIC DEVELOPMENT

TECHNOLOGICAL advance is next only to capital accumulation in causal importance to economic progress. Adam Smith stressed 'specialization' as the key to promoting the 'wealth of nations'. Marx regarded technological progress as the 'mainspring' of the capitalistic stage of development. Böhm-Bawerk equated 'roundabout' methods of production with industrialization. Schumpeter described the whole process of historical development largely in terms of 'innovation'. Keynes predicted a future state of 'quasi-stationary' affairs in which 'change and progress would result only from changes in techniques, taste, population and institutions'. All these economists emphasized the causal importance of technological progress for economic and social evolution with varying degrees of insight.

Beginning with Harrod and Domar we have a suggestive shift of emphasis to more operational treatments of the technological role in economic growth. However, they postulate 'neutral technological advance' so as to work with constant technological parameters, which are analytically convenient but practically inconvenient for development programming in different times and places. Joan Robinson, in her stimulating 'Notes on the Economics of Technical Progress', suggested more flexible technological parameters in growth analysis, for 'it is instructive to consider also the implications of *having* different ratios'.[1] These and other writers on economic growth are largely concerned with the demand aspect of technology and only incidentally with the productivity aspect of it, however.[2]

---

[1] See her *The Rate of Interest*, etc., p. 63.

[2] For a typical example of preoccupation with the demand aspect see J. Duesenberry, 'Innovation and Growth', *American Economic Review*, May 1956. For a criticism of such preoccupation see H. R. Bowen, 'Technological Change and Aggregate Demand', *American Economic Review*, December 1954. On the other hand, there is much that is instructive to underdeveloped economies in technological discussions of Japanese economists, such as found in Y. Takata (ed.), *Studies in Growth Economics*.

This is because they are preoccupied with the stabilization problem of advanced economies, not with the development problem of technologically backwards economies.

The present chapter is intended to analyse the effects of *non*-neutral technological changes on an underdeveloped economy's productive capacity, and also to indicate various influences on the flexible technological parameters involved.

TECHNOLOGICAL EFFECTS ON LABOUR PRODUCTIVITY

Let us first analyse the effects of labour-saving and labour-using techniques on net national output, leaving the particular reasons for their adoptions for later consideration. For this purpose we shall take as given non-labour productive factors, relative factor prices including the wage-rate, and the conditions of population growth and effective demand. On these assumptions, output can be considered a unique function of the quantity and productivity of labour, the latter reflecting technological change.

The Basic Relations

On the above assumptions, output will increase by an amount equal to

$$\Delta Y = \rho \Delta N, \tag{1}$$

where Y is potential output from full employment, N the amount of labour when fully employed, and ρ the average and marginal productivity of labour given by the prevailing state of technology. It is this productivity of labour which will be shown as varying over time in response to labour-saving and labour-using techniques. Here it suffices to state that a technologically advanced economy has a high ρ and that a technologically backward economy has a low ρ, that is, as a rule and on the average.

Next putting the ratio of an increase in the fully employed labour force to full-employment output equal to v we have

$$\frac{\Delta N}{Y} = v. \tag{2}$$

The ratio given by (2) reflects population growth and varies with the speed of the latter growth. It may be presumed that an 'overpopulated' economy has a large v and that an 'underpopulated' economy has a small v.

From (1) and (2) we have the rate of growth of full-employment output:

$$\frac{\Delta Y}{Y} = \rho v, \tag{3}$$

which shows that full-employment output is capable of growing at the rate ρv, the latter rate depending on technological advance and population growth.

Since the productivity of labour is the reciprocal of the labour-output ratio, $\rho = 1/a$ (where $a = N/Y = \Delta N/\Delta Y$), we may also express the rate of growth of full-employment output in the alternative form

$$\frac{\Delta Y}{Y} = \frac{1}{a}v = \frac{v}{a}, \tag{4}$$

which now shows that the rate of growth of full-employment output is capable of changing in inverse proportion as the labour-output ratio (a) changes, when the ratio of an additional labour force to full-employment output remains unchanged.

In order to isolate the effects of technological change we assume that the ratio of an increase in the fully employed labour force to output remains constant over time, that is, to be an invariant function of time:

$$v = v_t = \bar{v}. \tag{5}$$

However, the labour-output ratio is subject to change in response to the prevailing nature and direction of technological change, as we shall see subsequently.

The Effect of Labour-Saving Techniques

Given relative factor prices, we may regard industrial application of labour-saving or labour-using technology as autonomously given, that is, independently of market conditions.

We shall, however, explore a little later the economic as well as technological reasons for adopting labour-saving or labour-using techniques. The nature of a labour-saving technique may be seen thus: If the labour-output ratio is the product of the labour-capital ratio and the output-capital ratio, that is $N/Y = (N/K)/(Y/K)$ and if the productivity of capital (Y/K) is held constant, any fall in the amount of labour relative to given capital (a lower N/K) will reduce the labour-output ratio (a lower N/Y). Every invention and innovation tending to reduce the amount of labour per unit of capital (N/K) in a given production function could, therefore, be considered a labour-saving device.

Assuming no disturbing or offsetting forces to exist to change a steady fall in N/K and hence in N/Y, we may let the labour-output ratio $(a = N/Y)$ decrease at the constant rate g_a over time:

$$a = a_t = \frac{a_0}{(1+g_a)^t}, \tag{6}$$

where a_t is the dynamic labour-output ratio as a function of time, a_0 the initial value of that ratio, and g_a the constant rate of *decrease* of that ratio. Equation (6) implies the sequence:

$$a_0 = e,$$

$$a_1 = a_0/(1+g_a) = e/(1+g_a),$$

$$a_2 = a_1/(1+g_a) = e/(1+g_a)^2,$$

$$a_3 = a_2/(1+g_a) = e/(1+g_a)^3,$$

and so on.

Taking (5) and (6) into account and denoting $\Delta Y/Y$ by G_n, equation (4) can be reformulated as

$$G_n = \frac{\bar{v}}{a_0/(1+g_a)^t}, \tag{7}$$

which indicates that the rate of growth of full-employment output is capable of increasing in inverse proportion as the labour-output ratio decreases over time. In other words, a rising productivity of labour ($\rho_t = 1/a_t$) has the effect of increasing G_n, given a constant ratio of additional labour to output ($\nu_t = \bar{\nu}$).

The Effect of Labour-Using Techniques

Suppose, on the other hand, that the labour-using techniques are being adopted in such a way that the labour-output ratio rises over time at the constant rate g_a, according to the exponential relation

$$a = a_t = a_0(1+g_a)^t, \tag{8}$$

where g_a now signifies the constant rate of *increase* of the labour-output ratio.

Equation (8) implies the discrete movements defined as

$$a_0 = e,$$

$$a_1 = a_0(1+g_a) = e(1+g_a),$$

$$a_2 = a_1(1+g_a) = e(1+g_a)^2,$$

$$a_3 = a_2(1+g_a) = e(1+g_a)^3,$$

and so on.

In the light of (5) and (8), equation (4) can be rewritten as

$$G_n = \frac{\bar{\nu}}{a_0(1+g_a)^t}, \tag{9}$$

which tells us that the rate of growth of full-employment output is capable of decreasing in inverse proportion as the labour-output ratio increases over time, given a constant ν. This is merely another way of stating that a falling productivity of labour has the effect of decreasing G_n when the ratio of additional labour to output remains constant.

The Labour-Output Ratio as a Policy Parameter

If we take the position, as T. Haavelmo does at one point, that technological parameters 'actually are more related to human choice and human behaviour than to chemical formulae and laws of mechanics',[1] it is useful to contemplate the labour-output ratio as a policy parameter subject to deliberate manipulation within certain bounds. Instead of taking the labour-output ratio or the output-labour ratio as a 'given' technical datum to which to adapt everything else, why not adapt the existing labour-output ratio to some accepted values of G_n and ν? To ask this question is to suggest that technological parameters can be treated as matters of policy. Since there is no presumption in favour of the *actual* labour-output ratio (a') being always in equality with the *required* or equilibrium one (a) except by accident, it becomes necessary and desirable to make $a' = a$ by design, that is, insofar as it is feasible. From equation (3) we have the required value of the labour-output ratio consistent with the accepted levels of G_n and ν.

$$a = \frac{\nu}{G_n}, \quad \rho = \frac{G_n}{\nu}. \qquad (10)$$

Here a and ρ are respectively the required labour-output ratio and productivity of labour. What (10) implies is that the nature and direction of technological change must be deliberately influenced somehow to adapt the labour-output ratio to the rate of growth of full-employment output and the ratio of additional labour to output considered as given data. In other words, it contemplates the inequalities $a' \neq a$.

Suppose that a higher G_n is accepted as a target relatively to a given ν, as in an ambitious industrializing economy. Then the required labour-output ratio must fall, according to (10). This implies that the adoption of labour-*saving* devices should be encouraged to increase the productivity of labour. If the prevailing state of technology is such as to yield an actually large labour-output ratio (a') instead, the above change in G_n necessitates technological improvements such that the actual labour-output ratio is lowered to the level of the required figure (a). This may well be the characteristic case of underdeveloped economies. However, labour-saving devices cannot be recommended without some allowance for the possibility that the other 'given' datum ν may rise to necessitate labour-using rather than labour-saving techniques. Suppose, this time, that

[1] See his *A Study in the Theory of Economic Evolution*, p. 49.

a higher ν is deemed acceptable relatively to a given G_n, as it might in an 'over-populated' economy. As a consequence the required labour-output ratio is larger than before the above change in ν, according to (10). The policy implication in this case is that labour-using techniques of production should be promoted—unless a lower rate of growth of output is accepted. But then the productivity of labour is lowered in consequence of adopting labour-using techniques. Thus in the case of 'over-populated' economies there is a potential conflict between a desire to increase the productivity of labour and a desire to avoid serious unemployment in the very course of rapid technological progress.[1] Nevertheless, the main point to be noticed here is that the labour-output ratio should be regarded as a possible policy parameter capable of deliberate manipulation in any technologically flexible economy, instead of considering it always as a given datum. This leads us to a survey of the various influences affecting the adoption of labour-saving and labour-using techniques.

Influences on Labour-Saving, Labour-Using Techniques

It is difficult to determine precisely the speed of change in the labour-output ratio, that is, g_a which we have taken as autonomously given. However, some light may be cast on determinants of g_a by the following outline of the major factors responsible for choosing labour-saving and labour-using techniques.

The most obvious reason why any market economy should wish to adopt labour-saving devices is that such devices generally have the effect of reducing the cost of production per unit

---

[1] Apropos, a Japanese economist puts the matter this way: 'Moreover, the tempo of productivity increase will also be damped down at least temporarily by the necessity to absorb the surplus population as much as possible into the production process. Though the modern techniques of production cannot be assumed to be completely elastic as regards the proportion of factors employed, there may be some case in Japan for adopting more labour-intensive devices at the expense of labour productivity'. (See H. Kitamura, 'Long-Run Projection of the Japanese Economy—A Critical Evaluation,' *Kyklos*, IX(2), 1956. However, as Joan Robinson has pointed out, 'technological unemployment' need not occur in an economy adopting labour-saving innovations *if* 'effective demand for commodities and capital goods rises step by step with the rise in output per head.' (See her *The Rate of Interest*, etc., p. 47).

of labour. The higher, therefore, is the average wage-rate, the greater will, *cet. par.*, be the tendency to discover and adopt labour-saving devices. The trend toward 'automation' in the United States is a good case in point, although the 'higher wage movement' of organized labour there is by no means the only motivating factor involved. In a non-market economy greater emphasis is likely to be placed on the possibility of increasing real income per unit of labour or of diminishing human drudgery (real cost), however. Another possible explanation for adopting labour-saving devices may be found in a high degree of labour immobility that could exist for lack of effective labour-exchange arrangements. Thus it is entirely conceivable for an economy with a large and growing labour population nevertheless to promote technological advance along labour-saving lines, largely because a potentially available labour force is not always actually available for employment at the right time and in the right place. Yet another possible reason for labour-saving adoptions is that *full-employment* booms exceed under-employment slumps on balance so as to make it both necessary and profitable to adopt labour-saving inventions and innovations, especially in economies with rather slow population growth and hence with a fairly inelastic supply of labour. In the case of open economies, one reason for adopting labour-saving techniques may lie in the close contacts of such economies with those possessing plenty of labour-saving know-how. Depending on the ability to import such know-how and the propensity to imitate the technologically advanced, an open economy may advance more or less rapidly in the direction of labour-saving adoptions. Japan after the 'Meiji Restoration' was a historical case in point. Generally speaking, the better is the understanding of the long-run advantage of labour-saving technology in terms of greater productivity over its short-run disadvantage in terms of frictional unemployment ('technological unemployment' in this instance), the stronger will be the propensity to innovate along labour-saving lines.

As for the possible reasons for labour-using adoptions, they are more difficult to find in this day and age of 'gadget-mindedness'. The classic case for labour-using techniques is built on the well-known fear of 'technological unemployment'. But few would seriously propose the permanent adoption of labour-using techniques for the sake of employment, when there exist alternative ways and means of alleviating unemployment without sacrificing productivity (i.e. by increasing effective demand in shorter periods and by accumulating real capital in longer periods). A more cogent reason appears to be that producers, especially in an 'overpopulated' economy, believe that low labour costs due to superabundant labour will by far offset the low labour productivity implicit in more labour-using techniques of production. Acting on such a belief, producers might adopt labour-using techniques in greater proportion than labour-saving techniques, with the net result that the labour-output ratio is increased for the whole economy. Another explanation has it that the absence of sharp competition among entrepreneurs makes them satisfied to have inefficient equipment with a low technological content. This explanation does not, however, apply to those underdeveloped economies facing keen foreign competition and having therefore to adopt labour-saving techniques in order to meet that competition and to earn the foreign-exchange necessary for developmental purposes. In all underdeveloped economies one compelling reason for using labour-using rather than labour-saving techniques seems to be the common lack of funds (ultimately real savings) for installing streamlined equipment with a high technological content. Schumpeter's theory of innovation as a function of 'credit' (i.e. money capital) has relevance here. General observation suggests that labour-using technological advance is a limiting case of the preponderant trend toward the rising productivity of labour everywhere.

TECHNOLOGICAL EFFECTS ON CAPACITY GROWTH

Alternatively we may investigate technological impacts on the growth of capacity output by taking labour as given. For this purpose it is convenient to assume that the interest elasticity of capital supply is equal to zero, but it is necessary to drop the usual assumption of the stability of the capital-output ratio. Instead, we propose to work with a flexible capital-output ratio as an index of *non*-neutral technological advance. We shall also indicate, after the formal analysis, the trend influences affecting the capital-output ratio in varying circumstances.

The Basic Relations

As in the case of labour productivity, we begin with the basic determination of the rate of growth of full-capacity output. Output due to an increment of real capital will, on the aforementioned assumptions, increase by an amount equal to

$$\Delta Y' = \sigma\Delta K, \tag{$1'$}$$

where Y' is potential net national output from full capacity or simply full-capacity output, K the amount of real capital when fully utilized, and δ the average and marginal productivity of capital in question (when 'marginal', it signifies the average productivity of *net investment*, since $\Delta K = I$).

Next we assume that there is a definite relation between net investment and output:

$$\delta = \frac{\Delta K}{Y} = \frac{I}{Y'}, \tag{$2'$}$$

where δ is the ratio of incremental capital to output or what we earlier referred to as 'the capacity to produce capital goods.' On the most favourable assumption $\delta = s$ (where s is the saving ratio), as we discussed in the previous chapter. It is on such an assumption that s appears as an explicit variable in the Harrod model. The investment ratio (δ) need not remain constant, but it is generally high in an advanced economy and low in an underdeveloped economy.

From ($1'$) and ($2'$) we have the rate of growth of full-capacity output:

$$\frac{\Delta Y'}{Y'} = \sigma\delta, \tag{$3'$}$$

which shows that the rate of growth of full-capacity output is directly proportional to the productivity of capital (σ) times the investment ratio (δ).

Inasmuch as the productivity of capital is the reciprocal of the capital-output ratio, $\sigma = 1/b = K/Y = \Delta K/\Delta Y$, equation (3′) can also be written in the form

$$\frac{\Delta Y'}{Y'} = \frac{1}{b}\delta = \frac{\delta}{b}, \tag{4'}$$

which indicates that the rate of growth of full-capacity output is capable of changing in inverse proportion as the capital-output ratio (b) changes, given a constant δ.

To bring out technological impacts in bold relief, we make the specific assumption that the investment ratio is an invariant function of time:

$$\delta = \delta_t = \overline{\delta}. \tag{5'}$$

So much for the repetitious yet necessary preparations. We are now ready to analyse the possible effects of capital-saving and capital-using techniques on productive capacity.

The Effect of Capital-saving Techniques

Suppose that capital-*saving* techniques are in vogue. If such techniques are being adopted at the constant rate g_b, the capital-output ratio will decrease exponentially:

$$b = b_t = \frac{b_0}{(1+g_b)^t}, \tag{6'}$$

where b_t is the dynamic capital-output ratio, b_0 the initial value of that ratio, and g_b the rate of *decrease* of that ratio. Equation (6′) represents, in effect, a rising productivity of capital, since $\sigma_t = 1/b_t$. It implies the following downward cumulative movements:

$$b_0 = c,$$
$$b_1 = b_0/(1+g_b) = c/(1+g_b),$$
$$b_2 = b_1/(1+g_b) = c/(1+g_b)^2,$$
$$b_3 = b_2/(1+g_b) = c/(1+g_b)^3,$$

and so forth.

Substituting (5') and (6') in (4') denoting $\Delta Y'/Y'$ by G_k, we get

$$G_k = \frac{\bar{\delta}}{b_0/(1+g_b)^t}, \tag{7'}$$

which tells us that the rate of growth of full-capacity output is capable of increasing in inverse proportion as the capital-output ratio decreases over time, provided that the investment ratio (δ) remains constant.

The Effect of Capital-Using Techniques

We now turn to the opposite case where the preponderant tendency is to adopt capital-*using* techniques of production, for reasons yet to be specified. If the capital-output ratio increases at the constant rate g_b, we have the compound-interest growth of that ratio:

$$b = b_t = b_0(1+g_b)^t, \tag{8'}$$

where g_b, this time, signifies the constant rate of *increase* of the capital-output ratio. Equation (8') can be amplified as before:

$$b_0 = c,$$
$$b_1 = b_0(1+g_b) = c(1+g_b),$$
$$b_2 = b_1(1+g_b) = c(1+g_b)^2,$$
$$b_3 = b_2(1+g_b) = c(1+g_b)^3,$$

et cetera.

Taking (5') and (8') into consideration, equation (4') can be expressed in the modified form

$$G_k = \frac{\bar{\delta}}{b_0(1+g_b)^t}, \tag{9'}$$

which equation tells us that the rate of growth of full-capacity output can decrease inversely with an increasing capital-output ratio, when the investment ratio remains constant. In other words, a falling productivity of capital gives rise to a secular reduction in G_k.

The Capital-Output Ratio as a Policy Parameter

Again it is useful to consider the capital-output ratio as a possible policy parameter, as we did in the case of the labour-output ratio. From equation (3′) we have the *required* capital-output ratio consistent with the given values of G_k and δ:

$$b = \frac{\delta}{G_k}, \quad \sigma = \frac{G_k}{\delta}, \qquad (10')$$

where b and σ are the required capital-output ratio and productivity of capital respectively. Since the actual value of the capital-output ratio (b') is likely to deviate from its required or equilibrium value (b) under *laissez-faire*, it may become necessary matters of public policy to influence the nature and direction of technological advance in order to make $b' = b$ given some accepted values of G_k and δ.

Should, for instance, a higher G_k be accepted as necessary and desirable in relation to a given σ, the required capital-output ratio must fall, according to equation (10′). If the prevailing state of technology is such as to establish a high actual capital-output ratio, the above acceptance of a higher G_k as a desideratum requires the deliberate adaption of the existing capital-output ratio the accepted values of G_k and σ, that is, to the equilibrium value of that ratio b. However, the lowering of the capital-output ratio, while implying a higher rate of growth of capacity output, nevertheless involves some conceptual and practical difficulties.

For example, a United Nations study suggests that an under-developed economy with a high rate of population growth and a low rate of saving would do well to gear its investment programming to 'quick-yielding projects' such as agriculture rather than to 'capital intensive' projects such as heavy industry.[1] One might, as N. Kaldor did, dismiss it simply by asserting that 'there is no basic alternative to heavy industry',[2]

---

[1] U.N. *Economic Bulletin for Asia and the Far East*, November 1955, esp. 'Problems and Techniques of Economic Development Planning and Programming with Special Reference to ECAFE Countries.'

[2] In an address on 'Economic Development in India with Special Reference to the Second Five-Year Plan', before the New York Metropolitan Economic Association meeting, December 1956.

but the confusion still remains to the detriment of a theoretically sound policy. Those 'quick-yielding projects' are preferred presumably because they 'obviously offer relatively lower capital-output ratios from the immediate point of view'.[1] These are attractive propositions to capital-poor, overpopulated, underdeveloped countries, to be sure, but it is by no means so obvious that lower capital-output ratios will necessarily result from gearing investment programming to 'quick-yielding' and 'labour intensive' projects. We may justify our scepticism as follows.

Let K be real capital, N employable labour, Y output, K/N the capital-labour ratio, K/Y the capital-output ratio, and Y/N the productivity of labour. Let K/N represent the degree of 'capital-intensity', so that a high K/N may be associated with a 'capital-intensive' industry or project and a low K/N with a 'labour-intensive' industry or project. The proposition that a less 'capital-intensive' project can entail a lower capital-output ratio would be valid only if the productivity of labour was assumed independent of capital-intensity. But this latter assumption is of doubtful plausibility, for observation and experience indicate that the productivity of labour varies in consequence of more or less 'capital-intensive' industrialization. We may clarify this matter by reference to the following relation between the capital-output ratio and other technological parameters:

$$\frac{K}{Y} = \frac{K/N}{Y/N}. \tag{11'}$$

which tells us that the capital-output ratio is directly proportional to the capital-labour ratio and inversely proportional to the productivity of labour. It is clear from (11') that a low capital-output ratio can be identified with 'labour-intensive' projects or innovations *if* the denominator of the ratio $(K/N)/(Y/N)$ is assumed to remain unaffected by a fall in its numerator. It is also clear that a *higher* rather than lower capital-output ratio will result from the productivity of labour (Y/N) rising less than in proportion to the coefficient of capital-intensity (K/N). Thus there is a theoretical possibility that the

[1] U.N., *ibid.*

capital-output ratio may fall not in spite but because of 'capital-intensive' industrialization.[1] Thus, too, it is important for both analysis and policy to recognize the capital-labour ratio (K/N) and the productivity of labour (Y/N) not only as independent variables in relation to the dependent variable K/Y but also as *inter*-dependent variables in relation to each other.

[1] To illustrate this possibility, it seems useful to consider the following numerical example:

Type of Technique Adopted	(1) Degree of Roundabout-ness	(2) Productivity of labour	(3) Capital-Output Ratio	(4) Saving Ratio	(5) Growth Rate
	(K/N)	(Y/N)	(K/Y)	(S/Y)	$(\Delta Y/Y)$
Initial	50/100	10/100	5	0·05	0·01
Capital-intensive	100/100	25/100	4	0·05	0·0125
Labour-intensive	25/100	4/100	6·25	0·05	0·008

$(3) = (1)/(2)$; $(5) = (4)/(3)$.

This example illustrates the possibility that an underdeveloped economy with a low saving ratio nevertheless may attain a high growth rate $(\Delta Y/Y)$ by adopting 'capital-intensive' techniques or by encouraging 'capital-intensive' industrialization (the second row is the case in point).

The reader will be interested in the following reactions of Mrs. Joan Robinson and Messrs. A. K. Sen and S. Sachi to the above illustration of mine that appeared as a part of my 'Techniques for Maximum Growth and Employment', *Economic Weekly* (India), March 9, 1957. For those reactions of Mrs. Robinson, *et al.* serve to reveal the confused nature of the controversy over the choice of technique as well as to indicate wherein Mrs. Robinson and others agree and disagree with the above illustration.

Mrs. Robinson, in her note to the *Economic Weekly* (April 27, 1957), states: 'He, ["Mr. K. K. Kurihara"] shows three techniques, each employing 100 men. The most capital-intensive requires 100 units of investment [capital, to be more perspicuous] and produces an output of 25 units. The next requires 50 units of investment for 10 units of output, and the last 25 units of investment for 4 units of output. From every point of view the first technique [the second row, in our numerical example] is superior to the other two. This line of argument can be used against, for instance, the Ambar Charkha which produces less output both per man and per unit of investment than a spinning mill, but it has no bearing on the choice between say, two types of looms, of which the less mechanized produces less output per man but more per unit of investment and the more mechanized, less per unit of investment and more per man.'

A. K. Sen, in his 'Man, Machine and Growth' (*Economic Weekly*, March 30, 1957), states: 'Prof. Kurihara is quite right in suggesting that minimization

Influences on Capital-Saving, Capital-Using Techniques

It is difficult but possible to delineate the trend influences[1] on the speed of change in the capital-output ratio (g_b). In what follows, however, we shall discuss only those influences which tend to necessitate or foster the adoption of capital-using techniques and hence to raise the capital-output ratio, leaving the opposite influences to the reader's inference. For we are primarily interested in indicating what may have to be done to overcome a high capital-output ratio as a limiting factor in economic growth, given a constant investment or saving ratio.

Our foregoing discussion suggests that one basic explanation for the needlessly high capital-output ratio of an underdeveloped economy is the *low* degree of capital-intensity which may reduce output in greater proportion than capital relatively to given

---

[1] On the theoretical levels, see W. Fellner, 'The Capital-Output Ratio in Dynamic Economics', *op. cit.*; J. Robinson, 'Notes on the Economics of Technical Progress', *op. cit.*; Y. Takata, *op. cit.*; S. Tsuru, 'A Note on Capital-Output Ratios', *Economic Review*, April 1956. On empirical levels, see Harvard Economic Research Project, 'Estimates of the Capital Structure of American Industries, 1947', June 1953; D. Creamer, 'Capital and Output Trends in Manufacturing Industries 1880–1948' (National Bureau of Economic Research *Occasional Paper* 41), 1954; M. Shinohara, 'The Difference of Capital-Output Ratios among Industries', *Economic Review*, October 1956; Y. Okazaki, 'On the Capital-Coefficient in Underdeveloped Countries—with Special Reference to the Cases of India and Japan', *Economic Studies Quarterly*, March 1957.

---

of capital-intensity need not minimize the capital-output ratio ... It is perfectly possible that a higher capital-labour ratio may give us a lower capital-output ratio provided (Y/N) rises more than in proportion to (K/N). This is actually a question of facts, and one cannot generalize one way or the other about the relationship between (K/N) and (K/Y) ... While Prof. Kurihara criticizes the assumption of labour productivity (Y/N), being independent of capital-intensity (K/N), he assumes that the saving ratio (S/Y), is independent of it (0·05 in all the three cases). But surely the saving ratio depends upon the ratio of wage bill to output, which again depends upon the productivity of labour (Y/N).'

S. Sachi, in his 'Prof. Kurihara on Choice of Techniques' (*Economic Weekly*, March 1957), states: 'Prof. Kurihara convincingly refutes this theory [that underdeveloped economies "should develop labour intensive industries as they had abundance of labour"] as many others had done it earlier ... There is hardly any question of choice in this situation [reference is to the above numerical example]; if the capital intensive investment pattern is not chosen, it would be out of sheer ignorance. However, the real problem of choice arises when one type of investment pattern gives a lower rate of growth initially, and a higher rate thereafter, than the other type. In this situation, which pattern to choose would depend upon political considerations and not upon economic analysis.'

labour. That is to say, an attempt to economize on capital relatively to labour (less 'roundaboutness') could result in a paradoxical increase in the amount of capital required to produce a given output. We have seen that this paradox is due to the possibility that a fall in capital per unit of labour (K/N) may increase rather than decrease the capital-output ratio (K/Y) if that fall in capital per unit of labour occasions a more than proportional fall in the productivity of labour (Y/N), as equation (11') indicates. Joan Robinson suggests another explanation when she says that 'where entrepreneurs buy capital goods from each other, a fall in the price of capital goods relatively to wage rates encourage the adoption of capital-using techniques'.[10] This may be especially true of those under-developed economies depending heavily on imported equipment and raw materials, in addition to the virtual absence of large 'integrated' industries to which a change in factor prices makes little difference. And the price of capital goods may fall in favour of underdeveloped economies, not only because international competition among the producers and exporters of capital goods tends to bid it down, but also because domestic population growth tends to put a downward pressure on the average wage rate. It is here that the traditional analysis becomes relevant. Consider the capital-labour ratio as the dependent variable in

$$\frac{K}{N} = f\left(\frac{P_k}{P_n}\right), \qquad (12')$$

where P_k is the average price of capital (on some definition) and P_n the average price of labour (money wage-rate). Then the elasticity of substitution of capital for labour can be expressed in the general form

$$e = \frac{P_k/P_n}{K/N} \cdot \frac{d(K/N)}{d(P_k/P_n)} = \frac{d(K/N)}{d(P_k/P_n)} \Big/ \frac{K/N}{P_k/P_n} \lessgtr 1, \qquad (13')$$

where e stands for the elasticity coefficient measuring the degree of ease with which capital is substituted for labour in response to a change in relative factor prices. If the productivity of labour is held constant, equations (12') and (13) in conjunction

[10] See her *The Rate of Interest*, etc., pp. 52–3.

G

with equation ($11'$) indicate that $e = 1$ is a force making for a constant capital-output ratio, $e > 1$ for a higher capital-output ratio under discussion, and $e < 1$ for a lower capital-output ratio. As for changes in the factor prices themselves, they depend on the relative scarcity of capital and labour, the structures of capital and labour markets, the comparative bargaining strength of organized capital and labour forces, and possibly public policies with respect to the distribution of a given national income among productive factors.

Another possible explanation for the generally high capital-output ratios of underdeveloped economies is the structural need for durable capital during the early phase of industrialization, such as steel, electricity, ship-building, and other 'capital-using' developments. A corollary of this is that new industries in 'young' economies tend to move in the direction of capital-using technological advance, partly because those economies have not yet reached a 'mature' stage where 'scientific management' (managerial and administrative) and other capital-saving improvements are technically feasible. Also, extensive cultivation in agriculture, such as occurs in rapidly expanding areas, observedly calls for greater capital per unit of agricultural output.

A high interest rate is another important explanation for the capital-output ratio tending to be so high in an underdeveloped economy. This may sound a bit paradoxical, for common sense tells us that a high interest rate discourages the use of capital in the production process and so perhaps should lower the capital-output ratio. This seeming paradox would vanish on reflection, however. A high interest rate tends to discourage the use of capital *relatively to labour* (to lower K/N), since it has the effect of lowering the capitalized value of existing assets relatively to the expected 'supply price' of new assets and hence of making the latter assets appear more costly and less attractive than the former. In familiar Keynesian terminology, this means that the marginal efficiency of capital (the net profit-rate) is lower than the market rate of interest so as to discourage 'real' investment in durable equipment relatively to 'financial' investment in stocks, bonds, and other existing assets. The main point is that if 'roundabout' methods of production are discouraged (K/N is lowered, that is), by a prevailing high interest rate, output is likely to fall in greater proportion than capital and so to send up the capital-output ratio, according to equation ($11'$). Thus the expectation of a continuing high interest rate tends to promote less 'capital-intensive' (or more 'labour-intensive') techniques and, via the latter's decreasing impact on output, to make for a high capital-output ratio, given a constant wage-rate and a constant net profit-rate.

Lastly, the composition of output and the size and location of new industries may have something to do with the high capital-output ratio of an underdeveloped economy. If, for example, machine-made goods are preferred to hand-made goods, the composition of output can change in a way that would require more capital per unit of output. Also, if new plants and enterprises expand in size and yet are located in distance far from raw material sources (often found only in foreign countries), capital outlays may increase relatively to additional output in real terms, thus tending to send up the capital-output ratio for the economy as a whole.

CHAPTER VI

DUAL UNEMPLOYMENT IN UNDER-DEVELOPED ECONOMIES

KEYNES's 'general' theory of employment lacks generality in the respect that it leaves out of account that type of unemployment which exists for lack of real capital even when fully utilized, that is, even when effective demand is sufficient to justify full utilization of the existing capital stock. His theory of employment applies to a short-run situation where capital accumulation, population growth, technological advance and other fundamental conditions of supply are taken as given, and where therefore the volume of employment is uniquely determined by the level of effective demand. Thus Keynes's theory runs the risk of being applied in rationalizing the pyramid-building variety of unproductive employment policy just to stabilize or increase effective demand.

It is against this Keynesian background that Harrod calls attention to the long-run importance of productivity in considering employment stabilization; 'To secure full employment in the short run without regard to what may be necessary for securing a steady rate of progress is short-sighted'.[1] Harrod is credited for having provided the missing link between Keynes's short-run theory of employment and Marx's long-run theory of employment. For, as Joan Robinson has pointed out, 'though nothing is farther from his thoughts, Mr. Harrod has led us to Marx's theory of the reserve army of labour, which expands and contracts as the growth of population runs faster or slower than the rate or capital accumulation'[2]. She has christened this latter type 'Marxian unemployment', in contradistinction to 'Keynesian unemployment'.[3] Joan Robinson, moreover, has suggested that 'Marxian unemployment' is

[1] R. F. Harrod, Dynamic Economics, p. 74.
[2] J. Robinson, 'Mr. Harrod's Dynamics', *op. cit.*
[3] *Ibid.*

what 'exists in the backward, over-populated countries of the
east' as well as in 'war-shattered economies where unemployment results from the mere lack of equipment and material
to work with'.[1]

Thus Keynes's theory of employment has provided the central
point of departure from which to criticize a Ricardian world
of automatic full employment (*à la* Say's Law)[2] and to ponder
a Malthusian-Marxian world of 'overpopulation' and 'the
reserve army of labour'.[3] Furthermore, it would be a mistake
to dismiss Keynes's theory of employment wholly as inapplicable
to underdeveloped economies, not simply because short-runs
make up that Keynesian long-run in which 'we are all dead,'
but fundamentally because underdeveloped economies operating on the lines mainly of private enterprise cannot escape
the possibility of a cyclical shortage of effective demand. The
short-run presence of Keynesian unemployment alongside
long-run non-Keynesian unemployment enormously complicates an underdeveloped economy's full-employment policy,
since the short-run measures to meet the former are not
necessarily consonant with the long-run measures to meet the
latter.

[1] See her 'Marx and Keynes' in *Collected Economic Papers*, pp. 133–45.

[2] For attempts to extend Keynes's theory of employment to a growing advanced
economy, see Harrod, *Dynamic Economics*; Domar, 'Expansion and Employment',
op. cit.; J. Robinson, *The Rate of Interest*, etc., esp. Chap. 3 entitled 'The General-
ization of the General Theory'; M. Kalecki, *Theory of Economic Dynamics*, Rinehart, N.Y., 1954. esp. Part 6; B. Higgins, 'The Theory of Increasing Underemployment', *Economic Journal*, June 1950; R. Eisner, 'Underemployment Equilibrium Rates of Growth', *op. cit.*; D. Hamberg, 'Full Capacity vs. Full Employment
Growth', *Quarterly Journal of Economics*, August 1952; H. Pilvin, 'Full Capacity
vs. Full Employment Growth,' *ibid.*, November 1953 (with comments by Harrod
and Domar).

[3] Relevant to underdeveloped economies are: J. Robinson, 'A Theory of
Long-Run Development', *Economic Review* (Japan), October 1955, and also 'The
Choice of Technique', *Economic Weekly* (India), June 23, 1956; R. Nurkse, *Problems
of Capital Formation in Underdeveloped Economies*; A. and de I. M. Navarrete, 'Under-
employment in Underdeveloped Economies', *International Economic Papers*, No. 3,
1953; M. Morishima, 'Full Employment Policy in a Growing Economy', and
S. Fujita, 'Growth Theory and Superfluous Population', in *Studies in Growth
Economics* (Y. Takata, ed.); D. Ghosh, 'Technique of Production and Employment
in an Underdeveloped Economy', *Economic Weekly*, August 4, 1956; A. K. Dasgupta,
'Disguised Unemployment and Economic Development', *ibid.*, August 25, 1956;
K. K. Kurihara, 'Growth Analysis and the Problem of Capital Accumulation in
Underdeveloped Countries', *op. cit.*

The present chapter is broadly concerned with the dual nature of the unemployment problem in underdeveloped economies, and more particularly, with (a) the cyclical growth of Keynesian unemployment, and (b) the secular growth of non-Keynesian unemployment. Parametric operations for full and productive employment will be indicated in both cases. We shall also make some postscriptal observations on the implications of disguised unemployment.

THE CYCLICAL GROWTH OF KEYNESIAN UNEMPLOYMENT

An underdeveloped economy with capitalistic features is subject to cyclical unemployment of the Keynesian type within the short horizon of development programming (say, 5 years). For its effective demand, while it tends to exceed productive capacity over the long run, nevertheless may fall short of productive capacity in the short run. This possibility is strong, especially in those underdeveloped economies whose export income and private investment are quantitatively significant sources of aggregate effective demand. By way of demonstrating the relevance of Keynesian employment analysis as well as the limitations of Keynesian full-employment policy in underdeveloped economies, we shall begin with the discussion of the cyclical growth of involuntary mass unemployment.

The Supply of Labour
If population, technology, and factor prices are taken as given, it is possible to assume that there is always as much labour as is needed to keep the existing stock of capital fully utilized. In other words, we assume that the supply of labour is growing at the same rate as the rate at which labour is required to utilize the existing capital stock fully and continuously. This assumption will be removed when we come to consider the nature and origin of structural underemployment. To be exact, we assume that the following conditions are always satisfied:

$$N = N_r, \quad \Delta N = \Delta N_r, \tag{1}$$

where N is the amount of *available* labour governed by population growth and N_r the amount of *required* labour for fully utilizing the existing capital stock. The conditions given by (1), if satisfied, would assure that a shortage of labour could never be a bottleneck to full utilization of capital. They also imply that if the existing capital stock is less than fully utilized, that is, if idle or excess capacity appears, it is due to an insufficiency of effective demand. If the supply of labour is thus assumed to accommodate itself to any demand for labour, the appearance of Keynesian unemployment must be explained by reference to demand conditions. Here it is necessary to make a clear distinction between the demand for *required* labour and the demand for *actual* labour. Let us take up the first of these demands first.

The Demand for Required Labour

If effective demand (for output as a whole) is assumed to be high enough to warrant full utilization of the existing stock of capital, the amount of labour needed for that full utilization is given by

$$N_r = \beta K, \tag{2}$$

where K is the quantity of real capital when fully utilized and β the coefficient of labour intensity (reciprocal of the capital-labour ratio discussed previously) given by the prevailing state of technology. Equation (2) indicate a maximum potential volume of employment obtainable by fully utilizing the existing capital stock.

We know that capital and output are related in the form

$$K = bY', \tag{3}$$

where Y' is full-capacity output and b the average and marginal capital-output ratio. We also know that net investment (I) is equivalent to additional capital (ΔK) and is, in equilibrium, equal to savings, that is,

$$I = \Delta K = sY', \tag{4}$$

where s is the average propensity to save at full-capacity output.

From (3) and (4) we have an increment of fully utilized capital

$$\Delta K = \frac{s}{b}K, \tag{5}$$

from which follows the rate of growth of fully utilized capital (that is, by dividing both sides of which equation by K)

$$\frac{\Delta K}{K} = \frac{s}{b}. \tag{6}$$

Taking equations (2) and (6) into account, we can express the rate of growth of *required* labour in the form

$$\frac{\Delta N_r}{N_r} = \frac{\beta \Delta K}{N_r} = \frac{\beta \Delta K}{\beta K} = \frac{\Delta K}{K} = \frac{s}{b}, \tag{7}$$

which shows that the amount of required labour can grow at the same rate as the rate of growth of fully utilized capital, that is, at the rate s/b. If s/b is constant, equation (7) represents a steady line of progressive full employment consistent with full-capacity growth. But whether actual employment will or will not be on this steady line of full employment depends, not on the elasticity of labour supply which we are presently assuming to be infinite, but on the behaviour of effective demand which we have taken as given. This is where we must turn to the determination of the demand for *actual* labour.

The Demand for Actual Labour

Given the stock of real capital to equip labour, the amount of actually employed labour is a function of effective demand, that is,

$$N_e = \epsilon Y^0, \tag{8}$$

where N_e is the amount of *actual* labour demanded in response to real national income or effective demand, Y^0 the level of real national income or effective demand, and ϵ the technologically given ratio of employed labour to effective demand.

We know from Keynes's multiplier theory that effective demand can change by an amount equal to

$$\Delta Y^0 = \frac{1}{s'}\Delta I, \tag{9}$$

where ΔI is the autonomous investment multiplicand in real terms, including the unpredictable private investment and foreign balance mentioned a little earlier, and s' the marginal propensity to save. Here $1/s'$ is of course the multiplier. It is to be noticed that the marginal propensity to save (s') here is not so stable as the average propensity to save (s) appearing in equations (4)–(7).

If we suppose additional investment to be definitely related to effective demand, we can have

$$v = \frac{\Delta I}{Y^0}, \tag{10}$$

where v is the ratio of incremental investment to effective demand and may be as unstable as the factors affecting autonomous investment are variable (except in the case of public investment).

From (9) and (10) we have the rate of growth of effective demand

$$\frac{\Delta Y^0}{Y^0} = \frac{1}{s'}v = \frac{v}{s'}, \tag{11}$$

which rate is cyclically as variable as its determinants (s', v) are unstable.

In the light of (8) and (11) we may write down the rate of growth of *actual* labour demanded in the form

$$\frac{\Delta N_e}{N_e} = \frac{\epsilon \Delta Y^0}{N_e} = \frac{\epsilon \Delta Y^0}{\epsilon Y^0} = \frac{\Delta Y^0}{Y^0} = \frac{v}{s'}, \tag{12}$$

which reveals that actual labour demanded can grow at the rate v/s', that is, as rapidly as effective demand, when the ratio of actual labour to effective demand, (ϵ) is constant.

The Growth of Keynesian Unemployment

It is clear from the foregoing analysis that the basic condition necessary for the maintenance of 'full employment' in the Keynesian sense is given by

$$\frac{\Delta K}{K} = \frac{\Delta Y^0}{Y^0}, \quad \frac{s}{b} = \frac{v}{s'}, \tag{13}$$

If, however, a redundancy of capital or, what is the same, shortage of effective demand appears as a consequence of a temporary fall in private investment or export income (expressed in v), a discrepancy will emerge between required labour and actual labour demanded. For cyclical unemployment is measured by the difference between full employment that would obtain if the existing stock of capital was fully utilized and actual employment that the existing level of effective demand makes possible, as indicated earlier. In the present dynamic context the growth of Keynesian unemployment, as such, could therefore be expressed in the form

$$\frac{\Delta U^c}{U^c} = \frac{\Delta N_r}{N_r} - \frac{\Delta N_e}{N_e} = \frac{s}{b} - \frac{v}{s'}, \tag{14}$$

where $\Delta U^c/U^c$ is the rate of growth of Keynesian unemployment due to the excess of the rate of growth of capital over the rate of growth of demand (for output as a whole), and where the superscript c denotes the *cyclical* nature of the unemployment problem involved.

The growth of Keynesian unemployment expressed by equation (14) measures the degree of a cyclical deviation (downward) from the steady line of progressive full employment consistent with full-capacity growth. It reflects the cyclical growth of capitalism, whether in an advanced or underdeveloped economy.

However, an underdeveloped economy trying to satisfy the equilibrium condition given by equation (13) is under severe compulsion not to adopt measures that would defeat the long-run purpose of overcoming the more serious and fundamental problem of structural underemployment. With this reservation in mind, let us briefly explore operational possibilities for full and productive employment in the medium-long run.

Parametric Operations to Meet Keynesian Unemployment

Keynes looked upon autonomous investment (expressed in v) as a variable policy parameter, while viewing the marginal propensity to save (s') as a fixed parameter reflecting predetermined saving habits. In the present context, however, we shall consider both v and s' as variable policy parameters in order to enlarge the scope of policy manipulation. Moreover, it is necessary to disaggregate v and s' in order to see the alternatives open to an underdeveloped economy confronted with Keynesian unemployment.

We may disaggregate the ratio of additional autonomous investment to effective demand as follows:

$$v = \frac{\Delta I_p + \Delta I_g + \Delta E}{Y^0} = \frac{\Delta I_p}{Y^0} + \frac{\Delta I_g}{Y^0} + \frac{\Delta E}{Y^0} = v_p + v_g + v_e, \quad (15)$$

where I_p is domestic private investment, I_g government investment, E export income, v_p, v_g, and v_e respectively denoting $\Delta I_p/Y^0$, $\Delta I_g/Y^0$, and $\Delta E/Y^0$. Equation (15) gives us three investment policy parameters with which to operate on the leverage side of the multiplier process.

Likewise the marginal propensity to save can be disaggregated, that is,

$$s' = \frac{\Delta S_p + \Delta S_g + \Delta M}{\Delta Y^0} = \frac{\Delta S_p}{\Delta Y^0} + \frac{\Delta S_g}{\Delta Y^0} + \frac{\Delta M}{\Delta Y^0} = s'_p + s'_g + m, \quad (16)$$

where S_p is private savings, S_g government savings (i.e. budgetary surplus), M import expenditure, s'_p the private marginal propensity to save, s'_g the government marginal propensity to save, and m the marginal propensity to import. Equation (16) yields three saving parameters on the leakage side of the multiplier process.

Taking (15) and (16) into account, equation (11) can be rewritten

$$\frac{\Delta Y^0}{Y^0} = \frac{v}{s'} = \frac{v_p + v_g + v_e}{s'_p + s'_g + m}. \quad (17)$$

The long-run requirement that the growth of capital at the constant rate s/b be left undisturbed by medium-long run measures to meet Keynesian unemployment places some restrictions on possible parametric operations here. In the first place, the marginal propensity to save for the economy as a whole (s') cannot be lowered just to increase the multiplier temporarily, since a fall in s' may lead to a self-defeating fall in s and hence in the rate of growth of fully utilized capital. This means that the components of s' must be so manipulated as to leave s' as a whole constant, leaving the main burden on the leverage side. If s' is to remain constant, the private marginal propensity to save (s'_p), the government marginal propensity to save (s'_g), and the marginal propensity to import (m) must each be lowered by an amount equal to an increase in the other. Which particular component of s' is to be lowered is then a question that must be decided by reference to the least harm to *long-run productivity*.

As for the leverage side, the above-mentioned requirement means that the productivity of any component of v as well as its income-generating effect must be taken into account. Thus the aggregate ratio of additional investment to effective demand can be increased by simultaneously increasing v_p, v_g, and v_e with due regard to their productivity effects. In other words, the pyramid-building type of investment must be avoided in *all* cases. Otherwise the capital-output ratio (b) would increase as a consequence of a fall in the productivity of net investment, only to defeat the long-run purpose of keeping the growth of capital intact. As a matter of practical policy, however, the parameter v_e does not easily lend itself to domestic policy making inasmuch as it is largely dependent on foreign propensities to import. The relative weight to be given to v_p and v_g must be decided by reference to the degree of consistency with the long-run productivity counterpart of b (i.e. its reciprocal, σ) as well as to the extent to which *laissez-faire* is considered tolerable.

Thus Keynesian unemployment is much more difficult to meet in an underdeveloped economy than in an advanced economy which already has a high rate of growth of capital, and which therefore can afford to lower its marginal propensity to save or to raise its propensity to invest in unproductive yet employment-creating projects. Nevertheless the above disaggregative analysis indicates the possibility of coping with Keynesian unemployment in the medium-long run without impairing the long-run aim of increasing productive capacity.

THE SECULAR GROWTH OF NON-KEYNESIAN UNEMPLOYMENT

Far more serious than Keynesian unemployment due to the cyclical malbehaviour of effective demand is that non-Keynesian type of mass unemployment which is inherent in the under-developed, overpopulated structure of a developing economy, and which manifests itself largely in unproductive occupations known as 'disguised unemployment'. This is the type of un-employment which Harrod's juxtaposition of the natural and warranted rates of growth implies, and which Joan Robinson has chosen to call 'Marxian unemployment'. However, we consider it more perspicuous to call it 'non-Keynesian unem-ployment' or 'structural underemployment'. For Marx's 're-serve army of labour', while it may be due to the same funda-mental variables analysed by Harrod and Joan Robinson herself,[1] nevertheless seems to be a rhetorical expression to describe the historical fact that the depressing pressure of a redundant labour population on the wage-rate relative to the profit-rate tended to stimulate the rapid accumulation of capital.[2] Thus it appears that Marx considered 'the reserve army of labour' as a *sine qua non* of capitalistic development, even though he resented the 'exploitation' of labour involved.

---

[1] See her 'Marx and Keynes', *op. cit.*

[2] On the assumption that the marginal propensity to save out of profit-income is positive while the marginal propensity to save out of wage-income is zero. For explicity or implicit theorizing about Marx's 'reserve army of labour' in formal models, see S. Tsuru, *Essays on Marxian Economics* (Science Council of Japan Economic Series No. 8), Tokyo, 1956; M. Shinohara, 'Economic Progress and Price Structure', *Economic Review*, July 1954. For an informal observation see P. Sweezy, 'Keynes, the Economist', in *The New Economics* (S. E. Harris, ed.), Knopf, N.Y., 1948, esp. p. 107, where he states: 'Keynes treats unemployment as a symptom of a technical fault in the capitalist mechanism, while Marx regards it as the indispensable means by which capitalists maintain their control over the labour market.' On the other hand, Joan Robinson criticizes Marx for his neglect of the possibility of unemployment arising from 'the divorce between decisions to save and decisions to invest' emphasized by Keynes. (See her 'Marx and Keynes', *op. cit.*).

By contrast, our fundamental position is that the non-Keynesian type of unemployment is a basic *impediment* to industrialization because of the direct waste of otherwise productive manpower and the indirect encouragement its existence gives to marginal agriculture, cottage industries and other 'shock absorbers' of disguised unemployment at the expense of heavy industries.

With this general background, let us proceed to examine the nature and origin of non-Keynesian unemployment in the context of an underdeveloped economy. We begin with the analysis of the supply of available labour which we took as given in the preceding section.

The Supply of Labour
Given relative factor prices and the community's choice between work and leisure, the supply of labour may be considered as increasing by an amount equal to

$$\Delta N = \alpha \Delta P, \tag{18}$$

where N is the amount of labour supplied as before, P the size of the total population, and α the average and marginal 'propensity to work' based on the community's preference between work and leisure.

Next we may suppose a definite relation to exist between incremental population and available labour, that is,

$$\lambda = \frac{\Delta P}{N}, \tag{19}$$

where λ may be considered autonomously predetermined by the prevailing rates of births and deaths and possibly also by emigration policy. It may be presumed that an underdeveloped economy has a high λ for the reasons specified subsequently.

From (18) and (19) we have the rate of growth of *labour* population:

$$\frac{\Delta N}{N} = \alpha \lambda, \tag{20}$$

which represents the supply side of the problem of structural underemployment. Equation (20) tells us that the rate of growth of available labour is directly proportional to the propensity to work (α) times the ratio of additional population to available labour (λ). In other words, the supply of labour in a growing economy is a function of a culturally given parameter (α) and a demographically given parameter (λ).

The fundamental difficulty on the supply side is that most underdeveloped economies have a high rate of growth of available labour ($\Delta N/N$), both because they have no basic choice but to have a large fraction of the total population ready and willing to work (a high α) and because their demographic structure is usually such as to yield a high ratio of incremental population to available labour (a high λ). But whether the consequentially high rate of growth of labour supplied will or will not give rise to structural underemployment depends on the prevailing rate of growth of labour demanded. Let us turn to the demand side once more.

The Demand for Labour

As far as underdeveloped economies are concerned, the demand for labour is characterized by two fundamental difficulties, namely, (a) the slow growth of fully utilized capital, and (b) the decreasing impact of technological progress on the amount of labour demanded per unit of output in the very course of industrialization.

Capital must grow at the rate at which available labour is growing, if a growing labour force is to be fully and productively employed. And yet all underdeveloped economies have a low rate of growth of capital, not only because they have a low saving ratio (s), but also because they have a high capital-output ratio (b) for the reasons already discussed. Accordingly the rate of growth of required labour must be also low, as equation (7) clearly indicates. A low rate of growth of capital is in and by itself ominous enough, but there is yet another pressure on the rapid growth of required labour. Let us see how this comes about.

Equation (7) implies that productive capacity must also grow at the same rate as the rate at which required labour is growing. For given the constant ratio of required labour to capacity output, $N_r/Y' = a$, productive capacity must increase by $\Delta Y' = \Delta N_r/a$. Hence we have the rate of growth of productive capacity

$$\frac{\Delta Y'}{Y'} = \frac{\Delta N_r/a}{Y'} = \frac{\Delta N_r/a}{N_r/a} = \frac{\Delta N_r}{N_r} = \frac{s}{b}, \tag{21}$$

which shows that productive capacity, as well as fully utilized capital, must grow at the rate s/b.

If, however, the productivity of labour increases under the impact of technological progress, the labour-output ratio a will decline through time, as shown in the previous chapter. If so, the amount of required labour at any time is smaller than if the labour-output ratio did not decline, that is,

$$N_r(t) = \frac{a_0}{(1+g_a)^t}Y'_0, \tag{22}$$

where Y'_0 is the initial value of capacity output at $t = 0$ and g_a the constant rate of decrease of the labour-output ratio as before.

When account is taken of (21) and (22), it is necessary to modify equation (7) as

$$\frac{\Delta N_r}{N_r} = \frac{1+\dfrac{s}{b}}{1+g_a} - 1, \tag{23}$$

which indicates that if capital and output are growing at the rate s/b, while the labour-output ratio is decreasing at the rate g_a, the rate of growth of required labour $(1 + \Delta N_r/N_r)$ will equal only $(1 + s/b)/(1 + g_a)$. Thus equation (23) implies *secular technological unemployment*, which complicates the simple case of structural underemployment in conditions of neutral technology. It also implies an additional basic condition of full-employment equilibrium, as will be shown presently.

The Growth of Non-Keynesian Unemployment
If the rate of growth of available labour exceeds the rate of growth of required labour for the reasons mentioned above, we have the inequality

$$\frac{\Delta N}{N} = \frac{\Delta P}{P} > \frac{\Delta N_r}{N_r} = \frac{\Delta K}{K},$$

from which inequality follows the rate of growth of structural underemployment:

$$\frac{\Delta U^s}{U^s} = \frac{\Delta N}{N} - \frac{\Delta N_r}{N_r} = \alpha\lambda - \frac{s}{b}, \qquad (24)$$

where $\Delta U^s / U^s$ is the rate of growth of non-Keynesian unemployment, the superscript s indicating the *secular* nature of the unemployment problem involved. Equation (24) implies that the volume of structural underemployment will increase through time, according to the exponential form

$$U^s(t) = e^{(\alpha\lambda - s/b)t} U_0. \qquad (25)$$

Equations (24) and (25) intimate the persistent presence of disguised unemployment, for the majority of those becoming permanently unemployed for lack of capital equipment are subsequently absorbed in such unproductive occupations as subsistence farming, handicrafts, street vending, and domestic service—all of which require little or no capital equipment to work with. Disguised unemployment therefore is the specific form which structural underemployment takes not merely in underdeveloped economies but in the underdeveloped areas of an advanced economy (e.g. some southern parts of the U.S.) as well.

Thus we see that structural underemployment can appear and persist in an underdeveloped economy whose supply of labour tends to outrun its demand for labour, even if effective demand is high enough to keep the existing capital stock fully utilized and even if technological progress is neutral so as not to diminish the amount of labour required per unit of output. Structural underemployment, as such, is a drag on economic development in general and industrialization in particular, since it tends to perpetuate unproductive, inefficient enterprises as disguisers of non-cyclical, non-frictional unemployment.

Before discussing the operational possibilities of minimizing this non-Keynesian type of mass unemployment, it is useful to indicate two basic conditions of full employment to be satisfied in the long run, namely,

$$\frac{s}{b} = \alpha\lambda \qquad (26)$$

when the productivity of labour remains constant on the assumption of technological neutrality, and

$$\frac{s}{b} = \alpha\lambda + g_a \tag{27}$$

when the productivity of labour is rising to reduce the labour-output ratio through time. The right-hand side of equation (27) is an approximation to $(1 + \alpha\lambda)(1 + g_a) - 1$ at which rate capital and capacity must grow, when the labour-output ratio is decreasing so as to require less labour per unit of output, in order to avoid otherwise inevitable secular technological unemployment.

Parametric Operations to Meet Non-Keynesian Unemployment

The foregoing discussion makes it clear that an under-developed economy confronted with mass unemployment of the non-Keynesian type must broadly increase the rate of growth of capital $(\Delta K/K)$, decrease the rate of growth of population $(\Delta P/P)$, or do both. Specifically the elimination of structural underemployment or, positively speaking, the secular maintenance of full and productive employment requires appropriate operations with the structural parameters that determine those rates of growth of capital and population. Let us consider parametric operations in the light of the equilibrium conditions given by equations (26) and (27).

To increase the rate of growth of required labour, an under-developed economy must increase the saving ratio (s) and decrease the capital-output ratio (b), that is, in the circumstances characterized by $(\Delta P/P) > (\Delta K/K)$. This is easier said than done, especially when and where the standard of consumption is already so low as to make a rise in s difficult and the state of technology so backward as to make a fall in b (or a rise in the productivity of capital) also difficult. Here we see a potential conflict between labour's desire for full employment and its desire for greater current consumption—a conflict which does not exist in an advanced economy where it is oversaving (i.e. underconsumption) which makes for Keynesian unemployment. An attempt to increase the rate of growth of required labour through a rise in the saving ratio therefore involves an underdeveloped economy in a tendency to provoke labour's opprobrium against an economic system which allows a few to save more at the expense of mass consumption. To the extent, however, an underdeveloped economy increases s through measures that do not call for a greater sacrifice of already low consumption (e.g. fiscal and foreign-trade policies to be discussed later and separately), will it to that extent be able to increase the rate of growth of capital and hence the rate of growth of required labour without provoking popular resentment and without therefore upsetting political equilibrium.

As for a required fall in the capital-output ratio (b), an underdeveloped economy would have to increase the productivity of capital by making capital-saving technological improvements as well as by avoiding the wasteful use of plants and equipment. It will be shown later that a reallocation of capital to the more productive sectors could decrease the capital-output ratio for the whole economy. An attempt to reduce the capital-output ratio through a dear money policy must be ruled out as unpromising and unfruitful. For any decreasing effect that a dear money policy might have on the capital-output ratio could be completely offset by a possible rise in the money wage-rate (e.g. through trade-union action) or by a possible fall in the average price of capital goods (e.g. through market competition), that is, by factor price changes tending to encourage capital-using methods of production. Not only that, but a dear money policy is not consistent with the long-run aim of stimulating developmental investment activity. The reader may recall other suggestions about the lowering of the capital-output ratio in the preceding chapter on technology.

Another operational possibility can be seen in reducing the rate of decrease of the labour-output ratio (g_a) in equation (27). This means that an underdeveloped economy facing the possibility of secular technological unemployment would presumably have to resist labour-saving devices in order to minimize that addition to structural underemployment which cannot be absorbed in productive employment by accumulating capital at the rate $\alpha\lambda$. Two difficulties are discernible here. First, as noted in the last chapter, resistance to the adoption of labour-saving devices might result in such a significant fall in the productivity of labour as to necessitate a higher capital-output ratio, that is, via $K/Y = (K/N)/(Y/N)$. This is of course self-defeating, since capital must but cannot grow so fast when b is high as when it is low, given the saving ratio. Second, an implied fall in the rate of growth of labour productivity is inconsistent with the notion of the socially optimal rate of growth discussed earlier, since a rise, not a fall, in the rate of growth of labour productivity is what is needed to achieve a secularly rising standard of living. In the light of these difficulties it seems best to accept a positive constant g_a as given and then adapt the rate of growth of capital to $(\alpha\lambda + g_a)$ so that secular technological unemployment may be eliminated without sacrificing the productivity of labour and without lowering the standard of living.

Alternatively, an underdeveloped economy may try to reduce the rate of growth of population and hence the rate of growth of available labour by taking the rate of growth of capital as given. To be specific, an underdeveloped economy must, in the circumstances typified by $(\Delta P/P) > (\Delta K/K)$, decrease both α and λ. A fall in the propensity to work (α) implies that the community should be encouraged to prefer leisure to work so that a smaller fraction of the total population may be always able and willing to work. This involves an essentially cultural choice which may or may not be economically warranted. Surely the pressure to increase the rate of growth or required labour would be considerably reduced if those who should not or need not be regular members of the labour force (e.g. job seekers of the school age and the retirement age, housewives and mothers willing to work in hazardous industries, exceptionally talented scientists and artists having to earn their bread, and wealthy eccentrics wanting to gain a livelihood 'the hard way') were permanently removed from the labour market. If the productivity of labour is growing at the positive constant rate g_a, an underdeveloped economy can support a larger 'leisure class' and so reduce the otherwise large value of α. For a rising productivity gives effect to a shorter-hour, higher-wage movement.

Lastly, an underdeveloped economy may endeavour to

reduce the ratio of incremental population to available labour (λ) through birth control and other demographic experiments. Here some institutional difficulties must be faced, as population experts constantly remind us. The endeavour to reduce λ would include the encouragement of emigration, if and when feasible.[1] A negative effort to control population growth, however, may give way to a positive effort to accelerate technological progress in a broad sense, if the birth-rate is assumed to vary inversely with some index of know-how, as Haavelmo has suggested.[2] Moreover, the argument in favour of a large and growing population will become stronger rather than weaker as an underdeveloped economy irresistably advances toward a point where population growth can be looked upon as a stimulating source of investment-*demand* instead of as an annoying cause of structural underemployment.

A POSTSCRIPT ON DISGUISED UNEMPLOYMENT*

Before completing our employment discussion it seems useful to touch on R. Nurkse's view of disguised unemployment as a 'saving potential' in the context of an overpopulated underdeveloped economy.[3] According to this view, full mobilization of the disguised unemployment would increase net investment *without reducing consumption*. This Nurkse offers as a compromise

---

* This is part of my 'Techniques for Maximum Growth and Employment', *op cit.*

[1] For example, Japan, though industrially advanced, shares the overpopulated feature of underdeveloped economies, and therefore encourages as much emigration as underpopulated economies (Brazil in the postwar period, for instance) are willing to accept.

[2] Haavelmo, *A Study in the Theory of Economic Evolution*, p. 43. Haavelmo does not elaborate on this assumption, but he may have in mind the observable fact that birth-control information is more widespread among educated families than among uneducated ones. However, it must not be supposed that information is identical with practice. Thus, for example, Japan with its high literacy rate nevertheless has a large and growing population to feed and to employ. All the same the argument in favour of more know-how stands unvitiated, since technological progress tends to lower the capital-output ratio via improvements in the quality of capital.

[3] See Nurkse, *Problems of Capital Formation in Underdeveloped Countries*. Also Buchanan and Ellis, *Approaches to Economic Development*; M. Srinivasan, 'Commonsense Made Difficult', *Economic Weekly* (India), October 13, 1956; A. K. Dasgupta, 'Disguised Unemployment and Economic Development', *ibid.*

between the classical notion of investment and consumption as inevitable *alternatives* and the Keynesian idea of investment and consumption as possible *complements*. For an underdeveloped economy with a large reserve of redundant labour but without redundant capital presumably stands between a classical world of *fully employed resources* having to allocate more of those resources to capital-goods production at the expense of less to consumer-goods production and a Keynesian world of *idle resources* offering to increase output of both capital goods and consumer goods. This 'neutral' position is a comforting thought, but it may prove illusory upon further reflection. Instead of repeating more or less familiar practical objections,[1] we may suggest some theoretical difficulties involved in the various arguments advanced in support of Nurkse's compromise between the classical and Keynesian views of the relation of investment and consumption.

The gist of these arguments seem to be as follows: Assume that all the disguised unemployed are 'employed' in the consumer-goods sector (usually specified as subsistence agriculture). Since the disguised unemployed are by definition marginal or unproductive labour, their withdrawal from the consumer-goods sector would leave output of consumer goods unaffected. Now let the disguised unemployed be shifted to the capital-goods sector, abstracting from the practical difficulties involved in such a shift. Since the marginal productivity of labour in the capital-goods sector is positive *ex hypothesi*, capital-goods output would increase as a result of adding the disguised unemployed to that sector's working force. Thus disguised unemployment is believed to be a 'saving potential' that materializes in net investment (or an addition to the existing capital stock due to the above-mentioned increase in capital-goods production), if and when the disguised unemployed are effectively and fully mobilized by the capital-goods sector. Thus, too, the

[1] My colleague, Professor Robert Alexander, called my attention to the fact, widely observable in Latin America, that the disguised unemployed in agriculture are so unaccustomed to industrial discipline that they commit absenteeism almost as a matter of course when they are 'productively' employed in factories. He also mentioned the fact that a significant block of disguised unemployment in Latin America finds its way into the armed services, implying that not all the disguised unemployed can be 'mobilized' by the productive sector of an underdeveloped economy.

impression is created that disguised unemployment is, after all, a blessing in disguise, instead of being a drag on industrialization. However, the following considerations may dispel this misleading impression.

When due account is taken of the specificity of the labour released from the consumer-goods sector, output of *fixed* capital, which is of crucial importance to industrialization, may not increase significantly. Granting that the disguised unemployed can be transferred to 'investment' projects requiring no special skill or equipment, such 'investment' projects of a labour-intensive nature can hardly be expected to turn out fixed capital in quantities and qualities that are of immediate and adequate use to industrialization. The most that could be expected of such labour-intensive projects is a limited amount of preliminary capital formation (e.g. swamp clearance for factory sites, dirt road-building for modern highways, and handicrafts serving as raw materials for machine-made manufactures). But it takes 'machines to make machines' on a scale large enough to speed up industrialization. And the disguised unemployed are an ineffective substitute for such 'machines to make machines'.

The assumption of constant consumption is thrown into question, not because the marginal productivity of redundant labour in the consumer-goods sector may be above zero, but because its propensity to consume is likely to rise at all levels of income after its shift to the capital-goods sector. This likelihood is plausible for two reasons. First, prior to their shift to the capital-goods sector the disguised unemployed are forced to such a low standard of consumption that they will almost certainly develop new stronger consuming habits after the shift. Second, the urban areas, where capital-goods industries are heavily concentrated, are observably far more conducive to a strong propensity to consume than the rural areas from which the disguised unemployed are supposed to come. Thus when due account is taken of the 'habit effect' and the 'taste effect', let alone the Pigou 'effect', the propensity to consume for the whole economy may well rise in consequence of urbanizing the previously unproductive but presently productive consumers—the disguised unemployed. In this event the pressure will increase for allocating to the consumer-goods sector those resources which might otherwise be used to increase output of capital goods.

If, moreover, the capital-goods sector adopts labour-saving techniques of production, as it is likely to do in the course of industrialization, the implied reduction in the amount of labour required per unit of output sets a limit to that sector's ability to mobilize the disguised unemployed fully and continuously. As already discussed, in a case of this sort capital would have to grow much faster to equip a labour force with a rising productivity than to equip a labour force with a constant productivity. Thus the tacit assumption of technological neutrality involved in the usual argument about disguised unemployment as a 'saving potential' becomes untenable and unhelpful. Even if we abstract out the above complication arising from technological progress, we are still left with the fundamental problem of population growth tending to outrun capital accumulation. A *growing*, not just a large, population aggravates the difficulty of increasing net investment without reducing consumption, since it implies more mouths to feed as well as more hands to employ. In an underdeveloped economy with a growing population, such an increase in net national product in excess of consumption as full utilization of the disguised unemployed may make possible would probably be 'eaten up' largely, if not wholly, by the genuinely unproductive addition to the population (e.g. a growing number of those normally considered *below* the 'productive age' of, say, fifteen years). Furthermore, the tendency of population growth to outstrip capital accumulation implies that the volume of disguised unemployment grows faster than can be absorbed productively by the very stock of capital that the disguised unemployed are supposed to help expand.

These considerations cast some doubt on the usefulness of the hypothesis of disguised unemployment as a source of capital accumulation. These considerations, together with our formal discussion, suggest that disguised unemployment, far from helping capital accumulation and economic development, is more likely to hinder them by giving 'aid and comfort' to dubious projects of an employment-generating rather than a capacity-increasing nature.

CHAPTER VII

THE REDISTRIBUTIVE ROLE IN ECONOMIC DEVELOPMENT

THE long-run discussion of income distribution in advanced economies is mostly centred around the question: what effect does economic growth have on the secular distribution of income?[1] This question is of secondary importance as far as underdeveloped economies are concerned, since those economies are in no position to take growth as given and then proceed to speculate on its possible effects on income distribution. The relevant question for underdeveloped economies seems to be rather this: given certain changes in income distribution for institutional, political and ethical reasons, what will be the probable effects of such changes on the growth of output and capital? The present chapter will be addressed partly to this latter question.

The other main question to be discussed here is that of resource reallocation in relation to economic development. For from a long view it is just as important to reallocate given resources and to redistribute given income productively as it is necessary to enlarge the size of productive resources and national income rapidly. Since an economy's growth rate tends to vary directly with the saving ratio and inversely with the capital-output ratio, we shall discuss specifically (a) the impact of income redistribution on the saving ratio, and (b) the impact of resource reallocation on the capital-output ratio or on its reciprocal, capital productivity.

However, the particular techniques[2] of income redistribution

---

[1] Cf. C. Clark, *The Conditions of Economic Progress*; S. Kuznets, 'Economic Growth and Income Inequality', *op. cit.*; M. Bronfenbrenner, 'Some Neglected Implications of Secular Inflation', in *Post-Keynesian Economics*. Since I discussed the redistribution effect on investment-*demand* in the last-named symposium with advanced economies in mind, I now propose to concentrate on the *supply* and *productivity* of capital in the context of underdeveloped economies.

[2] Some redistributing techniques will be specified in subsequent chapters.

and resource reallocation, which vary from one economy to another, will be subsumed in given changes in distribution parameters. It may nevertheless be presumed that income redistributions and resource reallocations are brought about through price movements, priority allocations, fiscal policies, anti-monopoly legislation, and collective bargaining—in most cases.

THE REDISTRIBUTION EFFECT ON THE SAVING RATIO

From classical economists down to the present it has been vaguely felt that the distribution of income (and wealth) looms large in the background of national capital accumulation as a dominant and persistent factor. The extent of the 'distribution effect' on economic progress, however, has been and still is a subject of controversy, if one may judge by the 'underconsumptionist' arguments from Mandeville's 'Fable of the Bees'[1] to Keynes's 'paradox of thrift'. As regards *advanced* economies in the *short* run, there seems little doubt that Keynes 'smashed . . . the last pillar of the bourgeois argument . . . into dust', to borrow Schumpeter's phrase,[2] by the demonstration that at less than full employment an increase in thrift, far from augmenting real capital, tends to diminish it. As regards *underdeveloped* economies in the *long* run, however, it is less certain that the Keynesian argument against presumably unmitigated 'evil' of the propensity not to spend is wholly valid and the classical argument[3] for supposedly unmixed 'virtue' of thrift

[1] Bernard Mandeville, in a pre-classical period, held the then heretical view that prosperity was promoted by spending rather than by saving—which view Adam Smith dismissed as an 'error' but which Keynes cites approvingly. (See Keynes's *General Theory*, esp. 'Notes on Mercantilism'.) The other 'underconsumptionists' in the history of economic thought include Lauderdale, Malthus Sismondi, Marx and Hobson. (See A. H. Hansen, *Business Cycles and National Income*, Norton, N.Y., 1951, Chap. 14. Hansen leaves out Sismondi and Marx, however.)

[2] J. Schumpeter, 'John Maynard Keynes, 1883—1946', *op. cit.*

[3] The classical argument is based on the belief that capital accumulation depends on the strength of individual propensities to save and that for a significantly large proportion of this capital accumulation the economy as a whole depends on the 'abstinence of the rich'. The argument carries with it the implication that income inequality is a *sine qua non* of economic progress. Apart from

entirely invalid. The following analysis may throw light on this classical-Keynesian controversy with particular reference to underdeveloped economics.

Income Inequality and the Saving Ratio

Suppose that a given real national income (Y) is exhausted by wage income (Y_w) and non-wage income (Y_π), so that

$$Y = Y_w + Y_\pi, \qquad (1)$$

where Y_w includes salaries (of 'white-collar' workers), while Y_π includes profits, dividends, rents, interest, and royalties. Although there is some overlapping in the real world, the *preponderant* source of income should determine which group is appropriate to each family or individual income recipient. Thus if a family income consists largely of wages and partly of dividends (on its stockholdings, e.g.) then the family in question should be considered as belonging to the wage income group. Thus considered, family incomes from marginal sources would cancel each other out to leave those from principal sources pure and simple.

From equation (1) we have the wage and non-wage distribution parameters

$$\frac{Y_w}{Y} = \eta, \ \frac{Y_\pi}{Y} = 1 - \eta, \qquad (2)$$

which are predetermined by the institutional factors of property and inheritance and modified by factor pricing and redistribution policies. For the purpose of this discussion any decrease in the wage distribution ratio η will be considered as an increase in income inequality and any increase in it as a decrease in income inequality. This idea of income inequality is based on the assumption that wage-salary earners make up the overwhelming majority of those receiving less than the national average

---

theoretical demonstrations to the contrary, the fact that most underdeveloped economies depend on government saving for a substantial part of developmental capital considerably diminishes the scope of income inequality for promoting saving. This fact is reinforced by the supplementary evidence of 'interdependent consumer preference' which, as will be discussed in the text above, further diminishes the practical importance of income inequality as a precondition of capital growth.

income while non-wage earners constitute the minority that receives more than the average income. In the specific context of an underdeveloped economy, moreover, it is safe to make the additional assumption that the so-called 'middle-class' receiving somewhat above the national average income is relatively small, implying extreme income disparities between the rich and the poor. Such an extremely unequal distribution of income is basically a reflection of heavy concentration of income-producing property.

Now total savings (S) out of a given real national income is divisible into those out of wage income (S_w) and those out of non-wage income (S_π), so that

$$S = S_w + S_\pi, \tag{3}$$

the right-hand side of which equation may be specified as separate saving functions of a long-run nature (implying the equality of average and marginal propensities to save):

$$S_w = s_w Y_w = s_w \eta Y, \tag{4}$$

and

$$S_\pi = s_\pi Y_\pi = s_\pi (1 - \eta) Y. \tag{5}$$

Here s_w is the average and marginal propensity to save out of wage income and s_π that out of non-wage income. It is to be noticed that $s_w \eta$ represents the average and marginal propensity of the wage group to save out of *national* income, while $s_\pi (1 - \eta)$ represents the average and marginal propensity of the non-wage group to save out of *national* income. As is customary, it is assumed that the wage group has a smaller average and marginal propensity to save than the non-wage group, that is, $s_w < s_\pi$. It is this difference which makes income redistribution meaningful.

Substituting (4) and (5) in (3) and rearranging, we have total savings as a function of income and distribution:

$$S = [s_w \eta + s_\pi (1 - \eta)] Y, \tag{6}$$

from which we derive the average propensity to save for the economy as a whole (s):

$$\frac{S}{Y} = s = s_w \eta + s_\pi (1 - \eta). \tag{7}$$

Equation (7) indicates that if the wage distribution ratio η permanently falls, the average propensity to save out of national income or the national saving ratio will rise, provided $s_w < s_\pi$. The implication of equation (7) for an economy's growth rate can be shown in the form

$$\frac{\Delta Y}{Y} = G_k = \frac{s_w \eta + s_\pi (1 - \eta)}{b}, \tag{8}$$

where G_k is the rate of growth of output (or capital) and b the capital-output ratio, as before. What equation (8) tells us is that the rate of growth of output is capable of increasing as a consequence of an increase in income inequality (expressed in a lower η), when the capital-output ratio remains constant. Equation (8) illustrates the classical case for progress through inequality and the 'abstinence of the rich'.

Thus it would appear as if classical economists had been correct in tacitly justifying income inequality as an indispensable prerequisite to economic progress. However, the above analysis is incomplete in two fundamental respects, in that it neglects the possibly offsetting influence of interdependent consumer behaviour on the saving ratio and in that it ignores the possibly lowering effect of resource reallocation on the capital-output ratio. In addition, one may doubt the feasibility of redistributing income in favour of non-wage receivers against wage-salary earners, especially in those underdeveloped economies which are dedicated to the democratic principle of equal opportunity.[1] Such practical difficulties aside, let us consider the relation of income redistribution and the saving ratio in the light of the recent discussion of 'interdependent consumer preferences'.

Income Equalization and the Saving Ratio
Duesenberry has, wittingly or otherwise, thrown into question the classical idea of progress through inequality by suggesting

[1] Apropos, an Indian economist states: 'We learn from economic theory [classical] that one way of increasing saving in the economy could be by redistributing income from the poor to the rich. . .It is difficult to say how far such a policy will be politically feasible and socially desirable in a democratic country at the present time'. (See D. Jha, 'Fiscal Policy and the Economic Development of Underdeveloped Countries', *Indian Journal of Economics*, July 1956.

that 'a decrease in inequality might *increase* the average propensity to save'[1] in a society subject to the institutional-psychological habits of 'keeping up with the Joneses'. Such a suggestion may have been intended to discourage the 'under-consumptionist' belief that a more equal distribution of income might increase consumer demand in an advanced economy liable to an insufficiency of effective demand. As far, however, as an underdeveloped economy is concerned, the above suggestion of Duesenberry has the possibly unintended effect of strengthening the Keynesian belief in the compatibility of greater equality and capital growth.

For the purpose of the following discussion we make one broad assumption, namely, that the underdeveloped economy in question has effective controls (e.g. selective tariffs and multiple exchange rates) over the importation of foreign goods deemed conducive to keeping up with the international Joneses.[2] This assumption permits us to isolate the relation of *domestic* income equalization (in the Lorenz-curve sense) and the consumption (or saving) ratio. The other relevant assumptions will be specified in due course.

Let a given real national income (Y) be exhausted by that part going to low-income families (Y_1), another part going to middle-income families (Y_2), and the remainder going to high-income families (Y_3), so that

$$Y = Y_1 + Y_2 + Y_3, \qquad (9)$$

the distribution ratios of which are

$$\frac{Y_1}{Y} = \mu, \quad \frac{Y_2}{Y} = \epsilon, \quad \frac{Y_3}{Y} = 1 - \mu - \epsilon. \qquad (10)$$

---

[1] See J. S. Duesenberry, *Income, Saving and The Theory of Consumer Behaviour*, Cambridge, 1949, p. 44. Also see H. G. Johnson, 'The Effects of Income Redistribution on Aggregate Consumption with Interdependence of Consumers' Preferences', *Economica*, May 1952. Both of these writers are concerned with advanced economies, not with the implication of income equalization for the problem of economic growth in underdeveloped economies.

[2] See R. Nurkse, *Problems of Capital Formation in Underdeveloped Countries*, pp. 577-9. Nurkse applies Duesenberry's 'demonstration effect' to underdeveloped economies in an effort to explain the latter economies' difficulty of increasing domestic savings in the conspicuous presence of the rich international Joneses, implying the desirability of international homogenization, of narrowing the wide gap between the consumption standards of developed and underdeveloped economies.

Next we divide total real consumption expenditure (C) into that part made by low-income families (C_1), another part made by middle-income families (C_2), and the remaining part by high-income families (C_3), that is:

$$C = C_1 + C_2 + C_3. \tag{11}$$

Here it is necessary to specify the consumption habits of each group of families in order to allow for the 'interdependence effect' of redistribution. It will be assumed that the consumption of groups 1 and 3 depends only on their respective family incomes, while that of group 2 depends in part on the incomes of groups 1 and 3 in addition to its own income. In other words, middle-income families are assumed to be subject to 'emulation' in the sense that their consumption is positively influenced by the consumption of the other two groups of families. The exact extent to which changes in the consumption of groups 1 and 3 could influence the consumption of group 2 remains yet to be specified.

The right-hand side of equation (11) can then be expressed as three separate consumption functions of the forms:

$$C_1 = a_1 Y_1 = a_1 \mu Y, \tag{12}$$

$$C_3 = a_3 Y_3 = a_3 (1 - \mu - \epsilon) Y, \tag{13}$$

and

$$C_2 = \alpha C_1 + \beta C_3 = [\alpha a_1 \mu + \beta a_3 (1 - \mu - \epsilon)] Y. \tag{14}$$

Here a_1 is the average and marginal propensity of low-income families as a whole to consume out of low income, a_3 that of high-income families as a whole to consume out of high income, α the average and marginal propensity of middle-income families as a whole to emulate the consumption of low-income families, and β that of middle-income families to emulate the consumption of high-income families. Here $a_1 > a_3$, according to the usual assumption of the inverse correlation between the marginal propensity to consume and income. As for 'the propensity to emulate', it seems reasonable to assume that the middle-income group attaches far greater importance to the consumption of the high-income group than to that of the low-income group, or $\beta > \alpha$. This implies that the middle-income group increases its consumption as a result of a change in the consumption of the high-income group by a larger amount than the amount by which it increases its consumption as a result of a change in the consumption of the low-income group.

Combining (12), (13) and (14), equation (11) can now be made to read:

$$C = [a_1\mu + \alpha a_1\mu + \beta a_3(1-\mu-\epsilon) + a_3(1-\mu-\epsilon)]Y, \qquad (15)$$

from which we have the average propensity to consume for the entire economy (c):

$$\frac{C}{Y} = c = a_1\mu + \alpha a_1\mu + \beta a_3(1-\mu-\epsilon) + a_3(1-\mu-\epsilon), \qquad (16)$$

which indicates that if income is redistributed from group 3 to group 1 (expressed in a higher μ and a lower $1-\mu-\epsilon$, leaving ϵ constant), the national average propensity to consume (c) can *decrease* via the interdependence effects and income effects which such a redistribution produces. To be specific, equation (16) indicates that the redistribution will have such an *inter-dependence*-effect on the middle-income group as to reduce its average and marginal propensity to consume out of national income, $\alpha a_1\mu + \beta a_3(1 - \mu - \epsilon)$, such an *income*-effect on the high-income group as to reduce its average and marginal propensity to consume out of national income, $a_3(1 - \mu - \epsilon)$, and such an *income*-effect on the low-income group as to increase its average and marginal propensity to consume out of national income, $a_1\mu$, with the *ultimate* result that the national consumption ratio (c) is *decreased*. Thus even if the low-income group has a higher average and marginal propensity to consume out of low income than does the high-income group out of high income, $a_1 > a_3$, the implied increase in total consumption resulting from income equalization is more than offset by the adverse interdependence-effect due to $\beta > \alpha$.

Since the national saving ratio is given by $s = 1 - c$, the implication of equation (16) for the growth rate of an under-developed economy with a constant capital-output ratio (b) can be seen in the form

$$G_k = \frac{1 - [a_1\mu + \alpha a_1\mu + \beta a_3(1-\mu-\epsilon) + a_3(1-\mu-\epsilon)]}{b}, \qquad (17)$$

which shows that the growth rate (G_k) is capable of increasing if the national saving ratio is increased as a consequence of the interaction of the interdependence-effect and the income-effect of income equalization described by equations (9)–(16).

The above discussion suggests that the classical argument about the 'abstinence of the rich' based on income inequality is as inconclusive as it is misleading.[1] It also suggests that an underdeveloped economy with strong egalitarian and welfare sentiment need not be so apprehensive about the supposed incompatibility of greater income equality with economic progress deduced by abstracting from the socio-psychological phenomenon of interdependent consumer preference, of 'keeping up with the Joneses'.

CAPITAL-OUTPUT RATIO

Let us turn to the consideration of whether or not resource reallocation, however brought about, will have the effect of reducing the capital-output ratio or, what amounts to the same, of increasing the productivity of capital. Such a consideration presupposes the prevalence of great disparities in the ownership and control of economic resources among different sectors or industries and the existence of different productivities within a given economy.

Capital Reallocation and Productivity

Suppose that an economy is divided into two sectors, agricultural and industrial. Then the total *physical* stock of capital when fully utilized (K) can be divided into agricultural capital (K_a) and industrial capital (K_i), so that

$$K = K_a + K_i, \qquad (18)$$

the distribution ratio of which is

$$\frac{K_a}{K} = \lambda, \ \frac{K_i}{K} = 1 - \lambda. \qquad (19)$$

[1] The present analysis seems to justify, at least partly, the scepticism of S. Kuznets: 'There is danger in simple analogies; in arguing that because an unequal income distribution in Western Europe in the past led to accumulation of savings and financing of basic capital formation, the preservation or accentuation of present income inequalities in the underdeveloped countries is necessary to secure the same result'. (See his 'Economic Growth and Income Inequality', *op. cit.*)

Let agricultural output (Y_a) and industrial output (Y_i) exhaust a given total full-capacity output (Y) so that

$$Y = Y_a + Y_i. \tag{20}$$

Taking labour as given, output can then be specified as a function of capital and distribution:

$$Y_a = \sigma_a K_a = \sigma_a \lambda K.$$
$$Y_i = \sigma_i K_i = \sigma_i (1 - \lambda) K. \tag{22}$$

Here the average and marginal productivity of industrial capital (σ_i) is assumed to be higher than that of agricultural capital (σ_a) on the ground that the industrial sector possesses superior technological know-how and innovational ingenuity than does the agricultural sector.

By substitution and rearrangement, we have the average productivity of capital for the whole economy:

$$\frac{Y}{K} = \sigma = \sigma_a \lambda + \sigma_i (1 - \lambda), \tag{23}$$

which indicates that the average productivity of capital in general (σ) is capable of increasing as a result of an increase in the capital distribution ratio $(1 - \lambda)$, provided $\sigma_i > \sigma_a$. In other words, a reallocation of real capital in favour of the industrial sector with a higher average and marginal productivity would reduce the capital-output ratio for the economy as a whole. The implication of such a reallocation-induced change in the capital-output ratio for an economy's growth rate can be seen in the modified growth equation of the form

$$G_k = \frac{s}{b} = s\frac{1}{b} = s\sigma = s[\sigma_a \lambda + \sigma_i (1 - \lambda)], \tag{24}$$

where s is the saving ratio and b the capital-output ratio, as usual. Equation (24) shows that even if the saving ratio remains constant, the rate of growth of output can increase in consequence of a reallocation of real capital from the agricultural sector to the industrial sector so long as $\sigma_i > \sigma_a$.

The same analysis and reasoning apply to an economy that can be divided into the private sector and the public sector with different productivities, though capital reallocation in this instance would involve greater political and philosophical difficulties. Capital reallocations as between heavy and light industries with different productivities or as between export and home industries would involve less difficulty, however. Our model represented by equations (18)–(24) could easily be modified to fit such inter-industry reallocations.

Labour Reallocation and Productivity

Taking capital and technology as given, let us this time consider the possible effect of reallocating labour from one sector of the economy to another on the assumption that there exist different types of labour with different productivities. We shall again abstract from the particular techniques of reallocating a fully employed labour force from one line of production to another.

Let a given total labour force when fully employed (N) be disaggregated into unskilled labour (N_u) and skilled labour (N_s), so that

$$N = N_u + N_s, \qquad (25)$$

the distribution ratio of which is

$$\frac{N_u}{N} = \tau, \quad \frac{N_s}{N} = 1 - \tau. \qquad (26)$$

As far as an underdeveloped economy is concerned, the presumption here is that the labour distribution ratio τ is extremely large, implying that skilled labour is almost as scarce as capital, owing to the low level of technology, the lack of widespread technical education, the absence of complicated equipment, and the relatively high cost of obtaining specialized training (e.g. of sending native students to foreign technical schools) or of acquiring the services of foreign technicians.

Next suppose that total output is divisible into the products of unskilled labour (Y_u) and those of skilled labour (Y_s), so that

$$Y = Y_u + Y_s, \qquad (27)$$

right-hand side of which may be specified as

$$Y_u = \rho_u N_u = \rho_u \tau N, \tag{28}$$

and

$$Y_s = \rho_s N_s = \rho_s(1-\tau)N. \tag{29}$$

Here ρ_u and ρ_s are respectively the productivity of unskilled labour and that of skilled labour (in both cases average and marginal productivities being equal on the assumption of constant returns to scale). Here, also, are made the assumptions that the marginal productivity of skilled labour is higher than that of unskilled labour, $\rho_s > \rho_u$, and that the unskilled are capable of adapting themselves to the requirements of the skilled sector. On these assumptions, a reallocation of fully employed labour to the Y_s sector would increase the average productivity of labour for the whole economy, according to

$$\frac{Y}{N} = \rho = \rho_u \tau + \rho_s(1-\tau). \tag{30}$$

Equation (30), while it shows the possibility of increasing the average productivity through a rise in the skilled-labour distribution ration $(1-\tau)$, nevertheless does not exclude the possibility that average labour productivity for the whole economy may rise also as a result of an increase in the sectoral productivity of unskilled labour (a higher ρ_u) due to better training, improved aptitudes, or acquired skill.

Taking (30) into account and recalling Y/N as an independent variable affecting the capital-output ratio, we may express the latter ratio in the modified form

$$\frac{K}{Y} = b = \frac{K/N}{Y/N} = \frac{K/N}{\rho_u \tau + \rho_s(1-\tau)}. \tag{31}$$

Designating the capital-labour ratio by θ, we can bring out the implication of equations (30) and (31) for the growth rate of an economy with a constant saving ratio (s) thus:

$$G_k = \frac{s}{\theta/[\rho_u \tau + \rho_s(1-\tau)]}, \tag{32}$$

which indicates the theoretical possibility of the overall growth rate (G_k) rising as a consequence of a rise in the skilled-labour distribution ratio $(1 - \tau)$ when the saving ratio (s) and the coefficient of capital intensity (θ) remain constant.

Thus industrialization programming would include plans to reallocate a given labour force in full employment to those sectors and industries possessing demonstrably high productivities of labour as well as of capital. A similar analysis could be made of the beneficial effect of reallocating natural resources (land) with different productivities. It must not be supposed, however, that the reallocation of fully utilized resources can be left to the working of the *laissez-faire* pricing mechanism, for in conditions of *laissez-faire* economic resources are likely to be diverted from longer term and hence riskier projects into immediately profitable yet not necessarily productive projects. National rosters of qualified, competent technicians and specialists for manpower mobilization, together with public labour exchanges, would greatly facilitate productive reallocations. Also, a national policy of encouraging the immigration of foreign technicians and specialists would help underdeveloped economies without very many such trained personnel.

CHAPTER VIII

THE MONETARY ROLE IN ECONOMIC DEVELOPMENT

THE present state of monetary thinking in the field of growth economics is reflected in the oft-heard complaint that economists and monetary authorities are still uttering 'polite platitudes' about the desirability of better banking facilities, non-political central bank policies, and flexible currency systems.[1] Yet at least two great modern economists, Keynes and Schumpeter, stressed the causally significant role of money (in some sense) in long-run economic stability and growth. Keynes considered public credit (i.e. government compensatory borrowing and spending and World Bank lending operations) as a *sine qua non* of both domestic stable growth and international economic development, while at the same time favouring a 'cheap money' policy as a helpful stimulant to vigorous investment in the long run. Schumpeter, on the other hand, regarded private credit as one of the strategic variables in economic development, as an indispensable adjunct to entrepreneurship and innovation. In the light of these monetary insights of Keynes and Schumpeter this chapter will explore the monetary role in economic development, as distinguished from the fiscal role to be separately considered in the next chapter.

Specifically the present chapter will discuss (*a*) the functional relations among credit, interest, and growth, and (*b*) the relation of inflation and development. For the purposes of

[1] See, e.g. C. R. Whittlesey, 'Relation of Money to Economic Growth', *American Economic Review*, May 1956. Also see J. G. Gurley and E. S. Shaw, 'Financial Aspects of Economic Development', *ibid.*, September 1955; R. F. Harrod, 'Is Interest Obsolete?' in his *Dynamic Economics* (Lecture 5); Joan Robinson, 'The Rate of Interest', in her *The Rate of Interest*, etc. (Chaps. 1–6); S. Pal, 'Some Aspects of Monetary and Fiscal Policies for Economic Growth in Underdeveloped Countries', *Indian Journal of Economics*, July 1956. Only the last-named writer is specifically interested in underdeveloped economies, though the analysis is largely historical and institutional.

this discussion we shall make the institutional assumption that the underdeveloped economy in question has a central bank, commmercial banks subject to the regulations of the central bank (by law or by custom), and a monetary authority who determines or influences the availability and cost of money in the public interest.

CREDIT, INTEREST, AND GROWTH

The availability of credit and the rate of interest could be shown as capable of affecting the rate of growth of output under specified conditions. Let us first consider the relation of credit and growth in isolation by taking the interest rate as given.

A 'Closed' Model

To show the effect of a change in the quantity of money on the real income growth of an economy considered as a 'closed' system, it is useful to modify Keynes's liquidity-preference theory in the following respects. First, we shall take only that part of a total quantity of money supplied and demanded to hold which depends on income, and which Keynes attributes to the 'transactions' and 'precautionary' motives, abstracting from the other part which depends on the interest rate and the underlying 'speculative' motive.[1] This modification enables us to deal only with a choice between money and commodities (instead of between money and securities) as well as to analyse the direct relation between money and income (instead of the indirect relation between them via the effect of a change in the interest rate on investment-demand). Second, we shall limit transactions to capital goods, neglecting consumer goods. This is a special case of a more general case (as in Keynes's theory) involving both business and personal transactions. This second modification enables us to concentrate on the relation of money

---

[1] Keynes writes $M = M_1 + M_2 = L_1(Y) + L_2(r)$ as a condition of monetary equilibrium, where M is a total quantity of money supplied, M_1 the amount of 'transactions' and 'precautionary' money supplied, M_2 the amount of 'speculative' money supplied, $L_1(Y)$ the amount of 'transactions' and 'speculative' money demanded which depends on money national income, and $L_2(r)$ the amount of 'speculative' money demanded which depends on the interest rate. (See *General Theory*, p. 199.) We are interested in variants of M_1 and $L_1(Y)$ here.

and investment, thus leaving consumption and saving un-affected by a change in the quantity of transactions-money.

On these modified assumptions, we may express a saving-investment equilibrium condition in the form

$$I = S + \Delta M_1 - \Delta L_1, \tag{1}$$

where I is a net investment, S savings, ΔM_1 an increase in the quantity of transactions-money supplied by the banking system, and ΔL_1 an increase in the quantity of transactions-money demanded by the business community.

Equation (1) indicates the possibility of investment exceeding savings, $I > S$, by an amount equal to the excess of additional transactions-money supplied over additional transactions-money demanded, $\Delta M_1 - \Delta L_1$. This possible case of a discrepancy between I and S is analogous to the Robertsonian case of 'today's' demand for investible funds exceeding 'today's' savings out of 'yesterday's' income by an amount equal to 'dishoarding' (savers lending more than they save).[1]

Next we may specify the variables of equation (1) as follows:

$$I = b\Delta Y, \tag{2}$$

$$S = sY, \tag{3}$$

$$\Delta M_1 = mY, \tag{4}$$

$$\Delta L_1 = \lambda Y. \tag{5}$$

Here Y is net national real income, b the capital-output ratio s the saving ratio, m the ratio of additional transactions-money supplied to income, and λ the ratio of additional transactions-money demanded to income. Here m may be regarded as a monetary-policy parameter to be manipulated by the banking system in response to the changing needs of the business community and in accordance with overall monetary objectives. As for λ, it may be viewed as representing the business community's desire to hold so much more or less transactions-money against any level of national expenditure (expressed in Y).

---

[1] See D. H. Robertson, 'Saving and Hoarding', *Economic Journal*, September 1933.

Taking equations (1)–(5) into consideration, equation (1) can be rewritten as

$$b\Delta Y = sY + mY - \lambda Y = (s + m - \lambda)Y, \qquad (6)$$

from which we obtain the rate of growth of output involving monetary parameters:

$$\frac{\Delta Y}{Y} = \frac{s + m - \lambda}{b}, \qquad (7)$$

which indicates that when s and b are held constant, the growth rate will rise if $m - \lambda$ is rising, and will be constant or falling according as $m - \lambda$ is constant or falling.

The policy implications of equation (7) for an underdeveloped economy with a low s and a high b are not hard to see. For such an economy should, according to equation (7), attempt to increase the supply of transactions-money ratio (m) relatively to the given demand for transactions-money ratio (λ) or to persuade the business community to decrease the demand for transactions-money ratio (λ) relatively to the given supply of transactions-money ratio (m). Thus there is scope for monetary 'quantity policy' in a growing economy, if and when its demand for funds for investment is always matched by savings plus the new credit created, as equation (1) implies.

An 'Open' Model

Turning now to an underdeveloped economy considered as an 'open' system with foreign economic relations, it is possible to indicate the operational significance of net foreign borrowing for economic development. For this purpose we shall make the simplifying assumption of balanced trade so as to treat capital movements between nations purely as autonomous or non-compensatory ones. This assumption also enables us to abstract out the complicating secondary problem of 'repayment', inasmuch as foreign-investment incomes and payments (net interest, dividends, etc. received or paid on past overseas investments) enter the current account of the external payment balance. That latter problem of 'repayment' is considered secondary to the primary problem of increasing domestic productive capacity with the help of foreign capital, as far as borrowing underdeveloped economies are concerned. It may be presumed, moreover, that most underdeveloped economies borrow autonomously (that is, irrespective of current trade balances) and preferably from the International Bank for Reconstruction and Development.

An underdeveloped 'open' economy's total 'investment' is, in equilibrium, equal to its total 'savings' in the special form

$$I_h + L_f = S_h + B_f, \tag{9}$$

where I_h is home net investment, L_f foreign lending, S_h home savings, and B_f foreign borrowing. All variables here are cast in real terms, as usual. The left-hand side of equation (9) represents the open economy's total 'investment' and the right-hand side its total 'savings'. It is safe to conjecture that L_f is zero or small in most underdeveloped economies for obvious reasons, although compensatory foreign lending (excluded from our L_f *ex hypothesi*) might be positive and large, at least temporarily, in some underdeveloped economies with export surpluses.

From (9) we have *home* investment in the form

$$I_h = S_h + B_f - L_f, \tag{10}$$

which indicates that home investment can exceed home saving, $I_h > S_h$, by an amount equal to the excess of foreign borrowing over foreign lending, $B_f - L_f$.

Again we may specify both sides of equation (10) as

$$I_h = \frac{\Delta Y}{\sigma}, \tag{11}$$

$$S_h = sY, \tag{12}$$

$$B_f = \gamma Y, \tag{13}$$

and

$$L_f = \delta Y. \tag{14}$$

Here σ is the average and marginal productivity of net investment as before, s the home saving ratio, γ the average and marginal propensity to borrow abroad, and δ the average and marginal propensity to lend abroad. It is reasonable to presume that an underdeveloped open economy has, as a rule, a low σ, a low s, a high γ, and a low δ.

Taking equations (11)–(14) into consideration, we can re-write equation (10)

$$\frac{\Delta Y}{\sigma} = sY + \gamma Y - \delta Y = (s + \gamma - \delta)Y, \qquad (15)$$

from which we have the rate of growth of output involving international monetary parameters:

$$\frac{\Delta Y}{Y} = \sigma(s + \gamma - \delta), \qquad (16)$$

where γ and δ are the monetary parameters subject to policy manipulation. Equation (16) suggests the theoretical possibility of an underdeveloped open economy's growth rate rising as a result of a rise in the average propensity to borrow abroad (γ) or of a fall in the average propensity to lend abroad (δ), when it has a constantly low s and a constantly low σ.

The 'open' model represented by (9)–(16) seems to justify Keynes's optimistic emphasis on the increasingly important role of World Bank lending operations for developing the resources and productive capacity of 'the less developed countries' and for 'raising the standard of life and the conditions of labour everywhere'.[1] It is recognized, however, that, while borrowing from the World Bank is generally considered economically most desirable and politically least objectionable, the capital requirements of an underdeveloped economy would probably call for private foreign investment, intergovernmental invest-ment, and foreign grants as well.[2]

---

[1] See his Opening Remarks at the First Meeting of the Second Commission on the World Bank for Reconstruction and Development, July 3, 1944.

[2] Underdeveloped economies tend, for understandable reasons, to place less and less reliance upon those additional sources of foreign capital. For example, one writer minimizes the importance of private foreign investment on the ground that it is excessively influenced by 'the profit motive', 'racial and political affini-ties', and 'geographical situation of the borrowing countries'. (See D. Jha, 'Fiscal Policy and the Economic Development of Underdeveloped Countries', *op. cit.*). J. Viner, apparently writing from the standpoint of advanced lending

Interest, Capital and Growth

The long-run importance of the interest rate, the other major weapon of monetary policy, to underdeveloped economies owes its basic explanation to (*a*) the preponderance of external financing (borrowing from the banking system or in the capital market instead of using accumulated business savings out of past undistributed profits) and (*b*) the urgent need for new durable plant and equipment with long planning horizons over which to discount future returns in terms of money. Let us see how the interest rate might affect roundabout investment decisions and hence economic development.

We begin by taking the interest rate as given by

$$r = L(pY, \overline{M}), \tag{17}$$

where *r* is the interest rate paid on money and debts, *L* the amount of money demanded, Y real income, $\overline{M}$ the amount of money autonomously supplied by the banking system, and *p* the average price of output (hence pY is money national income). Equation (17) of course is Keynes's liquidity-preference function proper.

The interest rate given by (17) enters the calculation of the net profit rate via

$$\pi = \frac{pY - wN}{qK} - r, \tag{18}$$

where Y is net national output, N labour input, K capital input, π the net profit rate, *p* the unit price of national output, *w* the unit price of labour input or the money wage-rate, and *q* the unit price of capital input. Equation (18) implies that the

---

countries, expresses a rather pessimistic view of the role of private foreign investment: '. . . through war losses, heavy taxation and socialization, the fund of disposable private capital potentially available for foreign investment has been drastically reduced in some at least of the countries which formerly were important exporters of capital.' (See his *International Trade and Economic Development*, p. 109). As for intergovernmental lending and borrowing, underdeveloped economies seem to fear the 'political strings' that it usually carries. Grants-in-aid are likewise subject to political influences, and they might not be so productive in effect as loans extended on more or less 'commercial principles'.

net profit rate will be the higher the lower is the interest rate paid on money and debts. Rational producers are supposed to maximize the net profit rate given by (18) subject to the production function

$$\frac{Y}{N} = f\left(\frac{K}{N}\right). \tag{19}$$

Here we may assume, as before, that an increase in the coefficient of capital intensity (K/N) expressing the degree of roundaboutness leads to a more than proportional increase in the productivity of labour (Y/N). Letting $\rho = Y/N$ and $\theta = K/N$, we may express this assumption in the form

$$\frac{d\rho}{d\theta} > 1, \tag{20}$$

which assumption we shall find important presently.

A treatment consistent with Keynes's capital theory is to consider the gross profit rate, that is, the net profit rate plus the interest rate, as the appropriate discount rate which equates the present discounted value of future returns to capital with the present cost of constructing or acquiring that capital:

$$qK = \frac{pY - wN}{\pi + r}, \tag{21}$$

the right-hand side of which represents the present discounted value of what Keynes terms the 'prospective yield' of new capital equipment and the left-hand side of which represents what he calls the 'replacement cost' of that equipment. If we specify K as durable and differentiate qK with respect to $pY - wN$, our discount rate $\pi + r$ becomes identifiable with Keynes's 'marginal efficiency of capital'. It is to be noticed that our 'prospective yield' is the product of expected net money national income (pY) minus expected money wages (wN), while our discount rate comprises two elements, namely, the net profit rate (π) measuring the degree of risk and uncertainty and the interest rate (r) measuring the extent of liquidity-preference.

From (21) we have capital income (cost from the standpoint of individual users of capital input) equal to net money national income minus wage income (cost from the standpoint of individual users of labour input):

$$(\pi + r)qK = pY - wN, \qquad (22)$$

dividing both sides of which by N and rearranging, we get

$$\frac{K}{N} = \theta = \frac{p\dfrac{Y}{N} - w}{(\pi + r)q} = \frac{p\rho - w}{(\pi + r)q}. \qquad (23)$$

Equation (23) tells us that the coefficient of capital intensity θ varies directly with the net prospective yield per capital unit $p\rho - w$ and inversely with the cost per capital unit $(\pi + r)q$. What is relevant here is that θ can rise as a consequence of a fall in the interest rate r, when p, ρ, w, and q remain constant. For it is r, alone among the parameters involved, which the monetary authority is capable of influencing directly. However, as Joan Robinson has indicated,[1] the stimulating effect of a low interest rate on the amount of capital used per unit of labour in the given production process could be offset by a fall in the unit price of output p, a fall in labour productivity, or a rise in the wage-rate w (all appearing in the numerator of θ) as well as by a rise in the net profit rate π[2] or a rise in the unit price of capital input q (both appearing in the denominator of θ, along with r). Moreover, we must allow for the possibility that autonomous technological changes may be of an offsetting nature.

In the light of assumption (20) it is possible to indicate the favourable implication of a 'cheap money' policy, if not

---

[1] See her *The Rate of Interest*, etc., pp. 51–53, esp. p. 65.

[2] This is true especially of producers having to purchase capital goods from others, since a rise in the net profit rate increases the purchase price of capital goods (q) relatively to the wage-rate (w) and so induces the former to substitute labour for capital in the production process.

counterbalanced by the above offsetting changes, for the growth rate of an economy $(\Delta Y/Y)$ with a constant saving ratio (s) by relating the coefficient of capital intensity to the capital-output ratio:

$$\frac{K}{Y} = b = \frac{K/N}{Y/N} = \frac{p\rho - w/(\pi+r)q}{\rho}, \qquad (24)$$

and hence

$$\frac{\Delta Y}{Y} = \frac{s}{b} = \frac{s}{[p\rho - w/(\pi+r)q]/\rho}. \qquad (25)$$

Equation (25) indicates that a low rate of interest, via its increasing effect on the coefficient of capital intensity (round-aboutness) and via the latter's increasing effect on the productivity of labour, would, *cet. par.*, decrease the capital-output ratio b and so increase the growth rate $(\Delta Y/Y)$, when the saving ratio s remains constant. Barring such other parametric changes and autonomous technological changes of an offsetting nature as mentioned above, there seems to be some scope for a 'cheap money' policy as an instrument of development programming, especially in those underdeveloped economies following the principle of profit maximization over the expected future useful life of durable capital equipment.[1]

INFLATION AND DEVELOPMENT*

During the thirties some economists opposed 'Keynesian' full-employment policy in the name of anti-inflation. Today we find some economists opposing, explicity or implicitly, development policy for fear of inflation. The opposition to both full employment and economic development through 'inflationary' financing arouses the suspicion that the economic argument

---

* This section was originally published under the title of 'A Note on Inflation and Development', *Riron Keizaigaku* (Economic Studies Quarterly), Japan, June 1957.

[1] Even in underdeveloped non-market economies roundabout investment decisions would probably involve some discount rate measuring the excess of expected 'return over cost'.

involved is a thinly disguised ideological attack on 'the interventionists, the socialists, the communists, the nationalists,
the protectionists, the bureaucrats, and the relatives of all of
them'.[1] There is some danger that 'anti-inflation obstruction-
ists' will mislead underdeveloped economies into letting price
stability take precedence of economic development. The
crucial theoretical question at issue is whether 'development
through inflation' is conducive to capital accumulation, as
economists of underdeveloped economies claim hopefully,
or inimical to it, as those of advanced economies allege fear-
fully. This note is intended to shed some light on this controversial question.

The Criterion of 'True Inflation'

It is important, at the outset, to distinguish between the
criterion of what Keynes termed 'true inflation' applicable to
an advanced economy and that which is applicable to an underdeveloped economy. As is well known, it is the *full-employment*
inelasticity of output relative to rising effective demand that
serves as the criterion of 'true inflation' in the Keynesian sense,
though Keynes allows for the possibility of some inflation even
before the full-employment level arising from specific bottle-

---

[1] The quotation is from F. Machlup, 'The Finance of Development in Poor
countries: Foreign Capital and Domestic Inflation,' *Riron Keizaigaku*, April 1956.
One might question the legitimacy of lumping together of interventionists, socialists, *et al.* in the same category of 'inflationists'. I myself am inclined to agree with
Keynes in thinking that the revolutionary danger of mass unemployment (and of
underdevelopment) is infinitely more harmful to democratic values than the
central controls accompanying inflation which J. A. Schumpeter so dramatically
emphasized in his last speech before his death.

Compare Keynes's statement: 'Whilst, therefore, the enlargement of the functions
of government, involved in the task of adjusting to one another the propensity
to consume and the inducement to invest, would seem to a nineteenth-century pub-
licist or to a contemporary American financier to be a terrific encroachment on
individualism, I defend it, on the contrary, both as the only practicable means of
avoiding the destruction of existing economic forms in their entirety and as the
condition of the successful functioning of individual initiative.' (*General Theory*,
p. 380). J. A. Schumpeter's statement: 'Parennial inflationary pressure can play
an important part in the eventual conquest of the private enterprise system by
the bureaucracy—the resultant frictions and deadlocks being attributed to private
enterprise and used as arguments for further restrictions and regulations.' (See his
posthumous paper 'The March into Socialism' *American Economic Review*, May
1950).

necks.[1] As far, however, as underdeveloped economies are concerned, the correct criterion of 'true inflation' is to be found in inelastic full-*capacity* output. For in those economies the lack of real capital, not of labour, is the ultimate bottleneck to 'real' expansion relative to 'monetary' expansion.

What this means in terms of secular analysis (beyond the short-run programming horizon of five years, e.g.) is that it is necessary to investigate whether the forces making for 'chronic inflation' do or do not also represent the forces making for price stability. To be specific, one must inquire whether the so-called 'inflationary financing' of investment may or may not have a greater capacity-increasing effect than an income-generating effect in the long run. Domar's 'dual character of investment' is relevant here, for he alludes to the possibility that an economy investing at the rate $\Delta I/I$, while experiencing monetary expansion via the 'multiplier effect', nevertheless may undergo even greater real expansion via the 'sigma effect'. It is to this possibility that Domar attributes the fact that 'inflations have been so rare . . . in peacetime'.[2] We cannot rule out such a possibility even for an underdeveloped economy, for a number of reasons. Let me outline some plausible reasons why a given rate of growth of investment may expand productive capacity sufficiently to counteract any inflationary effect that it may have so as to minimize the inevitability of secular inflation.

1. If an underdeveloped economy planning the growth of net investment at the rate $\Delta I/I$ gears its investment planning primarily to the construction of productive durable equipment, it will give full play to the 'sigma effect' in the long run and so offset the 'multiplier effect' involved to some extent, if not

[1] *General Theory*, pp. 296–302. Note especially: 'If we assume a sufficient interval for the quantity of equipment itself to change, the elasticities of supply will be decidedly greater eventually. Thus a moderate change in effective demand, coming on a situation where there is widespread unemployment, may spend itself very little in raising prices and mainly in increasing employment; whilst a larger change, which, being unforeseen, causes some temporary "bottle-necks" to be reached, will spend itself in raising prices, as distinct from employment, to a greater extent at first than subsequently.' (*Ibid.*, pp. 300–301).

[2] E. D. Domar, 'Expansion and Employment', *American Economic Review*. March 1947.

completely. This may mean in practice that an underdeveloped economy deliberately refrains from investing in investment projects of the pyramid-building or armament variety, which projects generate demand without contributing to the growth of productive capacity. Here we are concerned with the productivity of the component 'multiplicands' in the aggregate increment of net investment (ΔI) relative to absolute net investment (I). Thus in a mixed, open economy we would have to disaggregate $\Delta I/I$ into $\Delta I^p/I^p$, $\Delta I^g/I^g$, and $\Delta F/F$, where I^p stands for private net investment, I^g for government net investment, and F for a net foreign balance. If an underdeveloped economy is to minimize the danger of chronic inflation, it would have to assign greater weight to those particular component rates of growth of net investment which have the greatest productivity potentials. It may be presumed that the government rate of growth of net investment ($\Delta I^g/I^g$) lends itself most readily to deliberate choice in this regard.

2. Since capital accumulation and technological progress tend to go hand in hand, it is arguable that the higher rate of growth of net investment ($\Delta I/I$), the greater will be the possibility of the productivity of investment (σ, in Domar's notation) rising for any level of net investment. If so, productive capacity growing at the rate σI could conceivably exceed effective demand growing at the rate $\Delta I/\alpha$ (where α is also Domar's notation for the marginal propensity to save). Apropos, Joan Robinson suggests that 'the more machines there are in use the greater are the opportunities for improving the methods of production in the machine-making sectors of industry'.[1] An improvement in the quality of capital may well be a function of the quantity of capital, as Joan Robinson seems to imply. If this be true, one way to increase the value of the technological parameter σ is increase the quantity of capital or, in the present context, raise $\Delta I/I$ through appropriate monetary or fiscal policies. This is the line of thinking that seems to underline T. Haavelmo's observation: '. . . very often the parameters that we call technological, actually are more related to human

---

[1] See her 'Notes on the Economics of Technical Progress', in *The Rate of Interest*, etc., Macmillan, London, 1952, p. 63.

choice and human behaviour than to chemical formulae and laws of mechanics'.[1] Moreover, it is safe to assume that 'inflationary' booms are more conducive to innovations than deflationary slumps in predominantly private-enterprise economies, though one may not, as J. A. Schumpeter was inclined to do, overlook the increasing role of government in stimulating, and often financing, innovations with a view to maximizing productivity or minimizing cost (witness 'linear programming' research activities in American universities under government grants, for instance).

3. If the productivity of investment (σ) is thus increased, it is possible that the marginal propensity to save out of property incomes (esp. profits and dividends) may rise and the overall marginal propensity to save, with it (α). If so, the 'multiplier effect' would decline for any additional net investment so as to make effective demand grow at the *smaller* rate $\Delta I/\alpha$ relatively to any given productive capacity growing at the rate σI. In addition to this possible dis-inflationary impact of a rise in α there may result a long-run tendency toward a higher *average* propensity to save with all its beneficial implications for the growth of productive capacity. Even if a rise in the marginal propensity to save (α) comes about through autonomous 'thrift campaigns' instead, its long-run counterpart (the average propensity to save) may rise to the possible benefit of productive capacity. In those underdeveloped economies which have substandards of consumption the credit-financed growth of net investment at the rate $\Delta I/I$ may, via its increasing effect on individual incomes, well be the only practical way to *initiate* the habit of saving on the part of consuming units. If the system of investment (financial), whether in bonds or stocks, designed to accommodate a positive rate of growth of real investment worked for more than a hundred years so that 'to save and to invest became at once the duty and the delight of a large class', as Keynes observed,[2] a present-day underdeveloped economy can consider the $\Delta I/I$ rate of growth of real investment as the initiating factor in cultivating saving habits.

---

[1] See his *A Study in the Theory of Economic Evolution*, North-Holland Publishing Co., Amsterdam, 1954, p. 49.

[2] See J. M. Keynes, *Essays in Persausion*, p. 84.

For these reasons 'true inflation' can be averted in an economy investing at the positive constant rate $\Delta I/I$ through bank credits or government deficits. It is only by overlooking or underestimating the productivity effect of investment that one can become unduly alarmed at its multiplier effect on the behaviour of money national income. Domar's 'dual character of investment' serves as a useful reminder that the instability of general prices should never be exaggerated by a one-sided look at the income-generating aspect of investment to the neglect of its capacity-increasing aspect. It is interesting to observe, in closing this part of the analysis, that the capacity-increasing effect of investment is regarded in an advanced economy with an insufficiency of effective demand as something of a nuisance, whereas the same effect is considered in an underdeveloped economy as a welcome force making for secular growth and price stability.

The Specific Effect of Inflation on Capital Growth

We have shown the reasons why 'true inflation' need not occur or persist in an underdeveloped economy. However, for the sake of argument let us assume that some inflation results from credit-financed investment at the positive constant rate $\Delta I/I$. The question now is: What is the possible effect of inflation on the growth of capital? This is the crucial question to ask inasmuch as the growth of capital is generally considered the key to industrialization programming. This question can be answered in a number of ways.

1. One can at once agree that the limiting case of *hyper*-inflation would militate against private thrift, even as Keynes warned that the experience of such an inflation 'must modify social psychology towards the practice of saving and investment'.[1] Even barring such hyper-inflations, two things need be mentioned here, as far as the impact of inflation on 'the practice of saving and investment' is concerned. First, we have the observation: 'The repercussions of inflation, it is said, are less serious in a country where the volume of assets expressed in money terms—bonds, insurance policies, savings deposits—

---

[1] *Persuasion*, p. 91.

is relatively small.'[1] This of course applies to most under-developed economies where middle-class savers are numerically insignificant.[2] Second, and more important, one should have concrete information or projections concerning the relative importance of debt and equity financing, of external and internal financings, and of private and public savings. For inflation is known to react favourably on equity dividends, corporate and business profits, and government tax-revenues. In the overall scheme of developmental financing equity capital, undistributed profits, and budgetary surpluses[3] may play so preponderant a role as to render superfluous all apprehensions about the destructive effect of inflation on private saving.

2. It is frequently argued that inflation tends to stimulate the propensity to 'hoard' in such inflation-hedges as real estate, stocks, jewelery, and stable foreign currencies. This is to misemphasize the *disposition* of given savings, whereas the real question at issue has to do with the aggregate *size* of savings. Insofar as the allocation of given savings is at issue, a more fruitful line of criticism might be to point out the danger of given savings being dissipated in profitable yet unproductive projects from a long view. It is not, as some writers seem to imagine, 'profit inflation' but the profit system itself that is basically responsible for the malallocation of given savings. Thus Britain's 'amusement' (dog-race tracks, e.g.) and Japan's 'pachinko' (pinball) have been thrown into question as examples of misusing scarce capital during the postwar period of reconstruction. All this goes to reinforce Keynes's argument in favour of 'the State, which is in a position to calculate the marginal efficiency [read productivity in the present context] of capital-goods on long views and on the basis of the general social advantage, taking an ever greater responsibility for directly

[1] Cf., H. C. Wallich, 'Underdeveloped Countries and the International Monetary Mechanism', in *Money, Trade and Economic Growth* (in honour of J. H. Williams), Macmillan, N.Y., 1951.

[2] Cf., S. Kuznets, 'Economic Growth and Income Inequality', *American Economic Review*, March 1955.

[3] On the productive role of budgetary surpluses see my 'Growth Models and Fiscal-Policy Parameters', *Finance Publiques* (Netherlands), No. 2/1956.

organizing investment.'[1] The main point to be stressed here is that although a capital-poor economy should pay due attention to the productive allocation of limited savings, it should pay even greater attention to the more urgent problem of augmenting the size of savings. Then such a diversion of given savings to inflation-hedges as individual wealth-holders might effect as a measure of self-protection would not matter too seriously.

3. Another possible answer is that an inflation-induced redistribution of real income in favour of variable-income groups against fixed-income groups may strengthen the former's saving habits more than it weakens the latter's saving habits. This means that the marginal propensity to save out of variable-income becomes larger than that out of fixed-income in consequence of inflation-induced redistributions. Given such differential marginal propensities to save, it can easily be shown that each inflation-induced redistribution of real income would increase the average propensity to save for the economy as a whole. If the average propensity to save for the whole economy is thus increased, the presumption is that the rate of growth of productive capacity will increase, whether we follow Harrod's growth model or Domar's growth model.[2] There is room for debating just which income groups are to be included in the 'variable' category and the 'fixed' category respectively. It is safe to assume that profit-takers and dividend-receivers are the most important single group in the former category and that interest or/and rent earners are the dominant group in the latter. Whether wage income is to be regarded as variable or fixed depends on the relative bargaining strength of organized labour in a concrete economy. If inflation accelerates what Keynes calls 'the euthanasia of the rentier',[3] so much the better for the enthusiasm of the entrepreneur *et hoc genus omne*. If, in

[1] *General Theory*, p. 164. In addition, Keynes envisages the desirability of the State undertaking 'communal saving' if and when the private propensity to save should prove insufficient for required capital growth. (See *ibid.*, p. 376).

[2] See R. F. Harrod, *Towards a Dynamic Economics*, Macmillan, London, 1948; Domar, *op. cit.*

[3] *General Theory*, p. 376. Keynes assumes the investment-demand equation of the form $I = f(y,p,r)$ and the profit-maximization condition $e(I) = r$, where I is real investment, y yield of an additional capital asset, p replacement cost, r the interest rate, e the marginal efficiency of capital $(e = y/p)$.

other words, inflation has the effect of shifting real income in favour of profit-takers against interest-earners, *real* investment in capital equipment will be greater than *financial* investment in stocks and bonds—to the long-run benefit of capital accumulation and economic development.

4. Yet another answer may be seen in the possibility that the consuming public may gradually adjust their consumption expenditures downward in reaction to secular inflation, abstracting from a short-run propensity to spend more on consumer goods today in anticipation of a further increase in consumer-goods prices tomorrow. If, in other words, we assume with A. C. Pigou[1] that savings are directly related to the price level, and hence inversely related to the size of real cash balances (e.g. savings accounts, government securities, and other liquid assets—in short, consumers' 'nest-eggs'), rising prices will have the effect of discouraging consumption out of real income and hence of increasing real savings—the 'Pigou effect' *in reverse*. Pigou assumes the volume of assets to be held constant, $A = \bar{A}$, and the amount of private savings to be a decreasing function of the real value of assets, $dS/d(A/P) < 0$, where S is savings and P the price index. On these assumptions, total savings could conceivably rise for any given real income and interest, if general prices are allowed to decrease the real value of assets and so to increase the desire to build up larger 'nest-eggs' (not for 'amenity', as Pigou argues in the context of an advanced economy, but for security in the present context).

5. Lastly, it would be amiss to emphasize saving alone as if it represented the ability to produce capital goods as well as the ability to abstain from current consumption. For, irrespective of the community's attitude toward thrift, a developing economy's ability to produce capital goods could increase if its industrialization made for a more homogeneous output and for a more flexible industrial structure. This means that the specificity of equipment and labour associated with the otherwise heterogeneous composition of output is reduced so as to

[1] See his 'Economic Progress in a Stable Environment', *Economica*, 14/1947. The micro-economic rationale involved is that the decreased real value of money savings due to rising prices has the effect of increasing the marginal utility of additional savings for an individual consumer.

enable those productive resources released by not consuming to be used for producing capital goods without much difficulty. It also means that the structure of industry is characterized by less such rigidities and maladjustments as resource immobility, inefficient factor combinations, and scarcities of specialized skills and materials. An underdeveloped economy's trouble may well be that its ability to produce capital goods rather than its propensity to save is too low for the desired target rate of growth. If so, structural maladjustments rather than inflation are to blame. Is it not reasonable to assume that the environment of rising prices is conducive to structural improvements?

The foregoing discussion suggests both that the capacity-increasing character of capital accumulation is in and by itself a disinflationary force and that rising prices short of hyper-inflation, far from impeding it, may promote the growth of capital necessary for rapid industrialization. It also suggests that underdeveloped economies should be encouraged to develop their productive resources as rapidly as possible without fears of inflation, that is, without undue apprehensions lest price stability be thereby upset.[1]

---

[1] We may mention the following qualifying limitations on 'development through inflation' in some *specific* economies: (1) Latent unemployment may be absent or exhausted so as to exert little or no downward pressure on the money wage-rate and to aggravate the problem of price-wage spirals. (2) Fears of loss from the falling real value of money may become greater than hopes of gain by the windfall margin between selling prices and paying costs, to impair productive incentives. (3) A rise in forced saving due to inflation may be more than offset by a fall in voluntary saving due to loss of confidence in the stability of purchasing power of money. (4) Creditors may become so demoralized by the adverse effect of rising prices on their fixed-income positions as to purchase no more government bonds or new private debentures floated to finance developmental projects. (5) The 'money illusion' may give way to 'real' motives so as to make cost-of-living adjustments in wages, interest, rents, and even dividends the rule rather than an exception and hence to stimulate consumer demand at the expense of corporate saving and investment. (6) Increased taxes, priority allocations, foreign-exchange controls, and other anti-inflationary measures of public policy in inflating, borrowing countries may discourage direct and portfolio foreign investments by capital-rich countries to the detriment of the former's development financing. (7) Domestic inflation may cause imports to become a subtle means of perverse capital flight from underdeveloped to developed economies and exports to become more difficult than can be easily overcome by devaluation, and so to reduce foreign exchange reserves as a source of developmental capital.

This outline is not exhaustive but sufficient to warn against *over*-optimistic inferences from our general conclusions.

CHAPTER IX

THE FISCAL ROLE IN ECONOMIC DEVELOPMENT

FISCAL theory and policy have undergone historical shifts of emphasis from revenue to welfare and, more recently, from cyclical stabilization to secular growth. It is with the fiscal role in secular growth that this chapter is concerned. To be specific, we shall analyse separately (a) the fiscal role in the *maximum* growth of *underdeveloped* economies, and (b) the fiscal role in the *stable* growth of *advanced* economies.

FISCAL OPERATIONS FOR MAXIMUM GROWTH*

Conscious use of fiscal measures for the purpose of promoting economic growth is a rather recent development, partly perhaps as a reaction to the prewar Keynesian emphasis on the purely countercyclical aspect of fiscal policy and partly no doubt because of post-Keynesian growth analysis of the Harrod-Domar type that potentially lends itself to policy applications. The Harrod-Domar growth models are purely *laissez-faire* ones based on the assumption of fiscal neutrality and designed to indicate the conditions of progressive equilibrium for an advanced economy. Their policy implications are therefore the very opposite of what one might expect of an underdeveloped economy. Nevertheless, the Harrod-Domar models are important not only because they represent a stimulating attempt to dynamize and secularize Keynes's static short-run saving-investment theory, but also because they are capable of being modified so as to introduce fiscal-policy parameters as explicit

---

* This section is largely based on my 'The Fiscal Role of Government in Economic Development', *Indian Journal of Economics*, July 1956. The reader's attention is called to the following contributions in the same issue of that Journal: O. Prakash, 'Taxation Policy in a Transitional Economy', D. Jha, 'Fiscal Policy and the Economic Development of Underdeveloped Countries', M. S. Bhatia, 'The Role of Public Budgeting in an Underdeveloped Economy', S. Pal, 'Some Aspects of Monetary and Fiscal Policies for Economic Growth in Underdeveloped Countries'.

variables in the economic growth of an underdeveloped country. Such modifications will be made in the course of this discussion. We shall analyse, in this section, the fiscal roles of government as (*a*) an investor, (*b*) a saver, and (*c*) an income redistributor—in the development of the productive capacity of underdeveloped economies.

Government as Investor

To show the fiscal role of government as an investor, it is necessary to disaggregate real government expenditure (G) into government investment (I_g) and government consumption (C_g), that is,

$$G = I_g + C_g, \tag{1}$$

where I_g may, in the present context, be considered as representing public outlays for such productive projects and equipment as highways, harbours, bridges, schools, hospitals, and transportation-communications facilities, and C_g as representing public outlays for such unproductive items as consumer goods, social services, armaments, and pyramids. The choice between these two types of government expenditure is subject to the legislative constraint.

Next we shall assume that the national budget is balanced in order to isolate the role of government as an investor rather than as a saver, that is,

$$G = T, \tag{2}$$

where T is the amount of taxes in real terms. We shall specify taxes as a function of net real national income (Y):

$$T = zY; \quad z = \frac{T}{Y}, \tag{3}$$

where z is the government average (= marginal) propensity to tax or simply the tax rate subject to the legislative constraint.

To demonstrate the interaction of the private and public sectors, it is useful to specify the consumption and investment functions as follows:

$$C = C_p + C_g = a_p(Y - T) + a_g Y = a_p(1 - z)Y + a_g Y, \tag{4}$$

where C is total consumption expenditure in real terms, C_p private consumption, a_p the private average ($=$ marginal) propensity to consume out of disposable income ($Y - T$), a_g the variable average ratio of government consumption expenditure to national income, the rest being as defined before.

$$I = I_p + I_g = \Delta K_p + \Delta K_g = \frac{\Delta Y}{\sigma}, \qquad (5)$$

where I is total real net investment, and I_p private investment. Here since net investment is equivalent to an increment of capital, $I = \Delta K$, we may think of both private net investment (ΔK_p) and government net investment (ΔK_g) as varying directly with an increment of output (ΔY) and inversely with the average ($=$ marginal) productivity of investment (σ), as implicit in the Domar equation. (That is to say, $\Delta Y = \sigma \Delta K$, $\sigma = \Delta Y / \Delta K$, and $\Delta K = \Delta Y / \sigma$ are equivalents.)

In equilibrium, we know that total investment equals total income minus total consumption, so that we can write

$$I = I_p + I_g = Y - C_p - C_g. \qquad (6)$$

From (5) and (6) we have an increment of productive capacity in the form

$$\Delta Y = \sigma(I_p + I_g) = \sigma(Y - C_p - C_g). \qquad (7)$$

Taking (1)-(4) into account and dividing both sides of equation (7) by Y, we get the full-capacity rate of growth of output (G_k):

$$\frac{\Delta Y}{Y} = G_k = \sigma[1 - a_p(1-z) - a_g], \qquad (8)$$

which equation contains three explicit fiscal-policy parameters, σ, z, and a_g, capable of increasing the relevant growth rate through appropriate operations. Let us specify the operational significance of equation (8).

In the first place, equation (8) suggests that if the average productivity of investment (σ) is increased by gearing government investment (I_g) to as genuinely productive channels as feasible, the full-capacity growth rate tends, *cet. par.*, to rise. Thus when the *capacity*-creating aspect of investment is considered more important, as in any development analysis, than its *income*-generating aspect, as in Keynes's short-run multiplier theory, it is necessary to exclude from I_g the pyramid-building type of outlays. To the extent that government investment is thus confined to productive (though not easy to measure in the less obvious cases of outlays for public education and health), to that extent will the average productivity of investment (σ) rise, as equation (5) implies, and therefore will the full-capacity growth rate (G_k) also rise, as equation (8) indicates. Here there is some danger that the increasing effect of productive government investment on σ will be offset by the decreasing effect of unproductive, though profitable, private investment (e.g. in cabarets, theatres, sports stadia and amusement centres) on σ. Here direct controls (e.g. priority allocations) may have to come to the rescue.

In the next place, the full-capacity growth rate can also be increased by increasing the average tax rate (z). For an increase in z has the effect of decreasing private consumption expenditure out of disposable income, as equation (4) implies, and hence of increasing that part of real income which is available for government investment according to equation (6). In other words, an increase in z means an increase in total taxes (T) for any level of Y and therefore in total government expenditure according to equation (2). If the government average propensity to consume (a_g) is constant, along with a constant σ, an increase in G *pari passu* with an increase in T must mean a larger amount of government investment, according to equation (1). This second operation is in line with Keynes's suggestion about the State exercising 'a guiding influence on the propensity to consume partly through its scheme of taxation', albeit in a reverse direction (Keynes would presumably raise the propensity to consume in the context of an advanced economy).

Lastly, the full-capacity growth rate can be increased by decreasing the government average propensity to consume (a_g), given a constant z and σ. A decrease in a_g would have the effect of decreasing government consumption (C_g) and hence of increasing government investment, according to equations (4) and (6). Here it is recognized that an attempt to reduce a_g involves the practical difficulty of cutting down, for any level of Y, consumer subsidies, social services, defence expenditures, and other obviously unproductive but socially useful public outlays, especially if the underdeveloped economy happens to represent also a welfare-conscious, defence-conscious nation.

In sum, the government in its capacity as an investor could increase the full-capacity rate of growth through (a) an *increase* in the average productivity of investment σ, (b) an *increase* in the average propensity to tax z, and (c) a *decrease* in the government average propensity to consume a_g—all within the framework of a *balanced* budget.

Government as Saver

Turning now to the fiscal role of government as a saver, we must begin our analysis by dropping the assumption of a balanced budget. This is necessary because government saving presupposes a budgetary *surplus*, as will be shown below.

Assume that there are definite relations between real net national income and taxes, transfer payments, and government expenditure:

$$\frac{T}{Y} = z, \quad \frac{R}{Y} = r, \quad \frac{G}{Y} = g, \tag{9}$$

where R stands for transfer payments (including social insurance benefits, relief, subsidies and interest on public debt), r the government average (= marginal) propensity to transfer, and g the government average (= marginal) propensity to spend, the remainder being the same as before. Here z, r and g are fiscal-policy parameters subject to the legislative constraint. Two things must be noticed about equation (9). First, instead of breaking down government expenditure (G) into investment (I_g) and consumption (C_g), as we did when we considered the government's role as an investor, here we treat government expenditure as a whole. Second, transfer payments are explicitly introduced here as a measure of income redistribution, instead of subsuming them in net 'withdrawals' ($T - R$).

The typical budgetary positions may be characterized by

(a) $(z-r) = g$: budgetary balance,

(b) $(z-r) > g$: budgetary surplus,

(c) $(z-r) < g$: budgetary deficit.

Here the budgetary balance (a) is to be regarded as zero government saving, the budgetary surplus (b) as positive government saving, and the budgetary deficit (c) as negative government saving. Dynamic long-term fiscal policy includes appropriate shifts in these typical budgetary positions. As far as an *underdeveloped* economy is concerned, it is intuitively clear that the budgetary *surplus* is the relevant position to be achieved and maintained. For it is as supplementing deficient private saving that the fiscal role of government *as a saver* is to be contemplated.

Taking (9) into consideration, we may express the savings-investment relation for the whole economy in the form

$$b\Delta Y = sY + zY - rY - gY = (s + z - r - g)Y, \qquad (10)$$

where $s = S/Y$ or the private saving ratio (average = marginal) and b the capital-output ratio (average = marginal). The right-hand side of equation (10) represents total savings, private and government, and the left-hand side private induced investment.

From (10) we have the full-capacity growth rate which depends on the technical relation of private and government saving ratios to the capital-output ratio:

$$\frac{\Delta Y}{Y} = G_k = \frac{s + z - r - g}{b} = \sigma(s + z - r - g), \qquad (11)$$

which makes it clear that the full-capacity growth rate will rise as a result of a positive government saving ratio, $(z - r) > g$, all other independent variables remaining constant. However, as equation (11) suggests, there are in fact alternative fiscal operations on z, r, and g in order to increase the government saving ratio, if the private saving ratio is too low in relation to that which is required for the socially optimal growth rate G_m (discussed in Chapter 3). Accordingly the overall objective of making $G_k = G_m$ can be and must implemented by such specific fiscal operations as are consistent with the best judgment of the fiscal authorities regarding the relative weights to be given to z, r, and g.

Given the excess of the socially optimal growth rate over the full-capacity growth rate, $G_m > G_k$, developmental fiscal policy should be aimed at increasing G_k so as to make $G_k = G_m$ by maintaining a persistent budgetary surplus through (a) a *decrease* in the government average propensity to spend g, (b) an *increase* in the average propensity to tax z, or (c) a *decrease* in the government average propensity to make transfer payments r. Perhaps it is expedient to combine three operations in order to reduce the pressure on any one operation, however.

It should be noted that a persistent budgetary surplus, however brought about, is consistent with the fiscal role of government as an investor as well as a saver, for it is open to the fiscal authorities to reduce that part of total government expenditure, $gY = G$, which goes to the purchase of consumer goods (C_g) and thereby increasing government investment ($I_g = G - C_g$), as equation (1) implies. It should also be noted that the fiscal role of government as a saver is in line with Keynes's suggestion that if and when 'the individual propensity to consume' is so high as to make for smaller net saving and hence for a smaller supply of capital, 'it will still be possible for communal saving through the agency of the State to be maintained at a level which will allow the growth of capital . . .'[1] The magnitude of such 'communal saving' to be secured through a budgetary surplus depends on the estimated values of the actual private saving ratio (s) and the capital-output ratio (b) in relation to the socially optimal growth rate (G_m). If, for example, $G_m = \cdot 03$, $s = \cdot 05$, and $b = 5$, 'communal saving' will have to be $(s^r - s)Y$, where $s^r = bG_m = \cdot 15$ (required saving ratio for the optimal growth rate), that is, 10 per cent. ($= \cdot 15 - \cdot 05$) of any level of national income. In the absence of such 'communal saving' the economy would grow at the rate $s/b = \cdot 01$, instead of $s^r/b = \cdot 03$. In an 'open' system the above burden on

[1] *General Theory*, p. 376.

'communal saving' could be considerably lessened by capital imports.[1]

Government as Income Redistributor

In the above analysis we abstracted from the composition of the tax rate and the transfer rate, but it is necessary to show that different tax rates and transfer rates imposed on different income brackets are capable of changing the private saving ratio and hence of affecting the full-capacity rate of growth. Accordingly we now turn to the consideration of the fiscal role of government as an income redistributor in the general scheme of development programming.

Let real national income distributed be divided into that part going to low-income brackets (Y_1) and the rest going to high-income brackets (Y_2), that is,

$$Y = Y_1 + Y_2, \tag{12}$$

the distribution ratio of which is

$$\frac{Y_1}{Y} = d, \quad \frac{Y_2}{Y} = 1 - d. \tag{13}$$

Before going any further let us make the assumption that there are two distinct income groups between which no mobility exists, and between which absolute discrimination exists with respect to taxes, transfer payments, and saving propensities, all other income-earners outside those groups being ignored. This simplifying assumption is made to justify the constant but different ratios of taxes, transfer payments, and savings to income involved in the following discussion.

Let total taxes be broken down into those imposed on low-income brackets (T_1) and those on high-income brackets (T_2), the tax rate in the former being assumed to be lower than that on the latter according to the principle of ability to pay:

$$T = T_1 + T_2 = z_1 Y_1 + z_2 Y_2, \tag{14}$$

---

[1] Cf., my 'Growth Analysis and the Problem of Capital Accumulation in Underdeveloped Countries,' *op. cit.*

where z_1 is the average (= marginal) tax rate on low-income brackets and z_2 that on high-income brackets.

Likewise transfer payments can be divided into those going to low-income brackets (R_1) and those going to high-income brackets (R_2) the transfer rate for the former being usually higher than that for the latter, especially in welfare-conscious economies:

$$R = R_1 + R_2 = r_1 Y_1 + r_2 Y_2, \qquad (15)$$

where r_1 is the average (= marginal) transfer rate for low-income brackets and r_2 that for high-income brackets. Whether $r_1 \gtrless r_2$ depends on the relative importance attached to subsidies to Y_1 and Y_2 brackets.

The private savings of low-income brackets after taxes and transfer payments is:

$$S_1 = s_1(Y_1 - T_1 + R_1) = s_1(1 - z_1 + r_1)Y_1, \qquad (16)$$

where s_1 is the average (= marginal) propensity to save of low-income brackets out of disposable income. Similarly the savings of high-income brackets is:

$$S_2 = s_2(Y_2 - T_2 + R_2) = s_2(1 - z_2 + r_2)Y_2, \qquad (17)$$

where s_2 is the average (= marginal) propensity to save of high-income brackets out of disposable income. It is plausible to assume that high-income brackets have a higher marginal propensity to save than low-income brackets do, or $s_2 > s_1$.

From equations (12)–(17) we have the full-capacity growth rate which embodies fiscal redistribution effects on the private saving ratio:

$$G_k = \frac{[s_1(1 - z_1 + r_1)d + s_2(1 - z_2 + r_2)(1 - d)] + z - r - g}{b}. \qquad (18)$$

Here $s_1(1 - z_1 + r_1)d$ and $s_2(1 - z_2 + r_2)(1 - d)$ are the average (= marginal) propensities to save of low-income and high-income brackets out of national income.

Equation (18) indicates that even if the average propensities to save of two income groups out of disposable income (s_1, s_2) remain constant, variations in relative tax rates (z_1, z_2) relative transfer rates (r_1, r_2), and the distribution ratio (d, and hence

$1 - d$) are capable of changing the aggregate average propensity to save out of national income and therefore the full-capacity growth rate (G_k), independently of whether the government budget is balanced or unbalanced, $(z - r) = g$. To be specific, an attempt to increase the full-capacity growth rate so as to make $G_k = G_m$ would call for (a) a *decrease* in z_2, (b) an *increase* in r_2, (c) an *increase* in z_1, and (d) a *decrease* in r_1—in sum, a less progressive tax-transfer structure. Moreover, the same attempt would require a decrease in the distribution ratio d through less progressive inheritance or death duties and perhaps other methods.

It is frankly recognized that these fiscal operations to redistribute income from lower to higher brackets for the sake of greater private saving may come in conflict with any 'egalitarian' objective that an underdeveloped economy might entertain. It is also to be admitted that a fiscal redistribution of income against low-income brackets for high-income brackets might increase the community's desire to consume for emulative reasons and so decrease total private saving to the detriment of capital accumulation and output growth. For it is conceivable that wage-earning families or individuals receiving incomes a great deal lower than those received by profit-taking ones might well have a stronger incentive to 'keep up with the Joneses', which in turn might stimulate the latter to 'keep ahead of the Smiths'. If so, both private saving ratios (s_1, s_2) would fall, to offset any increasing effect that the above fiscal operations might have on the overall private saving ratio. It is partly by abstracting from this sociological impact ('demonstration effect', so-called) and partly on the assumption of full employment that one can concur in the classical justification of income inequality as a *sine qua non* of economic progress.[1]

FISCAL OPERATIONS FOR STABLE GROWTH*

We have seen that long-term fiscal operations in an underdeveloped economy should be designed primarily to maximize

---

* This part is mainly based on my 'Growth Models and Fiscal-Policy Parameters'. *Finances Publiques* (Netherlands), No. 2/1956.

[1] The reader is referred back to Chap. 7 on this point.

the rate of growth of productive capacity. By contrast, long-term fiscal operations in an advanced market economy are calculated principally to stabilize such a rate of growth. We shall turn to the consideration of the fiscal role of government *as a stabilizer* in the latter type of economy.[1]

The Instability of Dynamic Equilibrium

So that the specific parametric operations may be meaningful, we shall begin with an analysis of the inherent instability of dynamic equilibrium (with a positive constant rate of change) in pure *laissez-faire* conditions. Fundamentally an advanced market economy tends to diverge chronically from the path of steady progress because the rate of growth consistent with private saving and investment seldom coincides with the rate of growth compatible with population growth and technological advance. For the purpose of this discussion we may designate as the equilibrium rate of steady progress without fluctuation that rate of growth of output (real net) which is required to keep a growing labour population with an increasing productivity of labour fully employed. This is the maximum potential rate of growth attainable in any society. We may approximate such a rate as follows:

Taking the average real wage-rate as given and the ratio of

---

[1] A. H. Hansen is among the very first to give emphasis to the need for long-term fiscal policy in addition to purely countercyclical operations. (See his *Fiscal Policy and Business Cycles*, Norton, N.Y., 1941). The assumption of fiscal neutrality involved in the *laissez-faire* growth models of Harrod, Domar, Kalecki, and Haavelmo has served to bring out in bold relief fundamental insights into the turbulent growth of market economies. Of these model-builders, Harrod is the most policy-conscious, but Joan Robinson has critized his policy discussions as being 'without much dependence on his own new contributions'. (See her 'Mr Harrod's Dynamics', *op. cit.*).

Growth models with explicit fiscal-policy parameters have been few. An exeption will be found in J. G. Gurley, 'Fiscal Policy in a Growing Economy', *Journal of Political Economy*, December 1953. Gurley, while calling attention to the important aspect of growth economics neglected by other writers, nevertheless is open to criticism for his opacity concerning the instability conditions of dynamic equilibrium which fiscal policy is supposed to remedy, for neglecting redistribution effects of long-term fiscal operations on secular growth, and for concentrating on the cyclical rather than chronic instability of a growing economy (that is, on the instability arising from divergences of the 'actual' growth rate from the 'warranted' growth rate rather than that arising from divergences of the 'warranted' rate from the 'natural' rate, to use Harrod's distinctions).

labour to output as technologically fixed, we have the following relations:

$$\frac{N}{Y} = v, \quad N = vY, \quad Y = \frac{N}{v}, \tag{19}$$

where N is the amount of labour when fully employed, Y real net national output, and v the average (= marginal) labour-output ratio.

From (19) and since the average productivity of labour is the reciprocal of the labour-output ratio, the relation of output and labour can be expressed in the form

$$Y = \rho N; \quad \left(\rho = \frac{1}{v} = \frac{Y}{N} \right), \tag{20}$$

where ρ is the coefficient measuring the average productivity of labour. Here $\Delta Y = \rho \Delta N$ implied.

From (19) and (20) and by denoting the ratio of additional labour to output $(\Delta N/Y)$ as n, we have the 'full-employment' rate of growth of output (G_n):

$$G_n = \frac{\Delta Y}{Y} = \frac{\Delta N}{Y} \rho = n\rho, \tag{21}$$

which rate is equivalent to Harrod's 'natural' growth rate based · on the simplifying assumption of 'neutral technological advance' and hence on that of a fixed labour-output ratio corresponding to a fixed capital-output ratio. But for this assumption the 'socially optimal' growth rate (G_m) of the preceding section would be a better approximation. Since Harrod juxtaposes the 'natural' and 'warranted' growth rates for advanced economies, the 'full-employment' growth rate given by (21) rather than the more complicated 'socially optimal' growth rate would appear to be the appropriate concept to make use of. The realization and maintenance of the full-employment growth rate, as such, presupposes a certain rate of capital accumulation. On the favourable assumption that technical conditions and relative factor prices are such as to make real capital readily adjusted to a growing labour population, we can say that G_n is what guarantees the maintenance of full employment. But G_n does not necessarily guarantee full utilization of capital. This is where we must turn to the 'full-capacity' rate of growth or the 'warranted' rate in Harrod's terminology.

We know that the full-capacity growth rate is given by

$$G_k = \frac{s}{b} = s\sigma; \quad \left(\sigma = \frac{1}{b} = \frac{Y}{K} \right), \tag{22}$$

which presupposes an appropriate adjustment of labour population to a growing stock of capital. Assuming that there is always an elastic supply of labour, we may say that G_k is what guarantees full utilization of the existing stock of capital. But G_k does not necessarily guarantee full employment of labour, since population growth and technological advances are not in fact always such as to insure an elastic supply of labour consistent with the demand for labour to be combined with capital.

Suppose that the economy is actually growing at the rate G_n, that is, at the full-employment rate. Now there is no reason why the full-capacity growth rate G_k should always coincide with the full-employment growth rate, except by chance or by design. But for the sake of argument let us suppose that the economy is initially in what Joan Robinson calls 'the golden age' in which the rate of capital accumulation is in perfect harmony with the rate of population growth so that there is full employment of *both* capital and labour. The necessary condition for the maintenance of 'the golden age', as such, is:

$$G_k = G_n; \quad \frac{s}{b} = n\rho. \tag{23}$$

Equations (23)—equivalents—show the basic condition necessary for the maintenance of stable growth without chronic divergences. Suppose, however, that at some point of time beyond the initial period the saving ratio s falls permanently so that the full-capacity growth rate G_k falls below the full-employment growth rate G_n, according to (22). This endogenous shock of the form $G_k < G_n$ sets off a divergent tendency to secular *inflation*, since the saving ratio consistent with the full-capacity growth rate is now less than the rate of investment induced by the actual trends of population and technology, that is, $bG_k = s < bG_n$. The actual divergent path of secular inflation would be characterized by the rising trend of money national income, according to the mechanism of the form $dY_m/dt = f(I_m - S_m)$, where Y, I, and S are income, investment and savings and the subscript m denotes the variables measured in terms of money.

Conversely, suppose that the saving ratio rises permanently at some point of time. Then the full-capacity growth rate must rise above the full-employment growth rate, $G_k > G_n$. This excess of G_k over G_n entails an opposite divergent tendency to secular *stagnation*, since the saving ratio consistent with the full-capacity growth rate is this time greater than the rate of investment induced by the actual growth of population and of technology, that is, $bG_k = s > bG_n$. The divergent path of secular stagnation would be characterized by the declining trend of real income, according to the mechanism of the form $dY/dt = F(S - I)$. In the absence of counterbalancing policies the initiating disturbances due to permanent changes in the saving ratio (or, for that matter, in the capital-output ratio which we are holding constant here) would create ever widening growth gaps between G_k and G_n with time, the inflationary or stagnationary nature of chronic instability involved depending on $G_k \gtrless G_n$. Thus we can think of the instability condition of dynamic equilibrium in terms of an increasing growth gap, that is,

$$\Delta(G_n - G_k) = \psi(G_n - G_k), \qquad (24)$$

where the function ψ has the properties $\psi(0) = 0$ and $\psi' > 0$ (where $\psi' = dX/dt$; $X = G_n - G_k$).

Such, in brief, is the inherent nature of secular instability involved in a pure *laissez-faire* growing economy.

Government as Stabilizer

The above analysis seems sufficient to indicate the general objectives of dynamic fiscal policy for stable growth. For the implication for fiscal policy in the possible case of secular inflation due to $G_k < G_n$ is that the saving ratio should be increased through tax-expenditure operations so as to make $bG_k = s = bG_n$. Contrariwise, the saving ratio should be decreased if the economy is threatened with a tendency to chronic stagnation due to $G_k > G_n$. But to a consideration of specific parametric operations we must now turn.

Suppose that the full-capacity growth rate falls below the full-employment growth rate, $G_k < G_n$, owing to a permanent fall in the private saving ratio s at some time $t > 0$, according to equation (22). The long-term compensatory fiscal policy called for is to achieve and maintain a positive government saving ratio, if there is to be $G_k = G_n$. Conversely, should there be $G_k > G_n$ owing to a permanent rise in the private saving ratio, the fiscal policy required is to achieve and maintain a negative government saving ratio (i.e. to hold a budgetary deficit). For a persistent budgetary *surplus* has the effect of increasing the saving consistent with the full-capacity growth rate to a figure equal to the rate of investment induced by the actual trends of population and technology, while a persistent budgetary *deficit* has the opposite effect of decreasing the saving consistent with the full-capacity growth rate to that figure. In the light of equation (11) we may rewrite equation (23)

$$\frac{s+z-r-g}{b} = n\rho, \qquad (25)$$

which expresses the new condition of dynamic equilibrium to be satisfied by fiscal operations. Equation (25) indicates that if secular inflation is threatened by $G_k < G_n$, it can be averted by a persistent budgetary surplus $(z - r) > g$, and also that if secular stagnation is foreshadowed by $G_k > G_n$, it can be prevented by a persistent budgetary deficit $(z - r) < g$.

Equation (25), moreover, suggests that the fiscal authorities could have alternative operations on the fiscal-policy parameters z, r, and g to achieve a budgetary surplus or deficit in order to compensate for deficient or excessive private saving. If the full-capacity growth rate consistent with private saving is generally above the full-employment growth rate so as to threaten a constantly depressed economy, as Harrod suggests, the aim of making $G_k = G_n$ would require (a) a *rise* in the government average propensity to spend g, (b) a *fall* in the average propensity to tax z, or (c) a *rise* in the average propensity to transfer r—in short, through a continuous budgetary deficit. Thus if the rate of private capital accumulation tends to outstrip the rate of population growth and technical advance, as in developed economies, an attempt to maintain a budgetary deficit, far from being 'immoral', is perfectly consistent with the general objective of promoting stable growth with full employment of both labour and capital but without secular stagnation. The usual objections to the budgetary deficit would lose much of their force if a constantly buoyant economy could be maintained through a skilful combination of tax reduction, government expenditure, and transfer payments.

From equations (12)–(18) we learn that the fiscal authorities are also capable of manipulating tax and transfer rates in order to influence the private saving ratio and hence of stabilizing the full-capacity growth rate relatively to the given full-employment growth rate. Taking those equations into account, we may express the basic condition of dynamic equilibrium in the extended form

$$\frac{[s_1(1-z_1+r_1)d+s_2(1-z_2+r_2)(1-d)]+z-r-g}{b} = np, \quad (26)$$

which indicates that the overall private saving ratio could be increased by decreasing z_2 and r_1 and increasing r_2 and z_1, that is, by a less progressive tax-transfer structure, if secular inflation due to $G_k < G_n$ is to be averted. Conversely, it indicates that the overall private saving ratio could be decreased by increasing z_2 and r_1 and decreasing r_2 and z_1, that is, by a more progressive tax-transfer structure, if secular stagnation due to $G_k > G_n$ is to be prevented. These parametric operations of a disaggregative nature presuppose $s_2 > s_1$, as before.

We must also allow for the possibility that the capital-output ratio b may be deliberately altered through a policy of selective subsidies (subsumed in the transfer rate r) to the individual firms and industries most likely to adopt 'capital-using' or 'capital-saving' know-how, without thereby affecting the overall size of r. Such a policy of selective subsidies might be coupled with tax remissions in favour of industrial developments along 'capital-using' or 'capital-saving' lines, that is, with the manipulation of the composition of the tax rate z.

Finally, a more comprehensive long-term fiscal policy would consider the possibility of influencing the rate of population growth[1] and hence of altering the full-employment growth rate G_n as well, instead of concentrating on the exclusive operations on G_k. Realization of a more comprehensive long-term fiscal policy for stable growth depends not only on further theoretical analysis but also on how far the economic possibilities of fiscal policy can be made reconcilable with its political limitations.[2]

[1] In this respect, N. Kaldor states: 'What he [Harrod] did not allow for was that the "fundamental conditions" determining the natural rate of growth are not determined by Heaven—they are pliable (within wide limits) and can be pushed outwards or pulled inwards by the endogenous forces of the economic system.' (See his 'The Relation of Economic Growth and Cyclical Fluctuations', *Economic Journal*, March 1954). A similar view is expressed in Haavelmo's *A Study in the Theory of Economic Evolution*. But neither of them suggests that population growth or the labour-output ratio be considered as objects for fiscal policy, a suggestion that might have a strong appeal to overpopulated underdeveloped economies as well as to underpopulated advanced economies.

[2] For some of the political and institutional difficulties involved in fiscal operations, see H. R. Bowen and G. M. Meier, 'Institutional Aspects of Economic Fluctuations', in *Post-Keynesian Economics*.

CHAPTER X

FOREIGN TRADE AND ECONOMIC
DEVELOPMENT*

'OPEN' models are just as useful in broadening the analysis as 'closed' models are essential in deepening it. In the present chapter we shall build open models of economic development to clarify the technical relation between foreign trade and domestic growth. Specifically this chapter will discuss (a) the relation between foreign trade and demand growth, (b) the relation between foreign trade and capacity growth, and (c) parametric operations for equilibrium growth—in the particular context of an open economy whose demand tends to grow faster than its capacity and so to make for persistent inflation and imbalance.[1]

This specific treatment of the problem has been chosen so as to relate the present discussion to the post-Keynesian controversy over the relation of domestic growth and the balance of payments.[2] Two distinct approaches to that relation are discernible. One approach stresses the need for domestic progress regardless of its repercussions on the balance of payments, while the other approach emphasizes the need for balance of payments equilibrium whether that external balance is or is not conducive to internal growth. This difference of professional opinion seems to arise from one-sided preoccupation with the

---

* This is a somewhat modified version of my 'Economic Development and the Balance of Payments', *Metroeconomica*, Vol. X, April, 1958.

[1] Most economies outside of the dollar area are confronted with the postwar problem of promoting secular growth in the midst of domestic inflation and foreign balance of payments difficulties. See, e.g. U.N. Economic Commission for Latin America, *Economic Survey of Latin America* 1954, Columbia Univ. Press, 1955; also my 'Japan's Trade Position in a Changing World Market', *Rev. Econ. Stat.*, November 1955.

[2] Cf. 'Growth and the Balance of Payments: A Symposium', *Bull. Oxford Inst. Stat.*, February 1955; R. Nurkse, 'The Relation between Home Investment and External Balance in the Light of British Experience, 1945-55', *Rev. Econ. Stat.*, May 1956; F. Machlup, 'The Finance of Development in Poor Countries: Foreign Capital and Domestic Inflation', *Econ. Studies Quarterly* (Japan), April 1956.

income-generating aspect of foreign trade (demand aspect) or with the capacity-creating aspect of it (supply aspect).

An attempt will be made here to combine these two aspects of foreign trade with a view to clarifying the conditions necessary for balanced or equilibrium growth without internal inflation and external imbalance. Such an attempt may also shed additional light on the national and international measures for freer trade and higher living standards all around.

FOREIGN TRADE AND DEMAND GROWTH

Let us begin with the analysis of the technical relation between foreign trade and demand growth, taking the conditions of supply as given. To show the effect of foreign trade activities on the growth of effective demand, it is necessary to dynamize and secularize Keynesian multiplier theory as follows:

$$\Delta Y^d = \frac{1}{s' + m' - b'}(\Delta I + \Delta G + \Delta E), \qquad (1)$$

where Y^d is real net national income determined by effective demand or simply effective demand, I autonomous private net investment, G government expenditure, E autonomous exports (including invisible credit items), s' the marginal propensity to save, m' the marginal propensity to import, and b' the marginal propensity to invest. Here the multiplicands ΔI, ΔG and ΔE are exogenous parameters, while the marginal propensities to save, to import, and to invest s', m', b' are endogenous parameters. The relative significance of ΔI, ΔG, and ΔE depends on the type of economy envisaged. Observation indicates that the export multiplicand ΔE is quantitatively more significant in underdeveloped economies than in advanced ones.[1] Needless to say, the relative importance of ΔI and ΔG rests largely on the extent of departure from the *laissez-faire* tradition. The marginal propensities to save, to import, and to invest are not necessarily the same as their average counterparts; nor do they hold constant relations to national income.

[1] See H. C. Wallich, 'Underdeveloped Countries and the International Monetary Mechanism', in *Money, Trade and Economic Growth*, Macmillan, N.Y., 1951

The values of s', m', and b' are observedly quite different as between advanced and underdeveloped economies, however. Inclusion of b' here signifies the possible presence of induced investment, in addition to autonomous investment.

Dividing both sides of equation (1) by Y^d and rearranging, we get the rate of growth of effective demand (G^d):

$$G^d = \frac{\Delta Y^d}{Y^d} = \frac{\alpha + \beta + \gamma}{s' + m' - b'}, \qquad (2)$$

where $\alpha = \Delta I / Y^d$, $\beta = \Delta G / Y^d$, and $\gamma = \Delta E / Y^d$. Equation (2) shows that the rate of growth of effective demand is capable of varying directly with changes in autonomous investment, government expenditure, and export income all relative to national income, and inversely with the marginal propensities to save, to import, and to invest. It represents the demand side of a growing open economy. It also shows that an increase in exports relative to national income (γ) or a decrease in the marginal propensity to import (m') would, *cet. par.*, increase the rate of growth of effective demand. However, whether a higher or lower rate of growth of effective demand is to be achieved and maintained cannot be decided except with reference to the rate of growth of productive capacity which we are presently taking as given. We shall return to this matter later. Meanwhile it is interesting to see what implications equation (2) has for an open economy's balance of payments position.

Putting $\Delta I = 0$, $\Delta G = 0$, and $\Delta E = 1$, we may concentrate on the multiplier effect of a change in exports in order to compare this export change with induced imports. For we know that additional imports are induced by an export-generated increment of domestic income, according to

$$\Delta M = m' \Delta Y^d = m' \frac{1}{s' + m' - b'} \Delta E = \frac{m'}{s' + m' - b'} \Delta E. \qquad (3)$$

Starting from the initial position of balance of payments equilibrium, $E - M = \Delta R = 0$ (where M is real imports including invisible debit items and ΔR an increment or a decrement of foreign exchange reserves), the emergence of a favourable or adverse balance of payments can be seen in the following illustrations of equation (3):

If $0 < s' > b' = 0$, then $\Delta M < \Delta E$ (case of undercompensation).

If $0 < s' < b' > 0$, then $\Delta M > \Delta E$ (case of overcompensation).

If $0 < s' = b' > 0$, then $\Delta M = \Delta E$ (case of equal compensation).

The first of these cases is a Keynesian one based on the assumption of excess capacity having a nulifying or decreasing effect on induced investment, so that induced imports always fall short of any original increment of exports and foreign exchange reserves accumulate by an amount equal to

$$\Delta R_n = (\Delta E_{n-1} + E_0) - (\Delta M_{n-1} + M_0).$$

The second case exemplifies an unstable system with the marginal propensity to invest tending to exceed the marginal propensity to save, as in war-devastated or underdeveloped economies with a general shortage of capital or during the upswing phase of a trade cycle with its exhaustion of idle plant and equipment. In this second case of overcompensation foreign reserves decumulate according to

$$-\Delta R_n = (\Delta M_{n-1} + M_0) - (\Delta E_{n-1} + E_0).$$

The last case of equal compensation arises from the marginal propensity to save being equal to the marginal propensity to invest, so that there is neither accumulation nor decumulation of exchange reserves, $\Delta R = 0$. This last case may not be considered desirable from a purely domestic point of view, for it means not only that any increment of autonomous exports will sooner or later be dissipated in an equal increment of imports but also that foreign exchange reserves as a possible source of developmental capital are not at all increasing over time. It would be considered none the less desirable if a single economy started from the initial position of balance of payments *dis*quilibrium.

Such is the interaction and interdependence of foreign trade and demand growth. Concern with the expansion of exports as a source of demand is justified to the extent that the actual rate of growth of national income is determined by demand alone, as when the conditions of supply are given. Such concern is entirely in keeping with the Keynesian tradition which rejects the classical notion that supply creates its own demand. Nevertheless it is one-sided concern all the same, for foreign trade relations are capable of influencing the supply side of a growing economy as well. This is where we must depart from Keynesian preoccupation with effective demand and turn to classical emphasis on supply and productivity once more, albeit without Say's Law.

FOREIGN TRADE AND CAPACITY GROWTH

Taking the conditions of demand as given this time, we may proceed to analyse the other relation between foreign trade and capacity growth. Given the size of natural resources and of the labour population, an economy's aggregate supply or productive capacity depends mainly on the quantity and quality of real capital. We may express an increase in productive capacity due to full utilization of available capital in the form

$$\Delta Y^s = \sigma \Delta K = \sigma I, \tag{4}$$

where Y^s is net national output determined by productive capacity or simply productive capacity, K the quantity of capital when fully utilized, I net investment ($I_t = K_t - K_{t-1}$), and σ the marginal (= average) productivity of capital technologically given.

But an *open* economy's net investment is, in equilibrium, equal to savings in an unusual sense, that is,

$$I = S + M - E; \quad I + E = S + M, \tag{5}$$

where S is domestic savings, other variables being the same as before.

Substituting (5) in (4), we have increment of productive capacity involving exports and imports:

$$\Delta Y^s = \sigma(S + M - E). \tag{6}$$

Next we define S, M, and E in $S = sY^s$, $M = mY^s$, and $E = eY^s$, where s is the saving ratio, m the import ratio, and e the export ratio (i.e. the average propensities to save and to import and the ratio of autonomous exports to given domestic production). Taking these definitions into account and rearranging, we have the rate of growth of productive capacity (G^s):

$$G^s = \frac{\Delta Y^s}{Y^s} = \sigma(s + m - e), \qquad (7)$$

which represents the supply side of a growing open economy. Equation (7) indicates that the rate of growth of productive capacity obtainable by fully utilizing available capital is capable of varying in direct proportion as the productivity of capital (σ) changes and as the domestic saving ratio plus the trade balance ratio ($s + m - e$) changes. The operational significance of equation (7) may be seen in the following plausible numerical examples:[1]

If $\sigma = \cdot5$, $s = \cdot10$, $m = \cdot05$, $e = \cdot07$, then $G^s = \cdot04$

(advanced economy).

If $\sigma = \cdot2$, $s = \cdot05$, $m = \cdot015$, $e = \cdot10$, then $G^s = \cdot02$

(underdeveloped economy).

These examples indicate that an advanced economy with a high capital productivity coefficient as well as with a high saving ratio can achieve a high rate of growth of productive capacity through a positive foreign balance ratio ($e - m > 0$), while an underdeveloped economy with low productivity and low saving can achieve only a low rate of growth of productive capacity through a negative foreign balance ratio ($e - m < 0$). They also imply that if an advanced economy's capacity tends

[1] The values of σ are inferred from the average capital-output ratios attributed to advanced and underdeveloped economies. See, e.g. W. Fellner, 'The Capital-Output Ratio in Dynamic Economics,' *op. cit.*; I. Yamada, 'The Five-Year Economic Plan in Japan and the Analysis of Postwar Japanese Economy', *Economic Review*, July 1956; Y. Okazaki, 'On the Capital-Coefficient in Underdeveloped Countries', *Economic Studies Quarterly*, March 1957. Advanced economies usually have smaller capital-output ratios, thus implying larger productivity of capital coefficients based on superior technology. For comparative saving ratios see S. Kuznets, 'Economic Growth and Income Inequality', *op. cit.* As for the export and import ratios, the low productive and exporting capacity of underdeveloped economies is a presumption against their export ratios being constantly above their import ratios. For comparative export-import figures in absolute term, see H. Wallich, *op. cit.*

to grow faster than its demand, it must increase its positive foreign balance ratio and that if an underdeveloped economy's capacity tends to grow more slowly than its demand, it must increase its negative foreign balance ratio.

Thus the presumption is that an advanced economy usually experiences a favourable balance of payments represented by $eY^s - mY^s = \Delta R > 0$, while an underdeveloped economy customarily experiences an adverse balance of payments characterized by $eY^s - mY^s = \Delta R < 0$. This, however, is not to say that an underdeveloped economy must not try to develop its productive capacity without regard to balance of payments equilibrium, as the subsequent analysis will show to the contrary. Let us turn to the consideration of parametric operations for equilibrium growth without inflation and imbalance.

PARAMETRIC OPERATIONS FOR EQUILIBRIUM GROWTH

Balanced or equilibrium growth is the ideal line of advance which, if realized, would guarantee rising real income without being dissipated in rising prices and without being disrupted by chronic balance of payments difficulties. It is clear from the foregoing analysis that the basic condition to be satisfied for the realization and maintenance of equilibrium growth is

$$\frac{\alpha+\beta+\gamma}{s'+m'-b'} = \sigma(s+m-e) \text{ or } G^d = G^s. \tag{8}$$

Equation (8) implies that if $G^d = G^s$, money national income $(Y^d{}_m)$ will rise according to the exponential form

$$Y^d = \underset{m}{Y^d} = P(t)Y^s = \underset{m0}{Y^d}(1+g_m)^t,$$

where P is the price index at time t, $Y_{m0}{}^d$ the initial value of money income, and g_m the rate of increase of money income $(\Delta Y_m{}^d/Y_m{}^d)$. If the economy started from the initial position of equilibrium $G^d = G^s$, a sudden shock of the form $G^d > G^s$ at time $t > 0$ would give rise to an inflationary divergence from the steady path of full-capacity growth. The initiating shock of the form $G^d > G^s$ may be due to a more or less permanent rise in α, β, γ or B' or, alternatively to a similar fall in s' and m', as equation (2) indicates. A situation characterized by $G^d > G^s$ is indicative not only of a persistent tendency toward inflation but also of chronic balance of payments difficulties. For a high G^d implies the possibility of large induced imports, while a low G^s suggests the likelihood of small exports supplied.

This leads us to the question: how can an open economy characterized by the inequality of the form $G^d > G^s$ wipe out internal inflation and external imbalance that are implicit in that inequality? The general answer is that G^d must be reduced without at the same time reducing G^s, while trying to increase G^s without increasing G^d, if there is to be $G^d = G^s$. This is a tall order indeed, but nevertheless let us explore possible operations with the parameters of equations (2) and (7) so as to satisfy the condition expressed by equation (8).

The Control of Effective Demand

The operational possibilities of reducing G^d are necessarily limited by the basic objective of fostering domestic economic progress without upsetting foreign balance of payments equilibrium. With this restriction in mind, let us first contemplate possible reductions in exogenous parameters α, β, and γ, taking endogenous parameters s', m', and b' as given.

By how much autonomous investment, government expenditure, or expert income should fall for any given level of national income depends on the multiplier and the desired decrement of effective demand involved, for we know from equation (1) that the required contraction of any of those multiplicands is given by $\Delta I = \Delta Y^d/k$, $\Delta G = \Delta Y^d/k$, or $\Delta E = \Delta Y^d/k$, where $k = 1/(s' + m' - b')$. Let, for instance, $s' = \cdot 05$, $m' = \cdot 3$, $b' = \cdot 1$, $\Delta Y^d = 1$. Then autonomous investment considered as relevant source of demand will have to contract by an amount equal to $1/4 = \cdot 25$, according to $\Delta I = \Delta Y^d/k$. The same holds valid for any other multiplicand.

It is important that the choice of any particular source of demand for reduction must be guided by reference to possible repercussions on the balance of payments and the secular growth of productive capacity. As far as the balance of payments is concerned, an autonomous fall in exports relative to

M

any given level of demand (γ) could, *cet. par.*, reduce G^d without provoking external imbalance, provided s' increased relatively to b' at the same time. Inasmuch, however, as a change in γ has no direct influence on s', a reduction in γ as a particular way to dampen excess demand must be ruled out as inconsistent with the aim of maintaining balance of payments equilibrium. Moreover, since the demand for a single economy's exports is mainly a function of other economies' income levels, it is not usually open to a single economy to manipulate γ as it sees fit (with the possible exception of the U.S. which could considerably influence the foreign demand for its exports through large-scale loans and gifts, as was demonstrated by the Marshall Plan). As far as the secular growth of productive capacity is concerned, a fall in α or β need not reduce the productivity of capital (σ), if such a fall is effected at the expense of unproductive components of autonomous private investment and government expenditure (e.g. pyramid-building and armaments). If a fall in α or β is brought about through a 'dear money' policy, it may well have the effect of discourag-'roundabout' methods of production and hence of reducing the productivity of capital in the long run (this latter effect operating via the possibly decreasing effect of a lower capital-labour ratio on labour productivity, as in $Y/K = (Y/N)/(K/N)$).

Taking α, β, and γ as given, we may now consider possible operations with s', m', and b' for the same purpose of controlling effective demand, albeit with due regard for the balance of payments and the secular growth of productive capacity.

A rise in s' is capable of reducing G^d without defeating the purpose of promoting balance of payments equilibrium and of expanding productive capacity. For, on the one hand, $s' \gtreqqless b'$ makes for $\Delta M \lesseqqgtr \Delta E$, as our earlier analysis has shown, while, on the other hand, the same increase in s' tends to increase s and σ in the long run and so to raise G^s without much dependence on a large external deficit in terms of ratios, $m > e$. The necessary reservation to have here is that the measures for increasing s' may prove inexpedient inasmuch as they imply consumption austerity possibly beyond what is considered tolerable in some cases.

A rise in the marginal propensity to import, m', might also be contemplated, provided that the marginal propensity to save exceeds or equals the marginal propensity to invest. For $s' \geqq b'$ makes for $\Delta M \leqq \Delta E$, as mentioned above. In addition to reducing G^d, a rise in m' tends to increase m in the long run so to help increase G^s. Furthermore, if a higher m' has the 'substitution effect' of diminishing the demand for home-produced consumer goods, abstracting from any offsetting 'income effect', it will to that extent increase s' and s, thus reducing G^d and raising G^s still more.

A fall in the marginal propensity to invest, b', might also be considered as an alternative operational possibility. A fall in b' tends to decrease G^d without thereby worsening the balance of payments, for we have already seen that zero or small b' gives full play to the Keynesian case of 'undercompensation'. Moreover, insofar as a fall in b' is brought about through measures designed to enlarge the scope of innovational investment and to reduce excessive reliance on induced investment (à la the acceleration principle), it tends to increase σ in the long run and so to raise G^s.

Thus in inflationary circumstances arising from $G^d > G^s$, the growth of demand can be controlled so as to make $G^d = G^s$ through (1), a rise in s' (2), a rise in m' (3), a fall in b' (4), a fall in α (5), a fall in β, and/or (6) a fall in γ—without provoking balance of payments disequilibrium and without impeding the secular growth of productive capacity. The control of productive capacity remains yet to be discussed.

The Control of Productive Capacity

To increase the rate of growth of productive capacity is admittedly more difficult than to decrease the rate of growth of effective demand. This difficulty is all the greater because of the restriction imposed upon our parametric operations, namely, not to increase G^s in such wise as to increase G^d and to entail $\Delta R < 0$. With this restriction at the back of our mind, let us explore possible operations with the parameters of equation (7).

An increase in the productivity of capital (σ) has the advantage of accelerating G^s without the self-defeating accompaniment of rising demand and without the worsening of external balance.

For it signifies greater productive and exporting capacity through more efficient utilization of a given stock of capital rather than an increment of capital that might generate unwanted demand or necessitate unwanted imports. We may see it as follows.

Suppose that the total stock of capital (K) is partioned into that which is owned and utilized by home-biased industries (K_h) catering to domestic markets and that which is owned and utilized by export-biased industries (K_e), catering to foreign markets, so that

$$K = K_h + K_e, \tag{9}$$

the distribution ratio of which is

$$\frac{K_h}{K} = \eta, \quad \frac{K_e}{K} = 1 - \eta. \tag{10}$$

Next we define productive capacity (Y^s) as being made up of home-biased output $(Y_h{}^s)$ and export-biased output $(Y_e{}^s)$ so that

$$Y^s = Y_h{}^s + Y_e{}^s, \tag{11}$$

the right-hand side of which equation may be specified as

$$Y_h{}^s = \sigma_h K_h, \tag{12}$$

$$Y_e{}^s = \sigma_e K_e, \tag{13}$$

where σ_h is the average and marginal productivity of capital in the home-biased industries as a whole and σ_e the average and marginal productivity of capital in the export-biased industries. Here we shall assume $\sigma_e > \sigma_h$ on the plausible ground that decreasing-cost (increasing-return) industries are the ones that usually require expanding export markets (especially in the absence of expanding domestic frontiers and markets), in addition to the home market. This assumption is crucial for the present argument in favour of increasing the distribution ratio, $1 - \eta$, for the purpose of raising the productivity of capital for the whole economy as well as the productive capacity of the export-biased industries.

Taking equations (10), (12) and (13) into account, we can rewrite equation (11)

$$Y^s = \sigma_h K_h + \sigma_e K_e = \sigma_h \eta K + \sigma_e (1 - \eta) K. \qquad (14)$$

From (14) we have the average productivity of capital for the whole economy:

$$\frac{Y^s}{K} = \sigma = \sigma_h \eta + \sigma_e (1 - \eta), \qquad (15)$$

which indicates that the average productivity of capital for the whole economy is capable of increasing as a result of an increase in the distribution ratio $(1 - \eta)$, provided that $\sigma_e > \sigma_h$. It also implies that export-biased output is enlarged by that rise in the distribution ratio $(1 - \eta)$, that is, via $Y_e^s = \sigma_e (1 - \eta) K$.[1] Moreover, this increase in capital productivity coefficient (σ) has the added advantage of necessitating a smaller import ratio (m) to supplement the domestic saving ratio (s).

A rise in the saving ratio (s) could increase G^s without at the same time increasing G^d, if it tended to increase s' and so to decrease the rate of growth of effective demand. Also a higher domestic saving ratio, like a higher productivity of capital, makes for less reliance on imports as a supplement to domestic real capital, according to equation (7). It may be presumed that a higher saving ratio is brought about through a redistribution of disposable income in favour of high-saving income groups or through a persistent budgetary surplus.

A rise in the import ratio (m), if it also represents a rise in m', is capable of increasing G^s without increasing G^d. But from the standpoint of long-run balance of payments equilibrium it is a rise in the average propensity to import *capital goods* (m_i) which

[1] Such a rise in the capacity to produce exportable goods does not, however necessarily result in an increase in the demand for exports which depends on foreign incomes, relative prices, exchange rates, and possibly non-economic foreign policies. That R. Nurkse recommends such an increase in Britain's export industries is at best a reflection of the special circumstances in which the foreign demand for exports (from the U.K.) happens to coincide with what Britain is capable of supplying. But for many trading nations (e.g. Japan) it is not so much the lack of exporting capacity as the lack of foreign markets (demand) which is troublesome. Accordingly an increase in the productive capacity of export-biased industries, while it may contribute to overall productivity and growth, nevertheless can prove rather disappointing for lack of expandable foreign markets.

is to be encouraged, keeping the average propensity to import consumer goods (m_c) constant. For the import ratio is actually the sum of these propensities, $m = m_c + m_i$. This means that if $m =$ constant, m_i can be increased only at the expense of m_c and that if $m_c =$ constant, a rise in m signifies a rise in m_i. If a rise in m is due to a rise in m_i instead of in m_c, it will make a *direct* contribution to the domestic capital-goods industries.[1] In terms of trade policy this may mean that tariffs and other import controls should be so directed as to keep the average propensity to import consumer goods (m_c) from rising.

Lastly, a fall in e relative to given m would increase G^s without militating against the other aim of reducing G^d, since a fall in e may well represent a fall in γ in the shorter run. However, a fall in e may have a detrimental effect on balance of payments equilibrium. The most that a single economy can do to protect its long-run balance of payments position is to rely on the increasing effect of a rise in γ on e so as to avoid an otherwise large deficit ratio, $e - m < 0$ that would be needed to increase G^s. Beyond that a single exporting economy can merely hope that the rest of the trading world will increase their incomes or their average propensities to import, given relative prices and exchange rates. The extent to which e should fall relatively to given m depends on the prevailing values of σ and s, for as a less developed economy becomes more productive and more thrifty, it can develop its productive capacity without importing foreign goods and capital in excess of what it can pay by its own exports.

CONCLUDING REMARKS

To emphasize the demand side of a growing economy alone is to lose sight of the capacity-creating aspect of foreign trade which classical theory from Adam Smith's *Wealth of Nations* down to the present has taught. To stress the supply side alone

---

[1] This is not to say that imported consumer goods are unproductive, for they do have the indirect effect of contributing to the domestic capital-goods industries by releasing productive factors that would otherwise be used in producing consumer goods. But for those economies with relative factor immobility and inadequate exchange reserves it is of great practical importance to concentrate on the importation of capital goods.

is to ignore the income-generating aspect of foreign trade which Keynesian theory has shown and to repeat the classical error of assuming that supply creates its own demand. Accordingly the realization and maintenance of equilibrium growth with full employment (both of labour and capital) but without internal inflation and external imbalance requires that the rate of growth of effective demand and the rate of growth of productive capacity be brought into equality with each other. With the inflationary circumstances occasioned by $G^d > G^s$ in view, we have explored possible operations with the parameters of the growth of demand equation and the growth of capacity equation so as to make $G^d = G^s$, that is, ways and means of reducing G^d without thereby reducing G^s and of increasing G^s without simultaneously increasing G^d.

If the choice must be made between domestic growth and balance of payments equilibrium, most underdeveloped economies will probably prefer the former to the latter, and with reason. For capacity growth is a presumption in favour of gradually improving balance of payments, while excessive preoccupation with the balance of payments problem tends to encourage the one-sided growth of 'exchange-earning' industries at the expense of overall industrialization, as colonial history so abundantly illustrates.

Underdevelopment, like underemployment, is a strong presumption against free non-discriminatory trade, for underdeveloped economies are always tempted, to protect and often justified in protecting their indigenous industries against the competition, actual or potential, of foreign goods. This is the important element of truth in Friedrich List's theory of industrialization through protection[1] which all but free-trade purists would recognize, especially in the light of the understandable drive for 'international homogenization', to borrow Haavelmo's phrase.[2] It is just as unfruitful to hope for multilateral trade without developing the underdeveloped areas of the world as it is idle to preach the advantage of free trade without promoting universal full employment. This latter is what we have recently learned from Keynesian theory. In

[1] See his *Das nationale System der politishen Öknonomie.*
[2] T. Haavelmo, *A Study in the Theory of Economic Evolution.*

this regard, it is instructive to recall that Keynes definitely linked as International Monetary Fund to 'the policy of full employment' and considered it an increasingly important task of a World Bank 'to make the resources of the world more fully available to all mankind, and so to order its operations as to promote and maintain equilibrium in the international balances of payments of all member countries'.[1] Our analysis suggests that less developed economies have every reason to proceed with their industrialization programming without undue fears of balances of payments disequilibrium.[2]

[1] See Keynes's speech before the House of Lords, May 23, 1944, and his Opening Remarks at the First Meeting of the Second Commission on the World Bank July 3, 1944.

[2] We may make the following qualifying observations about the possible antinomy of industrialization: (1) The greater production and exportation of manufactured goods incident to industrialization may raise the income elasticity of foreign demand for imports (or exports of the industrializing economy in question) far beyond unity, $(\Delta M_w/M_w)/(\Delta Y_w/Y_w) > 1$, where M_w is imports of the rest of the world and Y_w its national incomes considered as a whole. The exporting economy is then likely to experience greater instability in its foreign balances and, more particularly, a serious loss of exports whenever national incomes in the rest of the world take a downturn. (2) If the industrializing economy's imports consist largely of capital goods, it is possible to consider imports as a function of the rate of change of income, that is, $M_k = \beta\Delta Y$, where M_k is imports of capital goods and β the capital-output ratio involved (the reciprocal of the productivity of imported capital goods). Dividing both sides of this import equation by Y, we get the import ratio: $M_k/Y = \beta(\Delta Y/Y)$, which shows that a rise in the rate of growth of domestic income is capable of increasing the import ratio above the given export ratio (E/Y)—unless the capital-output ratio (β) is reduced by the increased productivity of imported capital goods. (3) The higher money wage-rate accompanying increased labour productivity may increase the average export price (P_e) relatively to the average import price (P_m) so as to discourage exports and increase imports, the latter effect being via $\Delta M = m\Delta Y = mk't\Delta E$, where k' is the foreign-trade multiplier, $t = P_e/P_m$ or the terms of trade index, and E exports. Such a rise in t is often offset by a government subsidy to exporters or by a monopolistic agreement among exporters not to raise export prices, however. (4) The expansion of export-biased industries at full employment may increase general prices (including export prices) to the detriment of export trade, while the same expansion at less than full employment may increase domestic real income and induced imports, the net effect on the foreign balance being the more adverse the more price-elastic is the foreign demand for imports, and the higher is the domestic marginal propensity to import.

CHAPTER XI

EPILOGUE ON POST-KEYNESIAN GROWTH THEORIES

In this chapter we shall conclude with a comparison of the theory developed in the preceding chapters with other post-Keynesian growth theories, with a view to indicating wherein the major differences lie and wherefore those differences are relevant to the economic development of underdeveloped countries. The comparison will be made under two headings: (a) the developmental role of the State, and (b) the nature and mechanism of balanced growth.

THE DEVELOPMENTAL ROLE OF THE STATE

First and above all, the stabilizing role of the State associated with the name of Keynes must, in our view, be coupled with its developmental role in the specific context of underdeveloped countries and on a much larger scale than in the past. The Harrod-Domar-Robinson models of *laissez-faire* growth have the negative virtue of demonstrating how precarious and unfruitful it is to leave the secular growth of an economy to the vagaries of private saving and investment, to the accident of profit-motivated inventions and innovations, and to the working of unguided market forces. All these growth models have this positive lesson for underdeveloped economies, that the State should be allowed to play not only a stabilizing role but also a *developmental* role, if those economies are to industrialize more effectively and rapidly than the now industrialized economies did in conditions of *laissez-faire*.

To be more specific, an underdeveloped economy would have to take Harrod's *autonomous* investment ratio (k) much more seriously than he does himself in the context of an advanced economy. For in the context of an underdeveloped economy autonomous investment is not, as Harrod arbitrarily assumes, necessarily a merely income-generating, saving-offsetting armaments expenditure but possibly a capacity-increasing public-investment outlay. It is by underestimating the crucial role of autonomous investment that Harrod overestimates the 'required' rate of growth of income to induce private investment. Inclusion of autonomous public investment would greatly lighten the otherwise unbearable burden on induced private investment in the underdeveloped circumstances where private initiative and risk-taking are obviously too deficient to bring about productive investment in sufficient quantities, anyway. We have shown how Harrod's deflationary bias due to the exclusion of autonomous investment could be turned into an initiating basis for secular growth by introducing autonomous investment as an explicit public-policy parameter in growth equations. Autonomous investment, when specified as government investment, could be instrumental in creating external economies that are so helpful in stimulating private enterprise and in increasing general productivity. Autonomous investment of a public nature has the added advantage of being far more stable than autonomous investment of a private nature.

The dual character of investment stressed by Domar acquires a new meaning in the context of an underdeveloped economy that entrusts to the State the task of controlling saving and investment in a Keynesian manner. For it is only on the assumption of *laissez-faire* saving and investment that the capacity-creating aspect of investment can be decried as depressing the profitability of further investment, instead of being welcomed as a force making for greater productivity and price stability. An underdeveloped economy taking Keynes's suggestions about 'a somewhat comprehensive socialization of investment' and 'communal saving through the agency of the State'[1] at all seriously would be spared the constant fear of effective demand being greater or smaller than productive capacity to threaten inflation or deflation. We have applied those suggestions of Keynes in our discussions of the monetary and fiscal roles of government in economic development.

The importance of investment-demand and expanding

[1] *General Theory*, p. 378 and p. 376.

markets stressed by R. Nurkse[1] makes sense only under *laissez-faire*. Preclusion of the government role in economic development has led Nurkse to an over-pessimistic view of domestic investment on the one hand and to an over-optimistic view of a 'saving potential' on the other. For the 'demonstration effect', which Nurkse fears as an obstacle to an underdeveloped open eonomy's domestic investment is really academic if and when such an economy has effective import controls, while the mobilization of the disguised unemployed as a 'saving potential' is equally academic if and when the economy in question has no effective public-works programmes or public labour exchanges. Thus Nurkse's attempt to take a middle course between the classical extreme of decreasing consumption to increase saving and investment (on the assumption of full employment) and the Keynesian extreme of increasing consumption and investment simultaneously (on the assumption of less than full employment) could be successful only by abandoning *laissez-faire*, by letting the State play a more active role in externally controlling the 'demonstration effect' and internally improving public works programmes or public systems of labour allocation.

Notable exceptions are found in the growth discussions of A. H. Hansen, J. Robinson, and W. A. Lewis,[2] however. Lewis gives greater emphasis to the role of government in economic development than most writers do, though he would presumably implement that government role by a Keynesian policy of controlling the instruments of production rather than a Marxian policy of owning those instruments. Elsewhere Lewis has indicated how an underdeveloped economy with much underemployed labour could expand credit to finance relatively labour-using, quick-producing developmental projects without increasing inflationary pressures.[3] Joan Robinson's discussion

---

[1] See his *Problems of Capital Formation*, etc.

[2] See Hansen, *The American Economy*, McGraw-Hill, N.Y., 1957; Robinson, *The Accumulation of Capital*, Irwin, Homewood, 1956; Lewis, *The Theory of Economic Growth*, Allen & Unwin, London, 1955. Compare my reviews of Hansen's book and Lewis's book respectively in *Current Economic Comment* (November 1957) and *Econometrica* (January 1957).

[3] W. A. Lewis, 'Economic Development with Unlimited Supplies of Labour', *The Manchester School of Economic and Social Studies*, May 1954.

of capital growth has the subtle effect of discrediting the whole idea of leaving so important a problem as economic growth to 'the capitalist rules of the game',[1] for her model of *laissez-faire* growth demonstrates, even more convincingly than do the Harrod-Domar models, how precarious, capricious and insecure it is to entrust to private profit-makers the paramount task of achieving the stable growth of an economy consistent with the needs of a growing population and the possibilities of advancing technology. It is not at all surprising, therefore, that Joan Robinson has elsewhere suggested that an underdeveloped economy would have to represent also a 'socialist' State in order to programme its industrialization.[2] Judging from her statement: 'The problem of combining the necessary degree of control with the traditional methods of democracy is the dominating political problem of the present time',[3] one can only surmise that Joan Robinson's notion of a 'socialist' State designed for the industrialization of an underdeveloped economy is essentially the same as Keynes's 'system of State Socialism'[4] based on the central control of productive facilities and recommended for the stability of an advanced economy.

[1] See her *The Accumulation of Capital*.

[2] Her lecture before Hitotsubashi University (Japan), as reported in *Hitotsubashi Shinbun*, May 30, 1955. In this regard, it is interesting to hear an Indian economist state: 'We learn the same lesson from the history of economic development of Japan. We find that between 1868 to 1879 the Japanese government took the lead in creating all sorts of facilities to spur industrialization. They built shipyards, iron foundries, model factories equipped with western machines, railroads and telegraphs, and hired foreign experts to teach new techniques. Such impetus provided by the Japanese government was very largely responsible for Japan's economic development and reduced the time required for industrialisation by several decades. Today India is faced with a similar situation as Japan was in the latter part of the nineteenth century in her urge for rapid economic development. The government has therefore to take the lead and create an impetus for development in the country.' (D. Jha, 'Fiscal Policy and the Economic Development of Underdeveloped Countries', *Indian Journal of Economics*, July 1956).

[3] See her *Collected Economic Papers*, p. 113.

[4] *General Theory*, p. 378. There Keynes is careful to distinguish between what is sometimes called 'Keynesian socialism' and traditional socialism by stating: 'It is not the ownership of the instruments of production which it is important for the State to assume. If the State is able to determine the aggregate amount of resources devoted to augmenting the instruments and the basic rate of reward to those who own them, it will have accomplished all that is necessary. Moreover, the necessary measures of socialization can be introduced gradually and without a break in the general traditions of society.'

Hansen, while he deals specifically with an advanced economy, nevertheless has much to say that is highly instructive to underdeveloped economies.[1] The 'mixed public-private economy', together with 'the democratic welfare state', which Hansen advocates for the stable growth of the American economy, could be recommended even more strongly for the maximum growth of underdeveloped economies. For the principal weapon of a mixed economy, as Hansen sees it, is fiscal-monetary policies that could be used to speed up capital accumulation and technological progress as well as to stabilize effective demand, while a democratic welfare state could be viewed as providing not only 'built-in stabilizers' (social-insurance payments, farm-support programmes, public housing, mass education, etc., favoured by him in the context of an advanced economy) but also 'social capital' (e.g. schools, hospitals, public recreation centres, public libraries, public-welfare departments, and other publicly controlled amenities of life) so helpful in increasing general productivity. In the context of an underdeveloped economy, Hansen's 'mixed-economy, welfare-state' scheme of thought would probably have to include direct controls (priority allocation policies, price controls, and import controls, e.g.) as well as indirect fiscal-monetary policies. Moreover, the rapid industrialization of underdeveloped countries would possibly necessitate a somewhat broader interpretation of Hansen's 'mixed-economy, welfare-state' scheme as well as of Keynes's 'State Socialism' so as to include the government ownership and operation of some industries and enterprises that have a vital bearing upon the public welfare and the stimulation of private initiative (e.g. public utilities and banking facilities).

The main difference between Hansen and us is that he, in a more orthodox Keynesian manner, envisages the State primarily as a compensatory agency, while we have assigned to the State the additional task of maximizing productive capacity. For it is not the stabilization of effective demand which it is crucial for the State in an underdeveloped country to promote.

[1] For an extended discussion of Hansen's 'mixed-economy, welfare-state' scheme see my 'Professor Hansen on America's Economic Revolution', *Economic Journal*, September, 1958.

Rather the principal economic task of the State in such a country is one of directly or indirectly developing its productive capacity relatively to any given level or rate of increase of effective demand. To fulfil this latter task, it is necessary to 'mix' central control and central ownership in proportions appropriate to the task and consistent with the social philosophy of a particular underdeveloped country. The doctrinaire dichotomy between the dogma of exclusive control and the dogma of exclusive ownership is meaningless, anyway, in a society with democratic safeguards against the abu.es of central authority. But this is a matter in which technical economists must have the co-operation of political scientists, philosophers, sociologists and psychologists if they are to give underdeveloped economies technical advice that is meaningful and fruitful in terms of human values.

THE NATURE AND MECHANISM OF BALANCED GROWTH

It is fashionable for writers on economic development to bandy around the expression 'balanced growth', though most writers fail to make clear what exactly it is that is 'balanced' or to realize that 'balanced growth' is a contradiction in substance, if not in terms as well, as far as a *laissez-faire* economy is concerned. Nor do they always make clear the precise mechanism whereby 'balanced growth' (on some definition) is supposed to be achieved and maintained. Accordingly it seems useful to review critically various concepts of 'balanced growth' and the growth mechanisms involved in those concepts.

Modern growth economics started as an attempt to explain the turbulent nature of long-run growth and the unstable nature of short-run equilibrium, that is, to make operationally significant the intuitive insights of Keynes and Schumpeter into the cyclical growth of capitalism. Harrod and Domar broke fresh ground for calling attention to the dual character of investment making for the unstable growth of an advanced economy in conditions mainly of *laissez-faire*. The equality of saving and investment as a condition of equilibrium can be regarded as a sufficient condition only so long as the stock of capital is assumed to remain constant, as in Keynes's short-run theory of effective demand. But if the stock of capital is allowed to grow, as it must be in a longer period, then there arises the possibility of investment becoming positive or negative as a result of changing capacity and hence of upsetting the temporary equality of investment and saving. How to make saving and investment balanced in a growing economy with an increasing stock of capital thus became the principal problem which Harrod and Domar attempted to solve formally.

The essence of 'balanced growth' common to Harrod and Domar is that effective demand and productive capacity must be kept in balance somehow, if an economy is to maintain a steady growth of output without idle capacity or redundant labour. In Harrod's growth theory, a basic condition of stable growth is that net national real income (Y) must increase by the same amount as productive capacity, when the saving ratio (s) and the capital-output ratio (b) are given:

$$\Delta Y = \frac{s}{b} Y,$$

the right-hand side of which is an increment of productive capacity and the left-hand side an increment of effective demand. From this equation follows the familiar *required* rate of growth of income ('warranted' rate, in Harrod's terminology):

$$\frac{\Delta Y}{Y} = \frac{s}{b},$$

which tells us that income must grow at the constant rate s/b if productive capacity is to be fully utilized without excess or short capacity. For it is clear from the above equation that if $\Delta Y/Y < s/b$, as seems to be the prevailing tendency of advanced economies as a whole and as a rule, secular stagnation might result from effective demand growing more slowly than productive capacity, or $\Delta Y < s/bY$.

Applied to an underdeveloped economy, it is an inflationary bias that is latent in the opposite tendency of capacity growing more slowly than demand, $\Delta Y/Y > s/b$ implying $\Delta Y > (s/b)Y$ in shorter periods comprising the long run. If this inflationary tendency is to be minimized, an underdeveloped economy would have to take appropriate steps to decelerate the expansion of effective demand (ΔY) or to accelerate the expansion of productive capacity ($(s/b)Y$) or do both. However, it is not so much to diminish inflationary pressures as to accumulate real capital and to overcome secular underemployment that an underdeveloped economy would have to concentrate on the supply or capacity side of the above equation. In other words, an underdeveloped economy must not only equate the rate of growth of effective demand and the rate of growth of productive capacity for 'stable growth' but also equate the rate of growth of productive capacity and the rate of growth of population with an increasing productivity, that is:

$$\frac{\Delta Y}{Y} = \frac{s}{b} = n + h,$$

where n is the rate of growth of labour population, h the rate of growth of labour productivity, and hence $n + h$ the 'socially optimal rate of growth' discussed earlier in this book. There we showed that Harrod's 'natural' rate is a special case of the general case involving a *variable* productivity of labour (or a variable labour-output ratio), since his 'warranted' rate coinciding with his 'natural' rate could take care of full employment only if the labour-output ratio does not decrease (or labour productivity does not increase) to require less labour per unit of output. In other words, if productive capacity grew only at the same rate as labour population, as on the assumption of a constant labour-output ratio, an underdeveloped economy would experience both secular underemployment for lack of capital and a stationary standard of living for lack of increasing productivity. Thus our notion of 'balanced growth' for an underdeveloped economy involves the balancing of the growth rates of effective demand, productive capacity, *and* a labour population whose productivity is *increasing* over time (instead of remaining constant, as in Harrod's discussion of the 'natural' rate).

As for Domar's notion of 'balanced growth', he is more explicit than Harrod on the demand side of a growing economy, for Domar spells out the 'multiplier' aspect of the demand side while Harrod does not. On the supply side, Domar differs from Harrod mainly in using the reciprocal of the latter's capital-output ratio, that is, in using the productivity of investment. Thus implicitly starting with $Y = I/\alpha$ as the *level* of effective demand and $Y' = \sigma K$ as the *level* of productive capacity and hence $Y = Y'$ or $I/\alpha = \sigma K$ as a condition of *static* equilibrium (where Y is effective demand, Y' productive capacity, I net investment, K capital stock, α the marginal (= average assumed) propensity to save, and σ the marginal (= average assumed) productivity of investment), Domar explicitly moves on to the condition of dynamic equilibrium

$$\frac{\Delta I}{I} = \alpha\sigma,$$

which follows from $\Delta Y = \Delta I/\alpha$ on the demand side and $\Delta Y' = \sigma\Delta K = \sigma I$ on the supply side and hence from $\Delta Y = \Delta Y'$ or $\Delta I/\alpha = \sigma I$.

Domar's growth equation $\Delta I/I = \alpha\sigma$ comes to the same thing as Harrod's 'warranted' rate of growth, since from the former's $Y = I/\alpha$ we get

$$\frac{\Delta Y}{Y} = \frac{\Delta I/\alpha}{Y} = \frac{\Delta I/\alpha}{I/\alpha} = \frac{\Delta I}{I} = \alpha\sigma = \frac{s}{b}. \quad (\alpha = s, \ \sigma = 1/b).$$

Thus Domar's notion of 'balanced growth' is one of keeping effective demand and productive capacity balanced so that an economy may grow steadily without developing excess or short capacity. The advantage of Domar's formulation over Harrod's seems to be that the former explicitly includes an autonomous multiplicand (ΔI) on the demand side so as to permit its treatment as public investment, while its disadvantage seems to lie in the absence of Harrod's kind of a 'natural' rate to take care of full employment as well as full capacity without artificially assuming full employment as an initial condition. Domar's 'balanced growth' is, moreover, subject to the same sort of criticism as has been properly made against Harrod's assumption of fixed technological coefficients (e.g. a constant capital-output ratio, a constant capital-labour ratio, and a constant labour-output ratio). It was partly as meeting

N

such criticisms that we included a chapter dealing with dynamic technological parameters (Chap. 5 of this book). However, we have expressed considerable scepticism regarding the reliability of market forces and relative factor-price movements in making technological parameters variable in the desired direction. Contrariwise we have expressed some hope that public policy might deliberately influence the factors affecting technological coefficients autonomously of market conditions and by reference to other prevailing growth variables.

Harrod and Domar have made the essential nature of the growth mechanism operationally significant, for they stress the saving ratio and the capital-output ratio (or its reciprocal) as measurable strategic variables to investigate and possibly to manipulate for a desired rate of growth. Because of the universal character of these strategic variables, the growth mechanism discussed by Harrod and Domar is applicable to all economic systems, albeit with due modification. By contrast, Joan Robinson's growth mechanism involving, as it does, 'value and distribution' parameters of a specifically capitalistic nature, while it mirrors the historical development of capitalism more realistically, nevertheless has less applicability and hence lacks a universal appeal. We have conjectured that Joan Robinson might have intended to show how absurd and intolerable it would be for a present-day underdeveloped economy to adopt a pattern of development most unfavourable to labour in relation to other productive factors. The implication of Joan Robinson's theory of capital accumulation seems to be that public policy should be substituted for 'the capitalist rules of the game' for a pattern of economic development that is most likely to prove least harmful to the full-employment and high-consumption aspirations of wage-earning groups. Thus one may say that Joan Robinson has come up with a Keynesian variant of 'labourism'.

Most directly concerned with underdeveloped economies is R. Nurkse's theory of capital formation and 'balanced growth'.[1] Nurkse's notion of 'balanced growth' seems to be that an underdeveloped economy should balance the demand for investment and the supply of savings through a combination of domestic

[1] See his *Problems of Capital Formation in Underdeveloped Countries*.

policies and foreign-trade policies largely within the framework of a free society. His emphasis on the demand side of capital accumulation reflects a Keynesian reaction against the classical notion of supply creating its own demand. His concern with the expansion of investment-demand for the specific purpose of economic development in an underdeveloped country is a refreshing departure from the traditional tendency to regard an underdeveloped economy as a market or a raw-material source for advance economies. However, that concern with investment-demand has the effect of weakening his other concern with the supply of savings, which other concern is more fundamental in any *long-run* analysis, classical or Keynesian. Moreover, Nurkse's concept of investment-demand suffers from the lack of a clear distinction between 'induced' and 'autonomous' investment, thus leaving out the explicit role of government in directly organizing investment projects for developmental purposes. It remains debatable whether an underdeveloped economy can or cannot overcome its 'initial market difficulty' to induce sufficient private investment in productive equipment by leaving investment decisions mainly to private entrepreneurs. 'Balanced growth' (of income) is not, as Nurkse supposes, to be desired to induce private investment but to be desired for its own sake, as far as an underdeveloped economy is concerned. For, as we pointed out in our criticism of Harrod's excessive reliance on induced investment to the neglect of autonomous investment, Nurkse's complaints about an underdeveloped economy's restricted markets and low real income tending to inhibit the private inducement to invest would be unnecessary if autonomous public investment of a capacity-increasing as well as income-generating nature was allowed to play a greater role.

On the supply side of capital accumulation, Nurkse invokes the 'demonstration effect' tempered by disguised unemployment as a 'saving potential'. We have already discussed these points and so need not belabour them again. We may make a few additional observations here, however. First, Nurkse's treatment of population is limited to one of postulating disguised unemployment as a 'saving potential' without analysing the functional relation between population growth and capital growth, as we tried to do in our discussions of the socially optimal rate of growth and secular underemployment and as Harrod and Joan Robinson do in their discussions of 'progressive equilibrium' and 'golden-age equilibrium'. Second, the role of technological progress is almost completely neglected in Nurkse's discussion of 'balanced growth'. Such a neglect of the technological role has led Nurkse to give excessive emphasis to the need for capital accumulation, whereas a little more Schumpetarian interest in technology would have enabled him to see that an underdeveloped economy could decrease the capital-output ratio relatively to any given saving ratio to increase its growth rate. Third, Nurkse limits the role of fiscal policy to one of mobilizing existing savings, instead of assigning to it such varied roles as an additional 'saver', 'investor', 'innovator' and 'redistributor'. We have discussed these latter roles of fiscal policy as desiderata for underdeveloped countries lacking in private initiative, private voluntary saving and private innovation. Lastly, although Nurkse allows for capital imports as an additional source of developmental capital, his apprehensive discussion of the 'demonstration effect' and his hopeful discussion of disguised unemployment as a 'saving potential' seem to have perhaps the unintended effect of de-emphasizing reliance on foreign sources of capital. We have indicated greater scope for foreign borrowing in the Keynesian spirit of 'international homogenization' through the agencies of the United Nations. Despite these limitations, Nurkse's theory of economic development is important for the smashing emphasis it gives to the one and only really expansible factor of growth, namely, real capital.

It is as exploring the possibilities opened up by the growth discussions of Harrod, Domar, Hansen, Joan Robinson, Nurkse, Lewis, and other post-Keynesian writers that further studies and researches should be undertaken if the economic development of present-day underdeveloped countries is to be promoted to the benefit of all mankind. If the present volume has provided an additional impetus for such studies and researches, the author would not have written it in vain.

APPENDIX

THE UNITED NATIONS AND ECONOMIC
DEVELOPMENT*

As a sequel to its *National and International Measures for Full Employment*, the United Nations has offered a report on *Measures for the Economic Development of Underdeveloped Countries* prepared by A. B. Cortez (Chile), D. R. Gadgil (India), G. Hakim (Lebanon), W. A. Lewis (England), and T. W. Schultz (U.S.).[1] A perusal of the report at once reveals immense good-will, imaginative insights and broad comprehension. Despite these admirable aspects of the report, the technical reader will, it is to be feared, be less than satisfied with the theoretical basis of the various measures recommended. Perhaps the experts were too self-conscious of the previous criticism of those who had prepared the full-employment report as 'too much inclined to treat the questions before them as if they were mathematical problems'.[2] So much so that they may have gone too far in neglecting the operationally significant functional relationships involved. This is doubtless in part due to the vastly complex and difficult problem of economic development as an object for economic analysis. Inasmuch, however, as the report purports to deal with the economic development of underdeveloped countries, I feel justified in criticizing it, and perhaps implementing it, mainly from an economic point of view. In so doing I wish to concentrate on the analytical part of the report, relegating policy remarks to the background.

The report provides, at the outset, a working definition of underdeveloped economies in terms of low 'per capita real

* This is my review article originally published in *Indian Economic Journal* April 1954.
1 United Nations, Department of Economic Affairs, N.Y., May 1951.
2 Cf. United Nations' *Economic and Social Council Official Records*, Tenth Session, 358th Meeting, February 21, 1950, p. 98. For an analytical rather than methodological criticism see my 'The United Nations and Full Employment,' *Journal of Political Economy*, August 1950.

income', which most significantly distinguishes 'poor countries' from the United States, Canada, and other 'wealthy' countries. The state of underdevelopment, as such, is then shown to be related to (1) economic organization and planning, (2) technology, (3) population growth, and (4) capital, domestic and external. The report discusses these variables separately and in relation to one another, and always with a view to formulating practical policy recommendations.

Perhaps by way of stressing a harmful accompaniment of the state of underdevelopment the experts start out with a discussion of unemployment, particularly that category of unemployment which is due to the lack of capital equipment and other industrial facilities—in short 'structural unemployment'. They, therefore, see in 'industrialization' the most logical remedy for this type of unemployment. It is recognized that, by contrast, the most serious kind of unemployment in advanced economies is due to a familiar Keynesian deficiency of effective demand. As Mrs. Joan Robinson has pointed out, the so-called 'structural unemployment' is merely another expression for the Marxian category of unemployment due to the observed tendency of population to outrun capital accumulation[1]—a tendency which characterized the development of early capitalism and which now confronts industrially backward countries. However, the report fails to recognize the existence of the marginal case where a country may be sandwiched between the devil of 'Marxian' unemployment and the deep sea of 'Keynesian' unemployment. Japan is a case in point for her rapid industrialization was made possible by undercapitalization of agriculture relative to agricultural population—at the increasing risk of mass unemployment due to the instablity and deficiency of effective demand. In properly emphasizing economic development as 'the main remedy for underemployment', therefore, one should nevertheless have the Keynesian reservation: 'When a country is growing in wealth somewhat rapidly, the further progress of this happy state of affairs is liable to be interrupted, in conditions of *laissez-faire*, by the insufficiency of the inducements to new investment.'[2]

[1] See her 'Mr Harrod's Dynamics', *Economic Journal*, March 1949.
[2] *General Theory*, p. 335.

This is to be taken as a warning both against the practical tendency of *laissez faire* and the theoretical omission of investment as a decreasing function of capital.

The next discussion of 'the psychological and social prerequisites of progress' seems rather commonplace. Surely, underdeveloped countries need not be told that 'there cannot be rapid economic progress unless the leaders of a country at all levels—politicians, teachers, engineers, business leaders, trade unionists, priests, journalists—desire economic progress for the country', coupled with 'the public will to advance'. (p.16). Centuries of poverty, unemployment, and the sheer lack of social amenities have made all backward economies hypersensitive to their industrial backwardness—so hypersensitive that they tend to impute derogatory contents into the word 'backward' both when used innocently and when spoken unemotionally. The point is that as a result of long 'colonialism' in many underdeveloped areas of the world, 'industrialization' has become a household word and a winning political slogan, especially for intensely nationalistic Asiatic countries.[1] Behind what appears to casual observers to be a naïve nationalistic romanticism lies a deep-seated, determination and 'will to advance', first and above all, on the economic front. This popular will to advance economically is all the more strengthened by an irresistible urge to achieve or maintain political independence. In all these nationalistic aspirations underdeveloped countries are constantly inspired by the historical examples of American industrialization and independence and Japan's phenomenal industrial progress, and, for better or for worse, by Russia's bold economic experiments. The experts may be putting the cart before the horse when they argue that 'ancient philosophies have to be scrapped; old social institutions have to disintegrate; bonds of caste, creed and race have to be burst before there can be rapid economic progress'. (p. 15). It is more likely that these 'painful readjustments' will be made more as a consequence of 'rapid economic progress' than as a significant 'pre-condition' thereof. Too much stress on these supposed impediments would merely strengthen the superficial notion that underdeveloped countries are 'destined'

[1] See, e.g., my *Labour in the Philippine Economy* Stanford Univ. Press, 1945.

to remain 'backward' simply because their 'way of life' is 'backward'. If economic progress carries with it a tendency to break down all these social barriers, as seems to be the case, then underdeveloped economies may be justified in by-passing 'determinants of determinants' and going directly to the operationally more significant determinants, taking the former as given. However, one would not dogmatize on this point.

Discussion of 'economic organization' and 'development planning' strikes me as indulging in the luxury of disaggregation where the problem of aggregation is at issue and as misplacing emphasis on the composition of a given output when the size of output is the most arresting problem. One receives the impression that the experts apply rather mechanically the classical allocation principle to a situation that calls for economic organization and planning along macroeconomic lines. Thus they overstress the danger of 'misallocation of resources' as if the question of maximum output and full employment were already settled. Two things are of particular significance here, namely, the discussion of foreign trade in relation to development and the selection of Japan as a model of developmental planning to be followed.

As for the first of these, the report recognizes that the principle of comparative advantage has limited application in an under-employed, underdeveloped economy, thus justifying a measure of protection for indigenous 'infant' industries; that excessive dependence on foreign trade tends to make underdeveloped economies not only cyclically unstable but permanently pre-occupied with a few profitable commercial crops (e.g. primary commodities wanted by industrial economies) to the neglect of diversification and industrialization; that balance of payment difficulties may complicate and impede domestic economic development, thus inferentially endorsing some 'priority' controls to encourage 'foreign exchange earning' or 'foreign exchange saving' industries. Discussion of the role of 'bulk purchasing' and 'state trading' in economic development is conspicuous by its absence, however.

As for the second, the experts consider 'the developments in Japan in the last half-century' to be 'most instructive' in relation to 'comprehensive and integrated' developmental planning.

(p. 60.). What they neglect to observe here is that feudalistic paternalism—one of those 'old social institutions' which they mention as an impediment to development—and 'monopolistic organization of production'—which they consider inimical to developmental initiative—are the two important elements which helped rather than hindered the rapid economic development of Japan. In other words, it is necessary to be more specific about the nature of 'comprehensive and integrated' planning as far as Japan is concerned, for that planning has been based on the paternalistic governmental encouragement of many 'key' industries (e.g. steel manufacturing and textile exports) as well as on the government monopoly of basic transportation developments (e.g. railroads), coupled with initial government subsidies to private monopolies (i.e. '*zai batsu*', albeit for military reasons, often). J. A. Schumpeter's paradoxical dictum that monopoly rather than competition makes for industrial progress has, therefore, had a qualified testing in Japan. Moreover, it is doubtful that the future development of underdeveloped economies can advantageously proceed along the lines of integrated 'domestic and factory industry', for it is by no means clear whether Japan's rapid economic progress owes more to the government-sponsored 'rationalization' of factory industry or to the integration of 'domestic and factory industry'. I am myself inclined to attach greater significance to the former.

Turning now to the technological factor, the experts deplore the 'low level of technology' in underdeveloped countries almost as much as they explore the causal possibilities of technical advance for development. We are told that 'the first major obstacle to the general advance in technology in underdeveloped countries is . . . the lack of an educational and administrative structure through which the producers can learn the new technology'. (p. 29). One might argue, perhaps more cogently, that the presence of cheap abundant labour is even a greater obstacle to technical advance in general and industrial rationalization in particular, for producers lack the incentive to innovate along modern lines so long as they believe, rightly or wrongly, that low wages, incident to abundant labour more than offset the productive inefficiency of not so 'roundabout' methods involving more labour relative to capital. It seems misleading to play up, as the report seems to do, 'simple and inexpensive technological improvements' (e.g. use of fertilizers and better crop rotation) in the limiting case of agricultural production as if underdeveloped economies did not have to depend increasingly on relatively complicated and expensive technological applications in industry for greater productive efficiency and for higher living standards.

We are informed that 'in some underdeveloped countries, where labour is overabundant, the problem is rather to find fruitful new techniques which are capital saving'. (p. 31). This is presumably because the low wages accompanying abundant labour render 'labour saving' devices superfluous and make the economizing of scarce and expensive capital more urgent. It would be more to the point, however, to say that, where the population is overabundant, a desired increase in the growth rate of output is more feasible with a lower than with a higher capital-output ratio, given the saving ratio. For since an under-developed economy in the process of constructing 'capital-using' industrial bases (e.g. railroads) tends to require very much capital relatively to its limited ability to save, it stands to reason that such an economy should be interested in techno-logical improvements along 'capital-saving' lines. The report rightly stresses the urgent need for greater technical assistance to underdeveloped areas, but it has done the whole question of technical aid less than full justice by failing to relate it, in a functional way, to either a saving ratio or a capital-output ratio and hence to the technically feasible rate of progress. In short, unless the question of technology is demonstrated to be causally significant for the determination of the growth rate of output in relation to the given rate of population growth, the argument in favour of 'capital-saving' devices is less than convincing.

With respect to population, the report rejects traditional pessimism concerning the tendency of population to outrun production. Instead, it vigorously espouses the conviction that production can be made to grow faster than population growth. It is implicitly assumed that the standard of living is a function of per capita rate of output growth, that is, the growth rate of output divided by the growth rate of population. Insofar,

therefore, as the growth rate of output is functionally dependent
on a saving ratio, one sure way to raise living standards is by increasing the rate of capital accumulation *pari passu* with population growth. Where capital is extremely scarce relatively to
population growth, the report favours a negative policy of reducing fertility rates (p. 48), in addition to a positive policy
of increasing production ahead of population growth. There is
no such allusion to the population growth of underdeveloped
economies as a possible stimulant to the effective demand of
advanced economies, as Mr. Harrod makes.[1] The report later
makes it abundantly clear that if the saving ratio is too high
relatively to population growth, as in the case of the United
States, surplus capital should be made available to those need-
ing it, especially those overpopulated underdeveloped economies
(see p. 77).

The chapter on 'Domestic Capital Formation', with its
classical emphasis on the conflict between the scarcity of capital
and the progress of industry, stands in sharp contrast with the
Keynesian stress on the possible interference of super-abundant
capital with full employment. This is a logical dichotomy inasmuch as the former is apropos of underdeveloped economies,
while the latter is intended for advanced economies. In considering economic progress as 'a function, among other things, of
the rate of new capital formation', the report mentions or
implies such limitations and difficulties of capital accumulation
as a tendency to hoard rather than save and invest, lower per
capita incomes, underdeveloped savings institutions, middle-
higher income groups' tendency to conspicous consumption.
However, it fails to mention some important impediments to
capital formation, such as political instability tending to discourage thriftiness, postwar uncertainty to shift tastes away from
durable goods, relative resource-immobility from consumer-
goods industries to capital-goods industries, and a socio-ethical
attitude toward egalitarianism (as compared with a Puritanic
individualism which the reader of Max Weber knows as a
historical justification of economic inequality on the grounds
of capital formation). These latter impediments are due in part

[1] Cf., R. F. Harrod, *Towards a Dynamic Economics*, Macmillan, London, 1948,
pp. 106–15.

to the structure of industry and the composition of aggregate demand and in part to the deep-seated feudalistic traditions of co-operative life. When these obstacles are frankly recognized, the task of increasing the rate of capital accumulation is even more formidable than the report would indicate. Theoretically, this suggests that it might be necessary to make the growth rate of output a function, not of a simple saving ratio, but a variable expressing the capacity to produce capital-goods which is determined more by the structure of industry, etc., than by the community's desire to save. Then it would be easier to understand why postwar Japan, for example, which has a relatively high average propensity to save, has nevertheless failed to achieve a rate of capital accumulation commensurate with the postwar capital requirements.[1]

The report rightly stresses the crucial importance of 'forced saving' for developmental purposes in underdeveloped countries, where voluntary savings are so low for institutional-psychological reasons that governments are obliged to mobilize developmental capital by means of taxation, inflation, priority resource allocations, and foreign-exchange control (especially against capital flight). It reluctantly admits that 'it is probably not possible to have rapid economic development without some inflation'. (p. 42). This is partly because the alternative of compulsory fiscal reduction of consumption is intolerable where living standards are already extremely low but largely because the 'money illusion' incident to price inflation has the effect of increasing the supply of capital-goods before takers of paper profits and earners of paper wages have become disillusioned with their not so prosperous real-income position. Against the stimulating effect of inflation on capital accumulation is set the discouraging impact on voluntary savings of 'the lower and middle income groups'. This, however, is equivocal. In the first place, the lower and middle income groups in underdeveloped economies are unlikely to have enough savings to worry about higher prices reducing their real value. In the next place, it is rentiers, of all fixed-income groups, whose saving is likely to be most severely affected and whose marginal

[1] Compare K. Ohkawa, 'The Growth Rate of the Japanese Economy', *Keizai Hyoron*, February 1952.

propensity to save may be smaller than that of entrepreneurs anyway. In this case the 'redistribution effect' of higher prices due to developmental inflationary financing would not reduce total voluntary savings significantly.

The possibility of increasing capital accumulation without reducing consumption is recognized, especially in the case of countries having much superfluous agricultural labour whose shift to capital-goods industries is generally believed not to diminish the output of consumer-goods. No mention is made of such possible bottlenecks as the immobility of labour (due to inadequate transportation facilities, if not to family ties) and the lack of specialized 'know-how' that might be involved in mobilizing 'the underemployed', however.

In their argument in favour of capital imports to supplement deficient domestic capital the experts take due cognizance of many technical and non-technical difficulties that stand in the way. Thus they speak of 'hazardous guesses as to their present national income' and 'scanty' statistical information about underdeveloped economies. They do not, however, stress such conceptual difficulties as involved in the whole notion of 'saving'. For instance, Mr. Colin Clark has been criticized for overestimating Japan's saving ratio which includes many consumers' capital items (e.g., semi-durable clothing) that are ordinarily excluded. Use of such a broad concept of 'saving' based on *ex post* national wealth statistics would yield an upward statistical bias so that the country in question is mistakenly thought capable of exporting 'surplus' savings, instead of having to import capital. On the other hand, the neglect of the influence of the structure of industry and the composition of aggregate demand mentioned above would yield a downward statistical bias, since the country is erroneously considered capable of producing capital-goods *pari passu* with the community's propensity to save. These conceptual problems must be clarified before making even 'hazardous guesses' as to national incomes and derived domestic saving ratios. The report seems weak in yet another respect, namely, its failure, perhaps deliberate, to relate the capital needs of underdeveloped countries to the stagnation danger of advanced economies arising from a tendency to 'oversave' relatively to existing investment opportunities that are limited by the historically declining marginal efficiency of superabundant capital. (This oversight might be considered a strength rather than a weakness—by those who are dogmatically opposed to the Keynes-Hansen stagnation hypothesis). My point is merely that the report is less than convincing when it pleads for capital exports from advanced to underdeveloped economies without explicitly stating the economic advantages of such exports (e.g. an additional outlet for possibly excessive domestic saving and an eventual inflow of dividends and interest serving as export-multiplicand) to advanced economies that tend to deviate from the path of what Mr. Harrod terms 'progressive equilibrium' with full employment.

For historical and political, and to less extent economic, reasons the report sees little promise in private capital exports to underdeveloped economies. Instead, it places far more confidence in the desirability and feasibility of inter-governmental lending and multinational developmental financing. Emphasizing as they seem to do the merits of multinational lending, it is no surprise that the experts should refuse to be impressed by the traditional concern with 'the transfer problem', which they believe to be quite soluble in the course of successful development. The World Bank is criticized for its present tendency to base its lending policy more on 'a measurement of foreign currency needs' than on developmental needs. This may be considered as an implied criticism of the International Monetary Fund, since this latter agency is supposed to ease foreign exchange difficulties so that the Bank may concentrate on strictly developmental lending. The report, however, might be in turn criticized for not warning against the danger of deviating from the desideratum of multinational lending on a 'purely technical and non-political' basis stressed by Keynes, especially in these turbulent times of international tension and friction.

Nothing that has been said above should be construed as casting doubt on the generally excellent treatment of the problem by the United Nations' experts. As a general verdict, it might not be amiss to say that the report under review will continue to serve as the indispensable primer of economic development for many years to come, though its policy recommendations are of less permanent value to a dynamic world economy. But above all, what stands out in the whole report is a new spirit of international collaboration in the economic field —far beyond the narrow technical vision of economists and far above the 'imperialistic' horizons of prewar nationalists.

BIBLIOGRAPHY

Specific Writings on Underdeveloped Economies

ARNDT, W. H., 'External Economies in Economic Growth', *Economic Record*, November 1955.

BERNSTEIN, E. M., and PATEL, I G., 'Inflation in Relation to Economic Development', International Monetary Fund *Staff Papers*, November 1952.

BRONFENBRENNER, M., 'The High Cost of Economic Development', *Land Economics*, May–August 1953.

BUCHANAN, N. S., and ELLIS, H. S., *Approaches to Economic Development*, Twentieth Century Fund, N.Y., 1955.

CHENERY, H. B., and KRETSCHMER, K. S., 'Resource Allocation for Economic Development', *Econometrica*, October 1956.

CLARK, C., 'The World Will Save Money in 1950's', *Fortune*, July 1950.

HEIMANN, E., 'Marxism and Underdeveloped Countries', *Social Research*, September 1952.

HICKS, J. R., and U. K., *Report on Finance and Taxation in Jamaica*, Government Printer, Kingston, Jamaica, 1955.

HIGGINS, B., 'Economic Development of Underdeveloped Areas: Past and Present', *Land Economics*, August 1955.

KALDOR, N., *Indian Tax Reform: Report of A Survey*, Dept. of Econ. Affairs, Ministry of Finance, Delhi, 1956.

KALECKI, M., 'The Problem of Financing of Economic Development', *Indian Economic Review*, February 1955.

KURIHARA, K. K., 'Growth Analysis and the Problem of Capital Accumulation in Underdeveloped Countries', *Metroeconomica*, December 1954.
　　　'The Fiscal Role of Government in Economic Development', *Indian Journal of Economics*, July 1956.
　　　'Economic Development and the Balance of Payments', *Metroeconomica*, Vol. IX, No. 3, 1957.

KUZNETS, S., et al., *Economic Growth: Brazil, India, Japan*, Duke Univ. Press, 1955.

LEIBENSTEIN, H., *Economic Backwardness and Economic Growth*, Wiley, N.Y., 1957.

MACHLUP, F., 'The Finance of Development in Poor Countries: Foreign Capital and Domestic Inflation', *Economic Studies Quarterly* (Japan), April 1956.

o

MEIER, G. M., and BALDWIN, R. E., *Economic Development*, Wiley, N.Y., 1957.

MYRDAL, G., *An International Economy: Problems and Prospects*, Harper & Bros., N.Y., 1956.

NEISSER, H., *et al.*, 'Economic Growth in Underdeveloped Countries', *American Economic Review*, May 1952.

NURKSE, R., *Problems of Capital Formation in Underdeveloped Countries*, Blackwell, Oxford, 1953.

PENROSE, E. F., 'Malthus and the Underdeveloped Areas', *Economic Journal*, June 1957.

PRAKASH, O., (ed.), 'Fiscal and Monetary Policy—Special Number in Honour of the Late Lord Keynes, 1883–1946', *Indian Journal of Economics*, July 1956.

ROBINSON, JOAN, 'A Theory of Long-Run Development', *Economic Review* (Japan), October 1955.
    'The Choice of Technique', *Economic Weekly* (India), June 23, 1956.

SINGER, H. W., 'The Mechanics of Economic Development', *Indian Economic Review*, August 1952.

TINBERGEN, J., 'Problems concerning India's Second Five Year Plan', *Finances Publiques* (Netherlands), No. 2/1956.

TSURU, S., 'A Note on Capital-Output Ratio', *Economic Review* (Japan), April 1956.

UNITED NATIONS, *Measures for the Economic Development of Underdeveloped Countries*, N.Y., 1951.

VAKIL, C. N., and BRAHMANAND, P. R., *Planning for an Expanding Economy: Accumulation, Employment and Technical Progress in Underdeveloped Countries*, Vora & Co., Bombay, 1956 (Institute of Pacific Relations, N.Y., 1956).

VINER, J., *International Trade and Economic Development*, Free Press, Glencoe, 1952 (Oxford, 1955).

WALLICH, H. C., 'Underdeveloped Countries and the International Monetary Mechanism', in *Money, Trade, and Economic Growth* (in honour of J. H. Williams), Macmillan, N.Y., 1951.

General Writings on Economic Growth

BAUMOL, W. J., *Economic Dynamics*, Macmillan, N.Y., 1951.

CLARK, C., *The Conditions of Economic Progress* (2nd ed.), Macmillan, London, 1951.

DOMAR, E. D., *Essays in the Theory of Economic Growth*, Oxford Univ. Press, N.Y., 1957.

EISNER, R., 'Underemployment Equilibrium Rates of Growth', *American Economic Review*, March 1952.

FELLNER, W., 'The Capital-Output Ratio in Dynamic Economics', in *Money, Trade, and Economic Growth* (in honour of J. H. Williams), Macmillan, N.Y., 1951.

GOODWIN, R. M., 'A Model of Cyclical Growth', in *The Business Cycle in the Post-War World* (E. Lundberg, ed.), Macmillan, London, 1955.

GURLEY, J. G., 'Fiscal Policy in a Growing Economy', *Journal of Political Economy*, December, 1953.

HAAVELMO, T., *A Study in the Theory of Economic Evolution*, North-Holland Publishing Co., Amsterdam, 1954.

HAMBERG, D., *Economic Growth and Instability*, W. W. Norton, N.Y., 1956.

HANSEN, A. H., 'Economic Progress and Declining Population Growth', *American Economic Review*, March 1939.
    The American Economy, McGraw-Hill, N.Y., 1957.

HARROD, R. F., 'An Essay in Dynamic Theory', *Economic Journal*, March 1939.
    Towards a Dynamic Economics, Macmillan, London, 1948.

HICKS, J. R., 'Mr Harrod's Dynamic Theory', *Economica*, May 1949.
    A Contribution to the Theory of the Trade Cycle, Oxford, 1950.

HIGGINS, B., 'The Theory of Increasing Underemployment', *Economic Journal*, June 1950.

KALDOR, N., 'The Relation of Economic Growth and Cyclical Fluctuations', *Economic Journal*, March 1954.

KALECKI, M., *Theory of Economic Dynamics*, G. Allen & Unwin, London, Rinehard, N.Y., 1954.

KEIRSTEAD, B., *The Theory of Economic Change*, Macmillan, Toronto, 1948.

KEYNES, J. M., 'Economic Possibilities for our Grandchildren' (1930), in *Essays in Persuasion*, Rupert Hart-Davis, London, 1952.
    'Some Economic Consequences of a Declining Population', *Eugenics Review*, April 1937.
    'Sundry Observations on the Nature of Capital', in *General Theory*.
    'The Bank for Reconstruction and Development' (Opening Remarks at the First Meeting of the Second Commission on the Bank, July 3, 1944), reproduced in *The New Economics* (S. E. Harris, ed.), Knopf, N.Y., 1948.

o*

KURIHARA, K. K., *Introduction to Keynesian Dynamics*, Allen & Unwin (London) and Columbia Univ. Press (N.Y.), 1956.

'Growth Models and Fiscal-Policy Parameters', *Finances Publiques* (Netherlands), No. 2/1956.

KUZNETS, S., 'Economic Growth and Income Inequality', *American Economic Review*, March 1955.

LEWIS, W. A., *The Theory of Economic Growth*, Allen & Unwin, London, 1955.

LUNDBERG, E., *Studies in the Theory of Economic Expansion*, King, London, 1937.

ROBINSON, JOAN, 'Mr Harrod's Dynamics', *Economic Journal*, March 1949.

The Rate of Interest and Other Essays, Macmillan, London, 1952.

The Accumulation of Capital, Irwin, Homewood, 1956.

ROSTOW, W. W., *The Process of Economic Growth*, W. W. Norton, N.Y., 1953.

SCHUMPETER, J. A., *The Theory of Economic Development*, Harvard Univ. Press, 1934.

SMITHIES, A., 'Economic Fluctuations and Growth', *Econometrica*, January 1957.

SOLOW, R., 'A Contribution to the Theory of Economic Growth', *Quarterly Journal of Economics*, February 1956.

TAKATA, Y. (ed.), *Studies in Economic Growth* (contributions by Y. Takata, M. Morishima, S. Ichimura, S. Fujita, and T. Watanabe), Osaka Univ. Monograph No. 1, 1954.

INDEX

GEORGE ALLEN & UNWIN LTD
London: 40 Museum Street, W.C.1

Auckland: 24 Wyndham Street
Bombay: 15 Graham Road, Ballard Estate, Bombay 1
Bridgetown: P.O. Box 222
Buenos Aires: Escritorio 454–459, Florida 165
Calcutta: 17 Chittaranjan Avenue, Calcutta 13
Cape Town: 68 Shortmarket Street
Hong Kong: 44 Mody Road, Kowloon
Ibadan: P.O. Box 62
Karachi: Karachi Chambers, McLeod Road
Madras: Mohan Mansions, 38c Mount Road, Madras 6
Mexico: Villalongin 32–10, Piso, Mexico 5, D.F.
Nairobi: P.O. Box 4536
New Delhi: 13–14 Asaf Ali Road, New Delhi 1
Ontario: 81 Curlew Drive, Don Mills
Philippines: 7 Waling-Waling Street, Roxas District,
Quezon City
São Paulo: Caixa Postal 8675
Singapore: 36c Prinsep Street, Singapore 7
Sydney: N.S.W.: Bradbury House, 55 York Street
Tokyo: 10 Kanda-Ogawamachi, 3-Chome, Chiyoda-Ku